Public Control of Business

Public Control of Business

SELECTED OPINIONS BY

HARLAN FISKE STONE

Associate Justice, Supreme Court of the United States

Edited by Alfred Lief

HOWELL, SOSKIN & COMPANY, NEW YORK

40-9420

MANUFACTURED IN THE U. S. A. BY H. WOLFF, NEW YORK.

Table of Contents

Mr. Justice Stone

Mr. Justice Stone has always conceived of the law as a system whose logic must yield to the test of experience. When he was nominated for the Supreme Court of the United States by President Coolidge the liberal groups in the Senate raised their hands in horror at this "man who has spent all his life in the atmosphere of big business," this "attorney of Morgan and Company." Harlan Fiske Stone ascended the bench in the general belief that he was conservative and "safe." In the year 1940 he is regarded as a spokesman for the liberal doctrine of legal interpretation which the more stubborn of spokesmen for business and finance view with alarm. But those who know the clarity of his thought and the consistency of his doctrines realize that Stone has not shifted from a conservative to a liberal point of view. It is the world about him that has changed.

The political incident that brought Harlan Stone to the attention of the nation's politicians as a conservative hung, characteristically enough, not upon a broad issue of radical or tory doctrine, but upon a question of the functioning of government. It was during the campaign for the reëlection of President Coolidge in 1924 that Stone, Attorney General of the United States, went out to Des Moines to tell the farmers that the program of Senator Robert M. La Follette, Sr., would, if adopted, bring disaster. Not that the speaker stood in any serious fear of defeat for Coolidge. The La Follette Third Party was bound to lose. But it might throw the election into Congress, and the organization of the government would then be controlled by a defeated minority.

There had been distrust of Stone by the Progressives before this, but that was automatic and general distrust stirred upon the occasion of his appointment as Attorney General. His reputation lay principally in the field of legal education, and little was known of him besides his Wall Street law practice. "If the appointment of Mr. Stone was not dictated by Wall Street interests, and particularly by J. P. Morgan & Co., it will at least be completely satisfactory to them." Such was the greeting.

Not even the housecleaning of débris left by the Daugherty régime, the discharge of volunteer agents of the Federal Bureau of Investigation, such as Cornelius Vanderbilt, Charles D. Hilles, Fred W. Upham, Edward B. McLean, and T. Coleman duPont, nor even the efficient handling of a tremendous load of war-inherited litigation dispelled distrust. And when Coolidge, who thought Stone's work had done more than anything else to ensure his election, nominated him to the Supreme Court, the storm broke briefly.

"He has breathed the mephitic air of the Department of Justice, permeated as it is to this very day with the influence of Daugherty," cried Senator Thomas J. Walsh, of Montana. And it was Senator George W. Norris, of Nebraska, shocked by other Coolidge appointees, who declared that Stone would be imbued with the ideas of big business. But there were only six votes against confirmation.

What was the reason for this attitude of the liberals? His friends may have remembered his rejection of Theodore Roosevelt's concept of "social justice" and of the crusade for "sociological jurisprudence." Some may have heard him in 1915 decry the notion that a judge should interpret popular sentiment; the judicial function was not political or legislative. The law was "better than its bad precedents" and benefited on the many occasions when precedents were overruled, "but I would not have what is normally a rare and exceptional exercise of the judicial power cultivated as a habit or resorted to by judges as a method of making effective their own individual notions of justice."

"The steady pressure of facts"—this was what developed new rules of law, Stone held. "The pressure of facts proven in court . . . rules formulated in the light of practical experience . . . and rarely, if ever, by political agitation or by the theories of social progress formulated outside the courtroom."

The man who deplored popular clamor and the impatient desire for speedy recognition of such theories, in the pre-war period of unrest, spoke out against the "red-raiding" which followed the war. The ruthless treatment of radicals by Attorney General A. Mitchell Palmer and his agents caused Stone, then dean of the Columbia University School of Law, to protest that aliens, too, had constitutional rights. In a long letter to a Senate committee in 1921—his first participation in a public cause—Stone denounced ruthless arrests without warrant, and summary deportations. The Constitution, he pointed out, guaranteed the protection of due process of law to "persons within the United States." Aliens, as well as citizens, were persons.

Thus it was not surprising that his initial act, upon becoming the head of the Department of Justice, was to get rid of Daugherty's intimate, William J. Burns; to abolish the snooping General Intelligence Division, and make the law-enforcement officers themselves amenable to law. But Stone was resolute enough not to heed newspaper criticism and dismiss all and sundry. He proceeded to reorganize at his own good pace and he had several others slated to go when Coolidge appointed him to the Court.

As a matter of fact, there have been few surprises in the public career of this self-reliant, deliberate, industrious New Englander, this factual scholar who conceived of the law as a doctrine shaped and necessarily affected by social experience.

In 1872, when Harlan Stone was born in Chesterfield, New Hampshire, the rise of corporate business enterprise and the nation's great economic expansion had barely begun. Young Stone, after two years of high school, wanted to be a scientific farmer. The family—it dated back to the Simon Stone who arrived at Massachusetts Bay Colony in 1635—was living on a farm in Mill Valley, a mile from Amherst. The boy was tall and strong. An accidental run-in with a teacher in a chapel rush at Massachusetts Agricultural College led to his expulsion and a change in his ambitions. He thought he might like being a doctor and he entered Amherst College, making up entrance requirements in the first year. This was a dogged period of struggle to find himself, and he came out of it with a decision to prepare for the profession of law.

On his own, young Stone worked his way by selling insurance and typewriters, and by tutoring. In the vigorous campus life almost every activity attracted him, except the physical. He concentrated on his studies, with time off for the presidency of the college Republican Club. Then he yielded to appeals to lend his 195 pounds to football, and he went down in school annals as the best Amherst center-rush ever had. The seniors of '94 voted him the class member likely to be the most famous.

To earn tuition for the Law School at Columbia, Stone taught physics and chemistry at Putnam High School in Newburyport. When he returned to Amherst for the commencement exercises of the class of '95 he heard one of the boys, Calvin Coolidge, whom he knew slightly, deliver a humorous oration.

While Coolidge made a quick study for the bar, Stone was paying his own way through Columbia by sandwiching in a job as history teacher at Adelphi Academy, in Brooklyn. His work at the law school so impressed Professor George F. Canfield that upon graduation in '98 a place was waiting for him in Canfield's law office. Three years later he became a partner. The firm was reorganized as Satterlee, Canfield & Stone, the first-named being Herbert L. Satterlee, son-in-law of J. Pierpont Morgan, Sr.

Meanwhile Stone had been lecturing at the law school with

much success. In 1903 he was made an adjunct professor, in 1905 a full professor. The law faculty prevailed upon Nicholas Murray Butler, Columbia's president, to name him dean. Stone accepted on condition that Butler make no appointments to the school without the advice and consent of the faculty. This ideal of democratic government was not so easily realized. The dominating president of the great university breached the agreement, and Stone resigned.

The next five years he devoted himself wholly to a lucrative law practice and to incidental directorships in corporations. At this time federal prosecution of trusts had become more insistent, and the efforts of states to meet new conditions by extension of their police powers had transformed the Fourteenth Amendment into a constitutional battleground. Labor was painfully organizing, fighting the injunctive process. Stone had confidence that courts would protect rights "temporarily obscured in times of political excitement." Courts were the bulwark of the minority against the tyranny of temporary majorities. In granting labor injunctions they properly restrained clearly illegal acts. And yet Stone honestly recognized that "the ability of limited groups of individuals to control great aggregations of capital through the stock control of corporations has given rise to most of the serious economic problems."

Constitutional law was not his field. When he returned to Columbia in 1910 as dean, on his original terms, he gave courses in personal property, mortgages, and equity. While Taft was still in the White House some of Stone's influential friends tried to get him a district judgeship. Because the salary was too small Stone might have declined it, if offered, but Taft rejected the suggestion. The dean continued his private connection simultaneously with strenuous upbuilding of the law school, its standards of admission and scholarship, and with persistent work for the advancement of legal education throughout the country. He lamented the lack of a worthy legal literature. Our law schools had done little to develop scholars and writers. Our lawyers and judges were too busy to develop philosophic thought.

With a world in turmoil, and repercussions of pacifism and intolerance on the campus, Dean Stone spoke for academic freedom—not for freedom to propagate doctrine, but for scientific truth. A teacher must be judicially minded, not partisan. This quality in Stone commended itself to Secretary of War Baker, who, in his own spiritual conflict as a former apostle of peace, selected him to serve on a board of inquiry to handle cases of conscientious objection. Stone visited army cantonments and examined several thousand drafted men who refused to perform military service. His difficulty was with non-religious objectors, whose sincerity was not obvious. But there was no sense in being arbitrary. "Liberty of conscience has a moral and social value which makes it worthy of preservation at the hands of the state," Stone reported. By a settled policy of violating conscience to protect itself, a government might ultimately lose its life.

After thirteen years as dean, with a distinguished chapter in legal education accomplished, and with a number of articles written for the *Columbia Law Review* which were repeatedly noted in court decisions, Stone decided in 1923 to drop pedagogy. He joined Sullivan and Cromwell as litigation expert—a Wall Street firm with a vast corporation and estate practice. It was then that Stone, in a book review, expressed his concept of the ideal system of jurisprudence as one which would take its form and draw its substance from changing social and economic conditions. Such a philosophy, he wrote, was not far removed from our native pragmatism and offered a solution for "many a knotty problem where history and logic do not point the way."

Early in '24, when President Coolidge was beset with Cabinet scandals and harassed by Senate investigations, Stone received a call to the White House. They had met infrequently since Amherst; last in 1919, when Coolidge was governor of Massachusetts. Stone was having breakfast with his father in a Boston hotel, and Coolidge walked in briskly and asked if he might sit at their table. There was no need for introductions as Father Stone had on occasion engaged Coolidge's legal services. During the entire meal the governor did not say a word. Through, he got up and left. He had only wanted company.

Now Coolidge had need for advice on the prosecution of oil frauds. He asked Stone to go over a list of names proposed for special counsel. Stone found objections of one kind or another to each, and finally mentioned Owen J. Roberts, of Philadelphia, saying that he did not know Roberts very well but had gained a good impression of him. If the President would call in Senator Pepper, of Pennsylvania, Pepper could give him more information, and if the appointment were acceptable to the Senator it would be all right with Stone. The idea was carried out the next day.

But at this meeting in the White House the talk drifted to erring Cabinet members and Stone said Coolidge should get rid of Daugherty. When they finished discussing the attorney-generalship, and as Stone was leaving, Coolidge suddenly asked, "Will you take it?" It became apparent that this was the main reason why the President had called him in.

Stone answered that he had not thought of the place for himself; that he was making a lot of money practicing law, more than a man should make, perhaps, and would take the job only as a public duty. And not for long. He specified that he would not stay the full term after 1924 in case Coolidge was reëlected. The arrangement satisfied the President, who was politically astute to recover prestige for the administration by divesting itself of a liability and taking on an able person never associated with politics.

About two months later Coolidge, in characteristic fashion, invited Stone to a White House breakfast with the Republican Senate leaders. The conversation was on speeding up the legislative program; nothing about Stone. It was the Coolidge way of letting the senators see that Stone was not the academic type.

The scheme bore fruit. Stone's name was sent in that afternoon, and the Republicans put through a quick confirmation.

Coolidge had reason to take pride in the Department that year. It disposed of 80,000 cases including prohibition enforcement, anti-trust actions, and litigation growing out of war-time transactions. In addition, Stone strengthened the morale and efficiency of the personnel and restricted it to legally authorized activity. The extension of governmental functions into new fields had enormously expanded administrative machinery, and Stone took care to prevent zeal in law enforcement from achieving results at the expense of private right and individual liberty.

On the other hand, Stone's respect for Coolidge increased. The President, for all his New Englander's suppression of emotion and cautious reticence, revealed administrative ability and was minutely informed on the doings of the executive departments. He would have made an excellent President in the 1840's or '50s, when the nation was not yet transformed from "isolated groups of agricultural pioneer communities . . . to an industrial state" and before "the domination of law and politics by inexorable economic forces."

The association of the two men led to the President's decision, not long after the successful election campaign, to give Stone the seat which Supreme Court Justice McKenna, aged and ailing, would relinquish. Stone's defense, in that campaign, of the Court's power to declare laws unconstitutional had been a sharp weapon in the fight with La Follette, who championed an amendment to empower Congress to repass congressional acts invalidated by the Court.

The La Follette proposal, Stone had said, was an attack on the fundamental principles of the Constitution. It would wipe out every vestige of state sovereignty, destroy executive authority to resist the encroachment of the legislative branch, and leave the judiciary helpless. "Only one branch of government would remain supreme, the one which responds most speedily to temporary and often fleeting changes in public opinion." The La Follette amendment would imperil every minority, he said. It would create in Congress "a centralized political organization not unlike that of the Roman Empire, where the centralized government, at first republican in form, drew to itself the actual regulation and control, in minutest detail, of every function of local government within the Empire."

When Stone went on the Court, Justice Holmes' conception of the Constitution was identical with his own: an instrument of government based on the suffrage of the people. He was glad to have, with Holmes, "the golden opportunity for the practice of a creative art—the moulding of our inherited legal doctrine." He regarded Holmes as "one of the most original and discerning intellects" of his time. Stone had not yet shed the belief, shared by many, that Mr. Justice Brandeis was an emotional reformer. But soon the new justice saw that Brandeis was as dispassionate a lawyer as himself, working to make the law responsive to the changed social forces and applying prodigious energy and exhaustive scrutiny to the facts and law of each case. Stone realized, too, that it required courage on the part of a judge to stand against the majority.

He fell in with the Brandeis habit of making careful examination of factual background and he himself brought to the Court a grasp of business, a broad knowledge of economic realities, which pitched him into disagreement with associates who adhered to traditional formulas. It nettled Chief Justice Taft to see Stone join in dissent with Holmes and Brandeis. It pleased Stone to think that the road hewn by Holmes and Brandeis eventually would be followed.

In a period of apparent prosperity, dissent was barely distinguishable from annoying idealism. The nation was getting along fine. Why bother? In the Court, however, that storm-center of controversy, alert minds sensed catastrophe. Stone, on a visit to the President in 1928, after Coolidge had withdrawn from the race, told him the decision was wise because the country was going to suffer the worst economic débâcle since the panic of '73. Coolidge was amazed, but after a little reflection brightened up and said, "Well, it's a good thing to get out while they still want you."

Later Stone was able to say: "The towering edifice of business and industry, which had become the dominating feature of the American structure, has been shaken to its foundations by forces, the full significance of which we still can see but dimly." The fortress of our civilization "developed unsuspected weaknesses and in consequence we are now engaged in the altogether wholesome task of critical reëxamination of what our hands have reared." He had strong words for those who engaged in anti-social business practices by reason of "the separation of ownership from management, the development of the corporate structure so as to vest in small groups control over the resources of great numbers of small and uninformed investors."

With the breakdown of states' attempts at regulation, with the accumulation of Court decisions thwarting legislatures and administrative bodies which were trying to cope with grave economic maladjustments, Stone at first attributed the differences in the Court mainly to appraisement of conditions which legislation sought to rectify. "We ought not to be completely absorbed in the technique of the law," he said. "The questions which come to us are rooted in history. . . . To grasp their significance our study must be extended beyond the examination of precedents and legal formulas by reading and research in fields extra-legal." Later the justice was more outspoken. He objected to judicial trespass on the functions of lawmakers and the injection of "our personal economic predilections."

Problems which only a generation before were for the individual to solve had become the burden of the nation. Private business had neglected its social responsibility.

The Court was under attack—from the Left, as usual. New federal efforts at regulation were blocked, and the cry went up for a reformation of the Court. Any thought of packing the Court, even the selection of a single judge because he was a "liberal," saddened Stone. He cherished the independence of the tribunal. Let those who wanted to use the Court as a political instrument ponder the fate of the supreme court in Germany!

It was important for the people to remember that the Court could and did reverse itself. Stone has seen many examples of the acceptance of the minority position, some of which came to pass even before the complexion of the Court changed. He has dealt a few finishing blows himself to obsolete principles. It was not enough to declare them wrong; it was essential to convince others, hence the technical thoroughness which he gave to each dissenting opinion.

The judicial labors of Mr. Justice Stone give the complete answer to unreconstructed businessmen, of whom Mr. Wendell Willkie is the most recent example, demanding a return to "free enterprise." Bitterly, Mr. Willkie says: "Mr. Roosevelt has won. The court is now his" and attributes to the newcomers a "revolutionary" upheaval of the American form of government in a recent series of majority opinions.

Specifically such critics point to decisions upholding the Labor Board's jurisdiction of contract shops (an opinion written by Justice Stone), the regulation of the marketing of farm products (an outgrowth of Stone's dissent into the first A.A.A. case), the taxation of state and federal employees' income (which resulted from a steady march of opinions by Stone), the reversal of minimum-wage invalidation (see Stone's dissent in *Morehead* v. *Tipaldo*), and the obligation of railroads to labor (see Stone's opinion on page 308, this volume).

In condemning the "new court" such critics have overlooked the statesmanship of the judge who took a cue neither from President Roosevelt nor from President Coolidge. Justice Stone's pragmatic approach to each question stands in contrast to the doctrinaire insistence of economic standpatters and their opponents alike. He has moulded principles of law out of the living fabric of the nation.

We are in a struggle, he has said, "to determine whether the giant economic forces which our industrial and financial world has created shall be under some larger measure of control."

We are "in one of the most critical periods of our history, when a major public problem is the choice of remedies for our economic ills and the mutual adjustment and reconciliation of those remedies with legal doctrine."

And finally, "The problems to which the machine and the corporation give rise have outstripped the ideology and values of an earlier day. The future demands that we undergo a corresponding moral adjustment."

Justice Stone makes plain, however, that his opinions upholding the constitutionality of statutes cannot be taken as an indication that he personally thinks the legislation wise or desirable; they are based wholly on his conception of the principles of government which are sanctioned or permitted by the Constitution.

In presenting the selection of opinions in this book made from Justice Stone's work of fifteen years on the Court, the editor of this volume assumes all responsibility. The treatment is designed for general readers and not for students of legal science; hence the omission of most citations and a condensation of the introductory passages. A preliminary statement of each controversy is followed by selected text.

Because of the close way in which Justices Holmes, Brandeis and Cardozo and Justice Stone worked in cooperation, it is desirable to point out when the three former justices ceased to be active on the Court. Justice Holmes retired January 12, 1932; Justice Brandeis, February 13, 1939; and Justice Cardozo's last opinion was delivered December 13, 1937.

ALFRED LIEF

Competition and Monopoly

TRADE ASSOCIATION ACTIVITIES

TWENTY-TWO firms making maple, beech, and birch flooring formed the Maple Flooring Manufacturers' Association, representing about seventy percent of the nation's production. The federal government, after enjoining other trade associations as unlawful combinations in restraint of interstate commerce, brought anti-trust proceedings against this group.

In prior cases Justices Holmes and Brandeis had dissented because they thought the facts showed the associations properly strove for intelligent competition. When the *Maple Flooring* case came up, shortly after Justice Stone's arrival on the Supreme Court, there was a majority in support of this concerted plan. Justice Stone wrote the majority opinion, summarizing the activities of which the government complained as follows:

The computation and distribution among the association's members of their average cost of all dimensions and grades of flooring; the compilation and distribution among members of a booklet showing freight rates on flooring from Cadillac, Mich., to more than 5,000 points of shipment in the United States; the gathering of statistics supplied at frequent intervals by each member to the association secretary, giving complete information as to the quantity and kind of flooring sold, prices received, and amount of stock on hand, these data being summarized by the secretary and transmitted to the members without revealing the specific sources of the information; meetings at which representatives of the members discussed the industry and exchanged views as to its problems.

Chief Justice Taft and Justice Sanford declared that the evidence brought this case substantially within the rules stated in the earlier decisions. Justice McReynolds, also dissenting, objected to the association's "artful gestures" and observed that "ordinary knowledge of human nature and of the impelling force of greed ought to permit no serious doubt concerning the ultimate outcome of the arrangements".

But Justice Stone pointed out it was neither alleged nor proved that there was any agreement among the members affecting production or maintaining prices, and that the evidence failed to establish uniformity of prices although the defendants conceded the dissemination of the information would tend to bring about uniformity through the operation of economic law. Instead, there was undisputed evidence that the members' prices were fair, reasonable, and usually lower than those of non-members. Justice Stone also wrote:

THE CONTENTION of the government is that there is a combination among the defendants, which is admitted; that the effect of the activities of the defendants carried on under the plan of the association must necessarily be to bring about a concerted effort on the part of members of the association to maintain prices at levels having a close relation to the average cost of flooring reported to members; and that consequently there is a necessary and inevitable restraint of interstate commerce; and that therefore the plan of the association itself is a violation of § 1 of the Sherman Act, which should be enjoined regardless of its actual operation and effect so far as price maintenance is concerned. The case must turn, therefore, on the effect of the activity of the defendants in the gathering and dissemination of information as to the cost of flooring, since, without that, the other activities complained of could have no material bearing on price levels in the industry, and it was to this phase of the case that the oral argument was mainly directed.

Having outlined the substantial issues in the case, it will now be convenient to examine more in detail the several activities of the defendants of which the government complains.

Computation and Distribution, Among the Members, of Information as to the Average Cost of Their Product.

There are three principal elements which enter into the computation of the cost of finished flooring. They are the cost of raw material, manufacturing cost, and the percentage of waste in converting rough lumber into flooring. The information as to the cost of rough lumber was procured by the secretary from reports of actual sales of lumber by members in the open market. From five to ten ascertained sales were taken as standard and the average was taken as the estimated cost of raw material. Manufacturing costs were ascertained by questionnaires sent out to members by which members were requested to give information as to labor costs, cost of warehousing, insurance and taxes, interest at six percent on the value of the plant; selling expense, including commissions and cost of advertising, and depreciation of plant. From the total thus ascertained there was deducted the net profit from wood and other by-products. The net total cost thus ascertained of all members reporting was then averaged.

The percentage of waste in converting the rough lumber into flooring was ascertained by test runs made by selected members of the association under the direction of the secretary of the association, in the course of which a given amount of rough lumber was converted into flooring of different sizes and the actual waste in the process ascertained and stated in terms of percentage. By combining the three elements of cost thus arrived at, the total cost per thousand feet of the aggregate of the different types and grades of flooring produced from a given amount of rough lumber was estimated. To this cost there was at one time added an estimated five percent for contingencies, which practice, however, was discontinued by resolution of the association of July 19, 1923. For the element of manufacturing and marketing cost, the first of these estimates prepared in the manner described was based upon an average of such cost for the first half of 1921. Other successive estimates were prepared on a like basis during the first, third, and fourth quarters of the year 1922.

In order to determine the cost of a given type or grade of flooring it was necessary to distribute the total cost of the aggregate of the different types and grades of finished flooring produced from a given amount of rough lumber among the several types and grades thus produced. This distribution was made by the officials of the association, and the estimated cost thus determined was tabulated and distributed among the members of the association. There is no substantial claim made on the part of the government that the preparation of these estimates of cost was not made with all practicable accuracy, or that they were in any respect not what they purported to be, an estimate of the actual cost of commercial grades of finished flooring fairly ascertained from the actual experience of members of the association, except that the point is made by the government that the distribution of cost among the several types and grades of finished flooring produced from a given amount of rough lumber was necessarily arbitrary and that it might be or become a cover for price fixing. Suffice it to say that neither the government nor the defendants seem to have found it necessary to prove upon what principle of cost accounting this distribution of cost was made, and there are no data from which any inference can be drawn as to whether or not it conformed to accepted practices of cost accounting applied to the manufacture of a diversified product from a single type of raw material.

The Compilation and Distribution Among Members of Information as to Freight Rates

Through the agency of the secretary of the association, a booklet was compiled and distributed to members of the association showing freight rates from Cadillac, Mich., to numerous points throughout the United States to which the finished flooring is shipped by members of the association. It appears from the evidence to have been the usual practice, in the maple flooring trade, to quote flooring at a delivered price and that purchasers of flooring usually will not buy on any other basis. The evidence, however, is undisputed that the defendants quote and sell on an f. o. b. mill basis whenever a purchaser so requests. It also appears that the mills of most of the members of the association are located in small towns in Michigan and Wisconsin and that the average freight rates from these principal producing points in Michigan and Wisconsin, to the principal centers of consumption in the United States, are approximately the same as the freight rate from Cadillac, Mich., to the same centers of consumption.

There is abundant evidence that there were delays in securing quotations of freight rates from the local agents of carriers in towns in which the factories of defendants are located, which seriously interfered with prompt quotations of delivered prices to customers; that the actual aggregate difference between local freight rates for most of the defendants' mills and the rate appearing in defendants' freight rate book based on rates at Cadillac, Mich., were so small as to be only nominal, and that the freight rate book served a useful and legitimate purpose in enabling members to quote promptly a delivered price on their product by adding to their mill price a previously calculated freight rate which approximated closely to the actual rate from their own mill towns.

The government bases its criticism of the use of the freight rate book upon the fact that antecedent associations, maintained by defendants, incorporated in the freight rate book a delivered price which was made up by adding the calculated freight rate from Cadillac, Mich., to a minimum price under the so-called "minimum price plan" of previous associations, whereby the price was fixed at cost plus ten percent of profit. It is conceded that the present association does not include a delivered price in the freight rate book, but it is urged by the government that the circulation of the tables of estimated cost of flooring, together with a freight rate book, enables members of the association to fix a delivered price by adding to the estimated cost circulated among members, the calculated freight rate published in the freight rate book, and that the freight rate book used in conjunction with the published material as to estimated cost is merely a device whereby the defendants have continued the so-called minimum price plan formerly maintained by predecessor associations, which was a plan whereby the members cooperated in the maintenance of a fixed minimum price. Defendants maintain that the minimum price plan was never actually carried out by any predecessor association, and that it was formally abandoned in February or March, 1920, after the failure to secure the approval of the plan by the Federal Trade Commission, and was never revived or continued.

It cannot, we think, be questioned that data as to the average cost of flooring circulated among the members of the association, when combined with a calculated freight rate which is either exactly or approximately the freight rate from the point of shipment, plus an arbitrary percentage of profit, could be made the basis for fixing prices or for an agreement for price maintenance which, if found to exist, would, under the decisions of this Court, constitute a violation of the Sherman Act. But, as we have already said, the record is barren of evidence that the published list of costs and the freight rate book have been so used by the present association. Consequently, the question which this Court must decide is whether the use of this material by members of the association will necessarily have that effect so as to produce that unreasonable restraint of interstate commerce which is condemned by the Sherman Act.

The Gathering and Distributing Among Members of Trade Statistics

It is contended by the government that an analysis of the reporting system adopted by the defendants shows that there is no information withheld by one member from another, and that every member is perfectly familiar not only with the summaries which show the exact market condition generally, but also with the exact condition of the business of each of his fellow members. An examination of the record discloses that this is not an accurate statement of the statistical information distributed among members of the association, certainly not within any recent period of the history of the successive associations. At the time of the filing of the bill, members reported weekly to the secretary of the association on forms showing dates of sales made by the reporting member, the quantity, the thickness and face, the grade, the kind of wood, the delivery, the prices at which sold, the average freight rate to destination, and the rate of commission paid, if any. Members also reported monthly the amount of flooring on hand of each dimension and grade and the amount of unfilled orders. Monthly reports were also required showing the amount of production for each period and the new orders booked for each variety of flooring. The association promptly reported back to the members statistics compiled from the reports of members including the identifying numbers of the mills making the reports, and information as to quantities, grades, prices, freight rates, etc., with respect to each sale. The names of purchasers were not reported, and from and after July 19, 1923, the identifying number of the mill making the report was omitted. All reports of sales and prices dealt exclusively with past and closed transactions.

The statistics gathered by the defendant association are given wide publicity. They are published in trade journals which are read by from ninety to ninety-five percent of the persons who purchase the products of association members. They are sent to the Department of Commerce, which publishes a monthly survey of current business. They are forwarded to the Federal Reserve and other banks and are available to any one at any time desiring to use them.

It is to be noted that the statistics gathered and disseminated do not include current price quotations; information as to employment conditions; geographical distribution of shipments; the names of customers or distribution by classes of purchasers; the details with respect to new orders booked, such as names of customers, geographical origin of orders; or details with respect to unfilled orders, such as names of customers, their geographical location; the names of members having surplus stocks on hand;

the amount of rough lumber on hand; or information as to cancellation of orders. Nor do they differ in any essential respect from trade or business statistics which are freely gathered and publicly disseminated in numerous branches of industry producing a standardized product such as grain, cotton, coal, oil, and involving interstate commerce whose statistics disclose volume and material elements affecting costs of production, sales price, and stock on hand.

Association Meetings

The articles of the defendant association provide for regular meetings for the transaction of business on the third Wednesday of April, July and October of each year, and that special meetings may be called by the president or a majority of the board of trustees. During the year in which the bill of complaint was filed, meetings appear to have been held monthly. Minutes of meetings were kept, although it is not contended that they constituted a complete record of the proceedings. Trade conditions generally, as reflected by the statistical information disseminated among members, were discussed; the market prices of rough maple flooring were also discussed, as were also manufacturing and market conditions. Those members who did not produce rough flooring lumber improved the occasion of the monthly meetings to secure purchases of this commodity from other members.

The testimony is explicit and not denied that following the decision in *United States* v. *American Linseed Oil Co.*, 262 U. S. 371 (June, 1923), there was no discussion of prices in meetings. There was no occasion to discuss past prices, as those were fully detailed in the statistical reports and the association was advised by counsel that future prices were not a proper subject of discussion. It was admitted by several witnesses, however, that upon occasion the trend of prices and future prices became the subject of discussion outside the meeting among individual representatives of the defendants attending the meeting. The government, however, does not charge, nor is it contended, that there was any understanding or agreement, either express or implied, at the meetings or elsewhere, with respect to prices.

Upon this state of the record, the District Court, from whose decision this appeal was taken, held that the plan or system operated by the defendant had a direct and necessary tendency to destroy competition; that the methods employed by them had at all times a controlling influence to impeding the economic laws of supply and demand, and tending to increase prices, and to stifle competition; that the plan of the association was therefore inherently illegal; that in consequence the actual results flowing from such a plan and the execution of it are of secondary importance. The court accordingly decreed the dissolution of the defendants' association and enjoined them from engaging in activities complained of by the government.

In arriving at this result it was admitted that it was impossible to measure, either accurately or even approximately, the effect of the activities of the defendants upon prices, production and competition in the flooring industry, for the reason that there could be, in the nature of things, no satisfactory standards of comparison. The court found no agreement to fix prices and that in fact lower prices have usually been quoted by members than by non-members of the association. In reaching its conclusion, the court relied principally upon the necessary tendency or effect of the plan actually in operation and upon the past history of the association and its predecessors as indicating a probable purpose on the part of the members of the association to use the plan as a medium for effecting actual and undue restraint on interstate commerce, and it is urged here that the history of the successive associations organized by the members of the defendant association, or a majority of them, establishes a systematic purpose on the part of the corporate defendants to restrain interstate commerce.

It is pointed out that the articles of the association of January 1, 1913, embodied the so-called "allotment plan," which provided for an allotted percentage of the aggregate shipments of all members within a given period, to each member, with a provision for the payment of a bonus or allowance to each member which did not make its full allotment or percentage of shipments. This plan was abandoned in March, 1920. On July 1, 1916, the articles of association of that date adopted a minimum price plan which it is claimed continued in effect until about January 1, 1921. This plan contemplated the establishment of a minimum price of maple, beech, and birch flooring by members of the association, such prices to consist of the average cost and expense of manufacturing and selling the product, plus an average profit of ten percent. The plan provided drastic penalties for the sale of flooring at less than the minimum price so established. It is also charged that on January, 1921, the defendants, by agreement, established a minimum price basis for the sale of flooring for the ensuing year. Under this plan the average net profit was reduced from ten to five percent and penalties for noncompliance with the minimum price scale were abolished.

It is conceded, however, that each of these several plans was abandoned and that the present association, both by the terms of its articles of association and in actual practice, has confined itself to the activities which have already been described in some detail.

We think it might be urged, on the basis of this record, that the defendants, by their course of conduct instead of evidencing the purpose of persistent violators of law, had steadily indicated a purpose to keep within the boundaries of legality as rapidly as those boundaries were marked out by the decision of courts interpreting the Sherman Act. Whether, however, their general purpose was to become law-abiding members of the community or law breakers, it is not, we think, very material unless the Court either can infer from this course of conduct a specific and continuing purpose or agreement or understanding on their part to do acts tending to effect an actual restraint of commerce . . . , or unless, on the other hand, it is established that the combination entered into by the defendants in the organization of the defendant association, and its activities as now carried on must necessarily result in such restraint. As already indicated, the record is barren of evidence tending to establish that there is any agreement or purpose or intention on the part of defendants to produce any effect upon commerce other than which would necessarily flow from the activities of the present association, and in our view the government must stand or fall upon its ability to bring the facts of the present case within the rule as laid down in *American Column & Lumber Co.* v. *United States,* 257 U. S. 377, where it was said:

"It has been repeatedly held by this Court that the purpose of the statute is to maintain free competition in interstate commerce and that any concerted action by any combination of men or corporations to cause, or which in fact does cause, direct and undue restraint of competition in such commerce falls within the condemnation of the Act and is unlawful,"

—and within the rule laid down by the Court in *United States* v. *American Linseed Oil Co.*:

"In the absence of a purpose to monopolize or the compulsion that results from contract or agreement, the individual certainly may exercise great freedom; but concerted action through combination presents a wholly different problem and is forbidden when the necessary tendency is to destroy the kind of competition to which the public has long looked for protection."

It should be noted that the bill of complaint neither charges, nor does the government urge, that there was any purpose on the part of the defendants to monopolize commerce in maple, beech, and birch flooring. It is not contended that there was the compulsion of any agreement fixing prices, restraining production or competition, or otherwise restraining interstate commerce. In our view, therefore, the sole question presented by this record for our consideration is whether the combination of the defendants in their existing association as actually conducted by them has a necessary tendency to cause direct and undue restraint of competition in commerce falling within the condemnation of the Act. In urging that such is the necessary effect, the government relies mainly upon the decisions of this Court in *Eastern States Retail Lumber Dealers' Association* v. *United States,* 234 U. S. 600; *American Column & Lumber Co.* v. *United States,* and *United States* v. *American Linseed Oil Co.*

It should be said at the outset that in considering the application of the rule of decision in these cases to the situation presented by this record, it should be remembered that this Court has often announced that each case arising under the Sherman Act must be determined upon the particular facts disclosed by the record, and that the opinions in those cases must be read in the light of their facts and of a clear recognition of the essential differences in the facts of those cases, and in the facts of any new case to which the rule of earlier decisions is to be applied.

In *Eastern States Retail Lumber Dealers' Association* v. *United States* the defendant members of the association had entered into a combination and agreement whereby members were required to report to the association the names of wholesale dealers in lumber who sold their product directly to consumers. The names of the offending wholesalers were placed upon a "black list" which was circulated among the members of the association. The name of a blacklisted wholesaler could be removed from the list only on application to the secretary of the association and on assurance that the offending wholesaler would no longer sell in competition with retailers. It was conceded by the defendants, and the court below found, that the circulation of this information would have a natural tendency to cause retailers receiving these reports to withhold patronage from listed concerns; that it therefore, necessarily, tended to restrain wholesalers from selling to the retail trade, which in itself was an undue and unreasonable restraint of commerce. Moreover, the Court said:

> "This record abounds in instances where the offending dealer was thus reported, the hoped for effect, unless he discontinued the offending practice, realized, and his trade directly and appreciably impaired."

There was thus presented a case in which the Court could not only see that the combination would necessarily result in a restraint on commerce which was unreasonable, but where in fact such restraints had actually been effected by the concerted action of the defendants.

In *American Column & Lumber Co.* v. *United States* the defendant association adopted a plan for the gathering from its members daily, and disseminating among them weekly, reports of all sales and shipments actually made, giving prices, names and addresses of purchasers, the kind, grade, and quantity of commodity sold and shipped. Its plan provided for a monthly production report giving production of members during the previous month; a monthly stock report showing stock on hand on the first day of the month; current price lists, followed by prompt information as to new price quotations as made. Monthly meetings were held at which the extensive interchange of reports was supplemented by further exchange of information as to production, at which active and concerted efforts were made to suppress competition by the restriction of production. The secretary of the association, in communications to members, actively urged curtailment of production and increase of prices. The record disclosed a systematic effort, participated in by the members of the association and led and directed by the secretary of the association, to cut down production and increase prices. The Court not only held that this concerted effort was in itself unlawful, but that it resulted in an actual excessive increase of price to which the Court found the "united action of this large and influential membership of dealers contributed greatly". The opinion of the Court in that case rests squarely on the ground that there was a combination on the part of the members to secure concerted action in curtailment of production and increase of price, which actually resulted in a restraint of commerce, producing increase of price.

In the *United States* v. *American Linseed Oil Co.* defendants entered into an agreement, with provisions for financial forfeitures in event of its violation, for the organization and maintenance of an exchange or bureau whose function it was to gather and distribute information, among the members, as to all price lists covering the product of members. Members agreed, under heavy penalties for violation, to furnish to the bureau a "schedule of prices and terms and adhere thereto—unless more onerous ones were obtained—until prepared to give immediate notice of departure therefrom for relay by the bureau to members". Members were required by the agreement to report by telegraph all variations of prices; the names of prospective buyers; the point of shipment; the exact prices, terms, and discounts; whether sales were made to jobber, or dealer, or consumer; in what quantity; and to report also by telegraph all orders received; to report daily all carload sales of product, giving full details; all such information being treated as confidential and concealed from the buyers. All information received was made available to members through the statistical surveys of the bureau.

It was provided that any subscriber who had offered his product to a prospective buyer, who did not purchase, should have the right to advise the bureau of the unsuccessful offer and to request the bureau to "bulletin" all its subscribers, asking specific information requiring any quotation for sale to such prospective buyer, and to make to subscribers a compilation report of the information secured by such "bulletin." Members were required to give the desired information. Each subscriber was required to furnish the bureau, upon request, information pertaining to any buyer of the product and might request the bureau to secure like information from all other subscribers "whenever it shall have an order or account with or inquiry from the buyer."

The plan as organized was actively carried out by the defendants, and the Court held that the plan as operated by the defendants was a violation of the Sherman Act in that "its necessary tendency was to suppress competition in interstate commerce". It was held that the agreement for price maintenance accompanied by free exchange of price information between competitors as to current prices of the product offered for sale; full details as to purchasers, actual and prospective; and the exchange of information as to buyers and those to whom offerings were made by sellers and of the terms of such offerings, could necessarily have only one purpose and effect, namely to restrain competition among sellers. The Court said:

> "If, looking at the entire contract by which they are bound together, in the light of what has been done under it the Court can see that its necessary tendency is to suppress competition in trade between the states, the combination must be declared unlawful. That such is its tendency, we think, must be affirmed."

It is not, we think, open to question that the dissemination of pertinent information concerning any trade or business tends to stabilize that trade or business and to produce uniformity of price and trade practice. Exchange of price quotations of market commodities tends to produce uniformity of prices in the markets of the world. Knowledge of the supplies of available merchandise tends to prevent overproduction and to avoid the economic disturbances produced by business crises resulting from overproduction. But the natural effect of the acquisition of wider and more scientific knowledge of business conditions, on the minds of the individuals engaged in commerce and its consequent effect in stabilizing production and price, can hardly be deemed a restraint of commerce, or, if so, it cannot, we think, be said to be an unreasonable restraint, or in any respect unlawful.

It is the consensus of opinion of economists and of many of the most important agencies of government that the public interest is served by the gathering and dissemination, in the widest possible manner, of information with respect to the production and distribution, cost and prices in actual sales, of market commodities because the making available of such information tends to stabilize trade and industry, to produce fairer price levels and to avoid the waste which inevitably attends the unintelligent conduct of economic enterprise. "Free competition" means a free and open market among both buyers and sellers for the sale and distribution of commodities. Competition does not become less free merely because the conduct of commercial operations becomes more intelligent through the free distribution of knowledge of all the essential factors entering into the commercial transaction. General knowledge that there is an accumulation of surplus of any market commodity would undoubtedly tend to diminish production, but the dissemination of that information cannot in itself be said to be restraint upon commerce in any legal sense. The manufacturer is free to produce, but prudence and business foresight based on that knowledge influences free choice in favor of more limited production. Restraint upon free competition begins when improper use is made of that information through any concerted action which operates to restrain the freedom of action of those who buy and sell.

It was not the purpose or the intent of the Sherman Anti-Trust Law to inhibit the intelligent conduct of business operations, nor do we conceive that its purpose was to suppress such influences as might affect the operations of interstate commerce through the application to them of the individual intelligence of those engaged in commerce, enlightened by accurate information as to the essential elements of the economics of a trade or business, however gathered or disseminated. Persons who unite in gathering and disseminating information in trade journals and statistical reports on industry, who gather and publish statistics as to the amount of production of commodities in interstate commerce, and who report market prices, are not engaged in unlawful conspiracies in restraint of trade merely because the ultimate result of their efforts may be to stabilize prices or limit production through a better understanding of economic laws and a more general ability to conform to them, for the simple reason that the Sherman Law neither repeals economic laws nor prohibits the gathering and dissemination of information. Sellers of any commodity who guide the daily conduct of their business on the basis of market reports would hardly be deemed to be conspirators engaged in restraint of interstate commerce. They would not be any the more so merely because they became stockholders in a corporation or joint owners of a trade journal, engaged in the business of compiling and publishing such reports.

We do not conceive that the members of trade associations become such conspirators merely because they gather and disseminate information, such as is here complained of, bearing on the business in which they are engaged, and make use of it in the management and control of their individual businesses; nor do we think that the proper application of the principles of decision of *Eastern States Retail Lumber Association* v. *United States,* or *American Column & Lumber Co.* v. *United States,* or *United States* v. *American Linseed Oil Co.,* leads to any such result. The Court held that the defendants in those cases were engaged in conspiracies against interstate trade and commerce because it was found that the character of the information which had been gathered and the use which was made of it led irresistibly to the conclusion that they had resulted, or would necessarily result, in a concerted effort of the defendants to curtail production or raise prices of commodities shipped in interstate commerce. The unlawfulness of the combination arose, not from the fact that the defendants had effected a combination to gather and disseminate information, but from the fact that the Court inferred from the peculiar circumstances of each case that concerted action had resulted or would necessarily result in tending arbitrarily to lessen production or increase prices.

Viewed in this light, can it be said in the present case that the character of the information gathered by the defendants, or the use which is being made of it, leads to any necessary inference that the defendants either have made or will make any different or other use of it than would normally be made if like statistics were published in a trade journal or were published by the Department of Commerce, to which all the gathered statistics are made available? The cost of production, prompt information as to the cost of transportation, are legitimate subjects of inquiry and knowledge in any industry. So likewise is the production of the commodity in that industry, the aggregate surplus stock, and the prices at which the commodity has actually been sold in the usual course of business.

We realize that such information, gathered and disseminated among the members of a trade or business, may be the basis of agreement or concerted action to lessen production arbitrarily or to raise prices beyond the levels of production and price which would prevail if no such agreement or concerted action ensued, and those engaged in commerce were left free to base individual initiative on full information of the essential elements of their business. Such concerted action constitutes a restraint of commerce and is illegal and may be enjoined as may any other combination or activity necessarily resulting in such concerted action as was the subject of consideration in *American Column & Lumber Co.* v. *United States* and *United States* v. *American Linseed Oil Co.* But in the absence of proof of such agreement or concerted action having been actually reached or actually attempted, under the present plan of operation of defendants we can find no basis in the gathering and dissemination of such information by them or in their activities under their present organization for the inference that such concerted action will necessarily result within the rule laid down in those cases.

We decide only that trade associations or combinations of persons or corporations which openly and fairly gather and disseminate information as to the cost of their product, the volume of production, the actual price which the product has brought in past transactions, stocks of merchandise on hand, approximate cost of transportation from the principal point of shipment to the points of consumption as did these defendants and who, as they did, meet and discuss such information and statistics without however reaching or attempting to reach any agreement or any concerted action with respect to prices or production or restraining competition, do not thereby engage in unlawful restraint of commerce.

Maple Flooring Mfrs' Ass'n et al. v. *United States*
268 U. S. 563 *Decided June 1, 1925*

DETERMINING REASONABLENESS OF RESTRAINT

CONFRONTED with a clear case of price-fixing by a trade association, the Court held that the test of an unreasonable restraint of trade was its effect on competition, not the character of the prices.

Here a group of firms controlling eighty-two percent of the business of manufacturing and distributing vitreous pottery for bathrooms and lavatories, and organized as the Sanitary Potters' Association, were indicted for combining to fix uniform prices and limit sales to so-called "legitimate jobbers." The trial judge had charged the jury that it might return a verdict of guilty without regard to the reasonableness of the prices; that the law clearly contemplated such an agreement by a combination controlling a substantial part of an industry as in itself an undue restraint. The judge refused to charge that "the essence of the law is injury to the public" and that not every restraint of trade "works an injury to the public".

After stating the facts, Justice Stone, speaking for the Court, said that the question to be considered was whether the trial judge correctly withdrew from the jury consideration of the reasonableness of the particular restraints charged.

THAT ONLY THOSE RESTRAINTS upon interstate commerce which are unreasonable are prohibited was the rule laid down by the opinions of this Court in the *Standard Oil* and *Tobacco* cases. But it does not follow that agreements to fix or maintain prices are reasonable restraints and therefore permitted by statute, merely because the prices themselves are reasonable.

Reasonableness is not a concept of definite and unchanging content. Its meaning necessarily varies in the different fields of law, because it is used as a convenient summary of the dominant considerations which control in the application of legal doctrines. Our view of what is a reasonable restraint of commerce is controlled by the recognized purpose of the Sherman Law itself. Whether this type of restraint is reasonable or not must be judged in part at least in the light of its effect on competition, for whatever difference of opinion there may be among economists as to the social and economic desirability of an unrestrained competitive system, it cannot be doubted that the Sherman Law and the judicial decisions interpreting it are based upon the assumption that the public interest is best protected from the evils of monopoly and price control by the maintenance of competition....

The aim and result of every price-fixing agreement, if effective, is the elimination of one form of competition. The power to fix prices, whether reasonably exercised or not, involves power to control the market and to fix arbitrary and unreasonable prices. The reasonable price fixed today may through economy and business changes become the unreasonable price of tomorrow. Once established, it may be maintained unchanged because of the absence of competition secured by the agreement for a price reasonable when fixed. Agreements which create such potential power may well be held to be in themselves unreasonable or unlawful restraints, without the necessity of minute inquiry whether a particular price is reasonable or unreasonable as fixed and without placing on the government in enforcing the Sherman Law the burden of ascertaining from day to day whether it has become unreasonable through the mere variation of economic conditions. Moreover, in the absence of express legislation requiring it, we should hesitate to adopt a construction making the difference between legal and illegal conduct in the field of business relations depend upon so uncertain a test as whether prices are reasonable—a determination which can be satisfactorily made only after a complete survey of our economic organization and a choice between rival philosophies.... Thus viewed, the Sherman Law is not only a prohibition against the infliction of a particular type of public injury. It "is a limitation of rights * * * which may be pushed to evil consequences and therefore restrained"....

That such was the view of this Court in deciding the *Standard Oil* and *Tobacco* cases, and that such is the effect of its decisions both before and after those cases, does not seem fairly open to question. Beginning with *United States* v. *Trans-Missouri Freight Rate Ass'n,* 166 U.S. 290; *United States* v. *Joint Traffic Ass'n,* 171 U.S. 505, where agreements for establishing reasonable and uniform freight rates by competing lines of railroad were held unlawful, it has since often been decided and always assumed that uniform price-fixing by those controlling in any substantial manner a trade or business in interstate commerce is prohibited by the Sherman Law, despite the reasonableness of the particular prices agreed upon. In *Addyston Pipe & Steel Co.* v. *United States,* 175 U.S. 211, 237, a case involving a scheme for fixing prices, this Court quoted with approval the following passage from the lower court's opinion:

"* * * the affiants say that, in their opinion, the prices at which pipe has been sold by defendants have been reasonable. We do not think the issue an important one, because, as already stated, we do not think that at common law there is any question of reasonableness open to the courts with reference to such a contract." . . .

In *Swift* v. *United States,* 196 U. S. 375, this Court approved and affirmed a decree which restrained the defendants "by combination, conspiracy or contract [from] raising or lowering prices or fixing uniform prices at which the said meats will be sold, either directly or through their respective agents". In *Dr. Miles Medical Co.* v. *Park & Sons Co.,* 220 U. S. 373, 408, decided at the same term of court as the *Standard Oil* and *Tobacco* cases, contracts fixing reasonable resale prices were declared unenforcible upon the authority of cases involving price-fixing arrangements between competitors.

That the opinions in the *Standard Oil* and *Tobacco* cases were not intended to affect this view of the illegality of price-fixing agreements affirmatively appeared from the opinion of the *Standard Oil* case where, in considering the *Freight Association* case, the Court said:

"That as considering the contracts and agreements, their necessary effect and the character of the parties by whom they were made, they were clearly restraints of trade within the purview of the statute, they could not be taken out of that category by indulging in general reasoning as to the expediency or non-expediency of having made the contracts or the wisdom or want of wisdom of the statute which prohibited their being made. That is to say, the cases but decided that the nature and character of the contracts, creating as they did a conclusive presumption which brought them within the statute, such result was not to be disregarded by the substitution of a judicial appreciation of what the law ought to be for the plain judicial duty of enforcing the law as it was made."

And in *Thompson* v. *Cayser,* 243 U. S. 66, 84, it was specifically pointed out that the *Standard Oil* and *Tobacco* cases did not overrule the earlier cases. The decisions in *Maple Flooring Ass'n* and in *Cement Mfrs.' Protective Ass'n,* 268 U. S. 588, were made on the assumption that any agreement for price-fixing, if found, would have been illegal as a matter of law. In *Federal Trade Commission* v. *Pacific States Paper Trade Ass'n,* 273 U. S. 52, we upheld orders of the Commission forbidding price-fixing and prohibiting the use of agreed price lists by wholesale dealers in interstate commerce, without regard to the reasonableness of the prices.

Cases in both the federal and state courts . . . have generally proceeded on a like assumption, and in the Second Circuit the view maintained below that the reasonableness or unreasonableness of the prices fixed must be submitted to the jury has apparently been abandoned. . . . While not necessarily controlling, the decisions of this Court denying the validity of resale price agreements, regardless of the reasonableness of the price, are persuasive. . . .

Respondents rely upon *Chicago Board of Trade* v. *United States,* 246 U. S. 231, in which an agreement by members of the Chicago Board of Trade controlling prices during certain hours of the day in a special class of grain contracts and affecting only a small proportion of the commerce in question was upheld. The purpose and effect of the agreement there was to maintain for a part of each business day the price which had been that day determined by open competition on the floor of the Exchange. That decision, dealing as it did with a regulation of a board of trade, does not sanction a price agreement among competitors in an open market such as is presented here.

The charge of the trial court, viewed as a whole, fairly submitted to the jury the question whether a price-fixing agreement as described in the first count was entered into by the respondents. Whether the prices actually agreed upon were reasonable or unreasonable was immaterial in the circumstances charged in the indictment and necessarily found by the verdict. The requested charge which we have quoted, and others of similar tenor, while true as abstract propositions, were inapplicable to the case in hand and rightly refused.

[The rest of the opinion, bearing on the questions of venue and admission of evidence, is omitted here.]

United States v. *Trenton Potteries Co. et al.*
273 U. S. 392 *Decided February 21, 1927*

WHAT CONSTITUTES AN UNFAIR METHOD

The Supreme Court was called upon to decide whether the Federal Trade Commission had exceeded its authority in ordering a candy manufacturer to cease and desist from a sales practice which the Commission held to be an "unfair method of competition". The company contended that the method in question did not hinder competition or injure competitors, since they were free to resort to it themselves; that the practice did not tend to create a monopoly or involve deception to consumers, and hence was not an "unfair method" within the meaning of the Federal Trade Commission Act.

The practice pursued by this manufacturer and many others was to sell "break and take" packages of assorted candies, competing with manufacturers of "straight goods" packages in the penny candy trade. The break-and-take assortments involved the element of chance as an inducement to children to buy. These candies were either smaller than those in straight-goods packages (which were sold without the aid of any chance feature) or inferior in quality. After summarizing the Commission's findings, Justice Stone concluded for the unanimous Court that there was no fixed category of unfair methods and that this one was properly condemned:

UPON THE RECORD it is not open to question that the practice complained of is a method of competition in interstate commerce and that it is successful in diverting trade from competitors who do not employ it. If the practice is unfair within the meaning of the Act, it is equally clear that the present proceeding, aimed at suppressing it, is brought, as § 5 of the Act requires, "in the interest of the public". The practice is carried on by forty or more manufacturers. The disposition of a large number of complaints pending before the Commission, similar to that in the present case, awaits the outcome of this suit. Sales of the break-and-take package by respondent aggregate about $234,000 per year.

The proceeding involves more than a mere private controversy. A practice so generally adopted by manufacturers necessarily affects not only competing manufacturers but the far greater number of retailers to whom they sell, and the consumers to whom the retailers sell. Thus the effects of the device are felt throughout the penny candy industry. A practice so widespread and so far-reaching in its consequences is of public concern if in other respects within the purview of the statute. . . . Hence we pass without further discussion to the decisive question whether the practice itself is one over which the Commission is given jurisdiction because it is unfair.

Although the method of competition adopted by the respondent induces children, too young to be capable of exercising an intelligent judgment of the transaction, to purchase an article less desirable in point of quality or quantity than that offered at a comparable price in the straight-goods package, we may take it that it does not involve any fraud or deception. It would seem also that competing manufacturers can adopt the break-and-take device at any time and thus maintain their competitive position.

From these premises respondent argues that the practice is beyond the reach of the Commission because it does not fall within any of the classes which this Court has held subject to the Commission's prohibition. . . . But we cannot say that the Commission's jurisdiction extends only to those types of practices which happen to have been litigated before this Court.

Neither the language nor the history of the Act suggests that Congress intended to confine the forbidden methods to fixed and unyielding categories. The common law afforded a definition of unfair competition and, before the enactment of the Federal Trade Commission Act, the Sherman Anti-Trust Act had laid its inhibition upon combinations to restrain or monopolize interstate commerce which the courts had construed to include restraints upon competition in interstate commerce. It would not have been a difficult feat of draftsmanship to have restricted the operation of the Trade Commission Act to those methods of competition in interstate commerce which are forbidden at common law or which are likely to grow into violations of the Sherman Act, if that had been the purpose of the legislation.

The Act undoubtedly was aimed at all familiar methods of law violation which prosecutions under the Sherman Act had disclosed. . . . But as this Court has pointed out it also had a broader purpose. . . . As proposed by the Senate Committee on Interstate Commerce and as introduced in the Senate, the bill which ultimately became the Federal Trade Commission Act declared "unfair competition" to be unlawful. But it was because the meaning which the common law had given to those words was deemed too narrow that the broader and more flexible phrase "unfair methods of competition" was substituted. Congress, in defining the powers of the Commission, thus advisedly adopted a phrase which, as this Court has said, does not "admit of precise definition, but the meaning and application of which must be arrived at by what this Court elsewhere has called 'the gradual process of judicial inclusion and exclusion.' " . . .

The argument that a method used by one competitor is not unfair if others may adopt it without any restriction of competition was rejected by this Court in *Federal Trade Commission* v. *Winsted Hosiery Co.*, 258 U. S. 483. . . . There it was specifically held that a trader may not, by pursuing a dishonest practice, force his competitors to choose between its adoption or the loss of their trade. A method of competition which casts upon one's competitors the burden of the loss of business unless they will descend to a practice which they are under a powerful moral compulsion not to adopt, even though it is not criminal, was thought to involve the kind of unfairness at which the statute was aimed.

The practice in this case presents the same dilemma to competitors, and we can perceive no reason for distinguishing between the element of chance as employed here and the element of deception involved in labeling cotton goods "Natural Wool", as in the *Winsted* case. It is true that the statute does not authorize regulation which has no purpose other than that of relieving merchants from troublesome competition or of censoring the morals of business men. But here the competitive method is shown to exploit consumers, children, who are unable to protect themselves. It employs a device whereby the amount of the return they receive from the expenditure of money is made to depend on chance. Such devices have met with condemnation throughout the community. Without inquiring whether, as respondent contends, the criminal statutes imposing penalties on gambling, lotteries and the like, fail to reach this particular practice in most or any of the states, it is clear that the practice is of the sort which the common law and criminal statutes have long deemed contrary to public policy. For these reasons a large share of the industry holds out against the device, despite the ensuing loss in trade, or bows reluctantly to what it brands unscrupulous. It would seem a gross perversion of the normal meaning of the word, which is the first criterion of statutory construction, to hold that the method is not "unfair." . . .

While this Court has declared that it is for the courts to determine what practices or methods of competition are to be deemed unfair . . . , in passing on that question the determination of the Commission is of weight. It was created with the avowed purpose of lodging the administrative functions committed to it in "a body specially competent to deal with them by reason of information, experience and careful study of the business and economic conditions of the industry affected," and it was organized in such a manner, with respect to the length and expiration of the terms of office of its members, as would "give to them an opportunity to acquire the expertness in dealing with these special questions concerning industry that comes from experience." . . . If the point were more doubtful than we think it, we should hesitate to reject the conclusion of the Commission, based as it is upon clear, specific and comprehensive findings supported by evidence.

We hold that the Commission correctly concluded that the practice was an unfair method of competition within the meaning of the statute. It is unnecessary to attempt a comprehensive definition of the unfair methods which are banned, even if it were possible to do so. We do not intimate either that the statute does not authorize the prohibition of other and hitherto unknown methods of competition or, on the other hand, that the Commission may prohibit every unethical competitive practice regardless of its particular character or consequences. New or different practices must be considered as they arise in the light of the circumstances in which they are employed.

Federal Trade Commission v. *R. F. Keppel & Bro.*
291 U. S. 304 *Decided February 5, 1934*

ESCAPE FROM A DISSOLUTION ORDER

To effect a merger of two competing manufacturing concerns a holding company was formed which acquired their voting stock in violation of the Clayton Act. After proceedings were begun by the Federal Trade Commission to compel divestment, the holding company was dissolved but the stock was disposed of in such a way as to accomplish a new merger. The Supreme Court held that the Commission lost jurisdiction upon the dissolution of the holding company. Justice Stone, however, maintained that the Commission still had power to prescribe restoration of competition. In a dissenting opinion based on knowledge of corporate practices he reëxamined the device described by Justice Roberts for the majority.

After a preliminary statement Stone said, with the concurrence of Chief Justice Hughes and Justices Brandeis and Cardozo:

IT IS NOW DECLARED that, however gross the violation of the Clayton Act, however flagrant the flouting of the Commission's authority, the celerity of the offender in ridding itself of the stock before the Commission could complete its hearings and make an order restoring the independence of the competitors leaves the Commission powerless to act against the merged corporation. This is the case, it is said, because the Clayton Act does not, in terms, forbid mergers, which may be formed by the stockholders of independent competing corporations; and, since the holding company was not the "sole and efficient agent in the accomplishment of the merger", which was effected upon the consent of the various classes of stockholders of the merged companies, it is concluded that the holding company, by its divestment of the stock, complied with the Clayton Act and in effect did "all the Commission could order", so there is no longer any ground for complaint. Further, notwithstanding the authority broadly conferred on the Commission "to enforce compliance" with § 7 "whenever * * * any person * * * has violated" its provisions, it is said that, as the statute in terms specifies only a single method by which compliance can be compelled—ordering the offender to divest itself of the stock—the Commission can make no other form of order.

Apart from the objection that the decision now reached is calculated to encourage hasty and ill-considered action by the Commission in order to avoid defeat of its jurisdiction by the adroit manipulations of offenders against the Clayton Act, I am unable to construe so narrowly a statute designed, as I think, to prevent just such suppression of competition as this case exemplifies.

1. It is true that the Clayton Act does not forbid corporate

mergers, but it does forbid the acquisition by one corporation of the stock of competing corporations so as substantially to lessen competition. It follows that mergers effected, as they commonly are, through such acquisition of stock, necessarily involve violations of the Act, as this one did. Only in rare instances would there be hope of a successful merger of independently owned corporations by securing the consent of their stockholders in advance of the acquisition of a working stock control of them. Hence the establishment of such control by the purchase or pooling of the voting stock, often effected in secrecy, is the normal first step toward consolidation. It is by this process that most corporate consolidations have been brought about, often by adding one consolidation to another through periods of years. . . . See Bonbright and Means, *The Holding Company,* pages 30, 50.

Unless we are to close our eyes to this open chapter in the record of corporate concentration, an examination of the legislative history of the Clayton Act and that of the earlier Sherman Anti-Trust Act can leave no doubt that the former was aimed at the acquisition of stock by holding companies, not only as itself a means of suppressing competition, but as the first and usual step in the process of merging competing corporations by which a suppression of competition might be unlawfully perpetuated. Thus one of the evils aimed at, the merger of competing corporations through stock control, was reached in its most usual form by forbidding the first step, the acquisition of the stock by a competing corporation, and by conferring on the Trade Commission authority to deal with the violation. It seems plain, therefore, that the illegality involved in acquiring the common stock of the competing companies, which was the first step toward the merger, was neither lessened nor condoned by taking the next and final steps in completing it. There is, then, no basis for contending that the Act has not been violated, or that the violation has been excused simply because events were pushed to the very conclusion that § 7 was designed to forestall.

2. It is also true that the holding company divested itself of the stock of the two competing operating companies before the

Commission had an opportunity to make its order; but it does not follow that it had done all that the Commission could command and that thus the statute was satisfied. Mere divestment of the stock is not enough. The manner of divestment is likewise subject to the requirements of the Clayton Act. This Court has recognized that the purpose of the Act is to restore the competition suppressed by the acquisition of the stock and has specifically held, over objections such as are now made, that the Commission has power not only to order divestment but to prescribe that it shall be done in a manner that will restore competition. . . .

Here the Commission has held that the divestment was not a compliance with the statute. In determining whether it was right in this conclusion, the manner of divestment and the activity of the holding company after the complaint of the Commission was filed and before the final merger of the two operating companies are of crucial significance.

When the complaint was filed, the holding company was in complete control of the two operating companies through ownership of their common stock, which alone had voting power. From the moment of the acquisition of the stock it had been, and it continued to be, a violator of the Clayton Act. Promptly after the complaint was filed it took measures to secure the fruits of its violation. It first proposed by letter to its stockholders a consolidation of the two operating companies, and at a special meeting its board of directors formulated a detailed plan for merger. This plan involved the organization of the two new holding companies, the transfer to them respectively by the first holding company of its respective holdings of the common stock in the two operating companies in exchange for the distribution by the new holding companies of their stock to the stockholders of the first holding company. Thus for each share in the first holding company owned by its stockholders they were to receive one share in each of the new holding companies. The original holding company was then to be dissolved and the four remaining companies, the two new holding companies and the two operating companies, were to be merged.

The plan, from the beginning, contemplated that the four companies should be bound by formal agreement to effect the merger. It was adopted at a specially called meeting of the stockholders of the first holding company and was carried into effect under its active direction and control. Before its dissolution, by exercising that control it had created the two new holding companies, committed all four of its subsidiary corporations to the merger both by their corporate action and by binding agreement, and had secured the approval of its action by its own stockholders. It will be observed that the original holding company did not divest itself of the stock of the two competing operating companies in the only manner by which competition could have been restored—by returning the stock to the respective stockholders of the operating companies, from whom it had been secured, or to their successors. Instead, it continued the suppression of competition by placing the stock of the two operating companies respectively in control of the two new holding companies, tied by contract to effect the merger, and by the method of distributing the stock of the new holding companies equally to its own stockholders it lodged common ownership and control of both the new holding companies in the two groups of stockholders of the original operating companies. The first holding company created the two new ones and throughout guided their policy, as it did that of the two operating companies. Acting in concert and in accord with the prearranged plan, all coöperated in executing it, and all, together with their creature, the merged company, were conscious beneficiaries of the violation of the statute.

By thus manipulating its illegally acquired stock control of the operating companies, the first holding company avoided such a distribution of stock as would have restored competition, and made easy the merger which, if the stock had been returned to those from whom it had originally been acquired, would have been difficult or impossible. Upon these and other facts, which need not now be detailed, the Commission made its finding, abundantly supported by evidence, that the course of action taken by the holding company was not to restore competition between the operating companies, but was "an artifice and subterfuge designed in an attempt to evade the Clayton Act, to perpetuate the elimination of competition", which it had brought about by the acquisition of the stock of the operating companies.

That the stockholders in the successive holding companies, who were the ultimate owners of the operating companies, consented to all this; that two-thirds of the nonvoting preferred stock of the operating companies which had never been lodged in the holding companies consented to it; that the merger might possibly have been effected in some other way, had competitive conditions been restored; all seems without significance. While under local statutes merger could not have been effected without the consent of the preferred stock, equally the consent of the stock acquired through violation of the Clayton Act and its active promotion of the merger were essential to the desired end. A prohibited act is no less illegal because its success involves the coöperation of other actors. It was the suppression of competition by the holding company, through the use which it made of the illegally acquired stock of the operating companies, and its manner of disposing of the stock so as to continue that suppression, which were violations of the Clayton Act and in conflict with the authority of the Commission. This was not any the less so because others consented.

Doubts whether the divestment effected by the first holding company was all that the Commission could have ordered are dissipated by our decision in *Federal Trade Commission* v. *Western Meat Co.*, 272 U. S. 554. There we upheld an order of divestment which directed that in transferring the stock the respondent corporation could not use it to acquire any of the property of the competing corporation, and that none of the stock could be transferred to anyone having any connection with or in any way under the influence of the offending corporation. Here we need not go so far.

3. There remains the question whether the Commission is now powerless to undo a consummation which, at an earlier stage,

it could have prevented. It is said, as a matter of statutory construction, that the grant to the Commission of specific power to command offenders to divest themselves of illegally acquired stock excludes the possibility of its ordering anything more or different, however incidental or necessary it may be to the exercise of the granted power.

It would seem that this point also had been settled by our decision in the *Western Meat Co.* case, where the offending company, through stock ownership, had acquired possession of the property and control of the business of a competitor. It wished to be free to divest itself of the stock without restriction, in order that it might acquire ownership of the competitor's property by transferring the stock to hands that would make merger easy. It was argued to us there, as it is here, that the statute provides only that the Commission may order divestment of the stock; that it does not say that the Commission can command relinquishment of the power, derived from stock ownership, to bring the competitor, or its property, under the control of the offending corporation, either directly or through transfer of the stock into friendly hands. But that argument was rejected, and the order directing divestment of both the property and stock by placing both in the hands of those not under the influence or control of the offender was upheld. This Court said:

> "Further violations of the Act through continued ownership could be effectively prevented only by requiring the owner wholly to divest itself of the stock and thus render possible once more free play of the competition which had been wrongfully suppressed. The purpose which the lawmakers entertained might be wholly defeated if the stock could be further used for securing the competitor's property. And the same result would follow a transfer to one controlled by or acting for the respondent."

No more here, than there, should it be said that the purpose of the statute must be defeated because the lawmakers did not attempt to provide with a meticulous precision how the Commission should proceed in every contingency that might arise. The dominating purpose of the statute is to restore to its original state the competition suppressed by the acquisition of the stock, and, just as we rejected a rigid literalism there in order to effect that purpose, and upheld an order which was but incidental, though necessary, to the effective exercise of the power specifically granted, so we should reject it now. Just as in that case we upheld the Commission's order directing the surrender of one of the fruits of wrongful stock ownership—the power to place a competing unit under the offender's domination—so should we now sustain the order commanding relinquishment of another of the fruits of that ownership—the accomplished merger.

Even if the question were a new one in this Court, no plausible reason has been advanced for interpreting this remedial statute as though it were a penal law. The Clayton Act was designed to prevent abuses growing from deficiencies due to the generality of the Sherman Anti-Trust Act. It sought to accomplish that end by conferring upon the Commission the power to strike at specific practices. In this, as in most schemes for regulation by administrative bodies, there must be a balance between the general and the particular. When the courts are faced with interpretation of the particular, administration breaks down and the manifest purpose of the legislature is defeated unless it is recognized that, surrounding granted powers, there must be a penumbra which will give scope for practical operation. In carrying such schemes into operation, the function of courts is constructive, not destructive, to make them, wherever reasonably possible, effective agencies for law enforcement and not to destroy them.

That the merged corporation is different from the original offender should lead to no different conclusion. It is but the creature and *alter ego* of the offender, created by the offender's exercise of power over the illegally acquired stock for the very purpose of perpetuating the suppression of competition which the Commission from the start had power to forbid. To declare that an offender, whose cause is pending before the Commission, can effect through its creatures and agents what it may not itself do, nullifies the statute.

Some scope may be given to the doctrine of *lis pendens* [control in a pending suit]. It is true that the Commission is an administrative body, and not a court. But it exercises many of the powers conventionally deemed judicial. It is authorized to bring offenders before it to determine whether they are violators of the Act and, if so, "to enforce compliance" by commanding that the violation cease. There is as much reason to believe that Congress did not intend to deny the Commission the authority to exercise effectively the granted power, and thus to preserve its jurisdiction until its function could be executed, as there would be were similar powers extended to a court of inferior jurisdiction. This is the more evident when it is remembered that obedience to the Commission's orders cannot be compelled without first subjecting them to the scrutiny of a court. Recognition of its authority involves neither departure from accepted principles nor any risk of abuse.

These considerations demand our rejection of the contention that an offender against the Clayton Act, properly brought before the Commission and subject to its order, can evade its authority and defeat the statute by taking refuge behind a cleverly erected screen of corporate dummies.

Arrow-Hart & Hegeman Electric Co. v. *Federal Trade Commission, 291 U. S. 587, 599* *Decided March 12, 1934*

LEASING WITH A TYING CLAUSE

A TYING clause in leases of patented machines was held to violate the Clayton Act by suppressing competition, Justice Stone pointing out that the lessor's patent monopoly had no bearing on the question of lawfulness.

The government had brought suit to enjoin the International Business Machines Corporation from leasing its tabulating and other machines upon the condition that the lessees use with these machines only tabulating cards manufactured by this company. Its machines and those of another defendant, Remington Rand, Inc., were subsequently the only ones on the market performing certain mechanical tabulations and computations, without intervening manual operation, by the use of cards bearing recorded data which were the subject of the tabulation and computation.

After minutely describing the devices manufactured by the International, Justice Stone noted the company's contentions: that the condition of its leases was not prohibited by the Clayton Act, that the condition did not tend to create monopoly, that its leases were lawful because the protection secured by the condition did not extend beyond the monopoly which it had acquired by patents on the cards and the machines in which they were used, and that in any case the condition was permissible under § 3 of the Act because its purpose and effect were only to preserve to the company the goodwill of its patrons by preventing the use of unsuitable cards which would interfere with the successful performance of the machines. Justice Stone said:

SECTION 3 of the Clayton Act, so far as it is applicable to the present case, provides that: "It shall be unlawful for any person engaged in commerce, in the course of such commerce, to lease * * * machinery * * * whether patented or unpatented, for use * * * within the United States * * * on the condition * * * that the lessee * * * shall not use * * * supplies or other commodities of a competitor * * * where the effect of such lease * * * or such condition * * * may be to substantially lessen competition or tend to create a monopoly in any line of commerce." The statute thus in precise terms makes unlawful a condition that the lessee shall not use the supplies or commodities of a competitor of the lessor if the effect of the condition "may be" to lessen competition substantially, or if it tends to create a monopoly.

Little need be said of the contention that the condition of appellant's leases does not infringe these prohibitions. It is true that the condition is not in so many words against the use of the cards of a competitor, but is affirmative in form, that the lessee shall use only appellant's cards in the leased machines. But as the lessee can make no use of the cards except with the leased machines, and the specified use of appellant's cards precludes the use of the cards of any competitor, the condition operates in the manner forbidden by the statute. . . . A different question is presented from that in the *Sinclair* case [*Federal Trade Commission* v. *Sinclair Ref. Co.,* 261 U. S. 463, 474], where a wholesale distributor of gasoline leased gasoline pumps to retail dealers with the stipulation that they should not be used for the pumping of gasoline of the lessor's competitors. As the only use made of the gasoline was to sell it, and as there was no restraint upon the purchase and sale of competing gasoline, there was no violation of the Clayton Act.

The conclusion of the trial court that appellant's leases infringe the monopoly provisions of the section does not want for support in the record. The agreed use of the "tying clause" by appellant and its only competitors, and the agreement by each of them to restrict its competition in the sale of cards to the lessees of the others, have operated to prevent competition and to create a monopoly in the production and sale of tabulating cards suitable for appellant's machines, as the District Court found. The commerce in tabulating cards is substantial. Appellant makes and sells 3,000,000,000 cards annually, 81 percent of the total, indicating that the sales by the Remington Rand Company, its only competitor, representing the remaining 19 percent, are approximately 600,000,000. It is stipulated that appellant derives a "substantial" profit from its card sales. The gross receipts from its machines during the past ten years have averaged $9,710,389 a year, and an average of $3,192,700 has been derived annually from the sale of its cards. These facts, and others, which we do not stop to enumerate, can leave no doubt that the effect of the condition in appellant's leases "may be to substantially lessen competition", and that it tends to create a monopoly, and has in fact been an important and effective step in the creation of a monopoly.

On the trial appellant offered to prove its ownership of patents which, it asserts, give it a monopoly of the right to manufacture, use, and vend the cards, separately and in combination with its sorting and tabulating machines, of which, it insists, they are a part. It argues that the condition of its leases is lawful because it does not enlarge the monopoly secured by the patents, and that the trial court erred in refusing to consider appellant's patent monopoly as a defense to the suit.

Appellant's patents appear to extend only to the cards when perforated, and to have no application to those which the lessees purchase before they are punched. The contention is thus reduced to the dubious claim that the sale of the unpunched cards is a contributory infringement of the patents covering the use of perforated cards separately or in combination with the machines. . . .

But we do not place our decision on this narrow ground. We rest it rather on the language of § 3 of the Clayton Act which expressly makes tying clauses unlawful, whether the machine leased is "patented or unpatented". The section does not purport to curtail the patent monopoly of the lessor or to restrict its protection by suit for infringement. But it does in terms deny to the lessor of a patented, as well as of an unpatented machine, the benefit of any condition or agreement that the lessee shall not use the supplies of a competitor. The only purpose or effect of the tying clause, so far as it could be effectively applied to patented articles, is either to prevent the use, by a lessee, of the product of a competitor of the lessor, where the lessor's patent, *prima facie,* embraces that product, and thus avoid judicial review of the patent, or else to compel its examination in every suit brought to set aside the tying clause, although the suit could usually result in no binding adjudication as to the validity of the patent, since infringement would not be in issue. The phrase "whether patented or unpatented" would seem well chosen to foreclose the possibility of either alternative.

When Congress had before it the bill which became § 3 of the Clayton Act, it was familiar with the decision of this Court in *Henry* v. *A. B. Dick Co.,* 224 U. S. 1, and with the contentions made in *United States* v. *United Shoe Machinery Co.,* 247 U. S. 32, 33, then pending before this Court; cases in which it was held that a tying clause could lawfully be extended to unpatented supplies for a leased patented machine. . . . One purpose of § 3 undoubtedly was to prevent such use of the tying clause. . . . But the debates on § 3, on the floor of the Senate, disclose that it was well known to that body that one of the contentions in the pending cause, *United States* v. *United Shoe Machinery Co.*, was that it was permissible, in any circumstances, for a lessor to tie several patented articles together. They show that the proponents of the bill were as much concerned that that practice should be prohibited as that the tying of non-patented to patented articles should be ended. . . . The phrase, "whether patented or unpatented," as used in § 3 is as applicable to the one practice as to the other. It would fail of the purpose which it plainly expresses if it did not operate to preclude the possibility of both, and to make the validity of the tying clause a matter to be determined independently of the protection afforded by any monopoly of the lessor. Such, we think, must be taken to be the effect of the section unless its language and history are to be disregarded. Under its provisions the lawfulness of the tying clause must be ascertained by applying it to the standards prescribed by § 3 as though the leased article and its parts were unpatented.

Despite the plain language of § 3, making unlawful the tying clause when it tends to create a monopoly, appellant insists that it does not forbid tying clauses whose purpose and effect are to protect the goodwill of the lessor in the leased machines, even though monopoly ensues. In support of this contention appellant places great emphasis on the admitted fact that it is essential to the successful performance of the leased machines that the cards used in them conform, with relatively minute tolerances, to specifications as to size, thickness, and freedom from defects which would affect adversely the electrical circuits indispensable to the proper operation of the machines. The point is stressed that failure, even though occasional, to conform to these requirements, causes inaccuracies in the functioning of the machine, serious in their consequences and difficult to trace to their source, with consequent injury to the reputation of the machines and goodwill of the lessors.

There is no contention that others than appellant cannot meet these requirements. It affirmatively appears, by stipulation, that others are capable of manufacturing cards suitable for use in appellant's machines, and that paper required for that purpose may be obtained from the manufacturers who supply appellant. The Remington Rand Company manufactures cards suitable for its own machines, but since it has been barred by agreement with appellant from selling its cards for use in appellant's machines, its cards are not electrically tested. The government, under the provisions of its lease, following its own methods, has made large quantities of the cards, which are in successful use with appellant's machines. The suggestion that without the tying clause an adequate supply of cards would not be forthcoming from competitive sources is not supported by the evidence. "The very existence of such restrictions suggests that in its absence a competing article of equal or better quality would be offered at the same or at a lower price." . . . Appellant's sales of cards return a substantial profit and the government's payment of fifteen percent increase in rental to secure the privilege of making its own cards is profitable only if it produces the cards at a cost less than fifty-five percent of the price charged by appellant.

Appellant is not prevented from proclaiming the virtues of its own cards or warning against the danger of using, in its machines, cards which do not conform to the necessary specifications, or even from making its leases conditional upon the use of cards which conform to them. For aught that appears such measures would protect its goodwill, without the creation of monopoly or resort to the suppression of competition.

The Clayton Act names no exception to its prohibition of monopolistic tying clauses. Even if we are free to make an exception to its unambiguous command . . . , we can perceive no tenable basis for an exception in favor of a condition whose substantial benefit to the lessor is the elimination of business competition and the creation of monopoly, rather than the protection of its goodwill, and where it does not appear that the latter cannot be achieved by methods which do not tend to monopoly and are not otherwise unlawful.

International Business Machines Corp. v. *United States*
298 U. S. 131 *Decided April 27, 1936*

Employer-Obligations to Labor

POWER TO SET MINIMUM WAGES

THE Supreme Court declared a New York minimum-wage law an unconstitutional impairment of freedom of contract, Justice Butler stating for the majority that the statute was essentially the same as the law for the District of Columbia which the Court had condemned in the *Adkins* case thirteen years before. Chief Justice Hughes saw a difference: the earlier law had been based on cost of living, the later one on value of service rendered. Justices Brandeis, Stone and Cardozo concurred in his dissent. But Stone insisted that the *Adkins* decision was never right, and Brandeis and Cardozo joined in his separate dissent. Wage regulation was not forbidden by the Fourteenth Amendment but was "an appropriate corrective for serious social and economic maladjustments." He said:

WHILE I AGREE with all that the Chief Justice has said, I would not make the differences between the present statute and that involved in the *Adkins* case the sole basis of decision. I attach little importance to the fact that the earlier statute was aimed only at a starvation wage and that the present one does not prohibit such a wage unless it is also less than the reasonable value of the service. Since neither statute compels employment at any wage, I do not assume that employers in one case, more than in the other, would pay the minimum wage if the service were worth less.

The vague and general pronouncement of the Fourteenth Amendment against deprivation of liberty without due process of law is a limitation of legislative power, not a formula for its exercise. It does not purport to say in what particular manner that power shall be exerted. It makes no finespun distinctions between methods which the legislature may and which it may not choose to solve a pressing problem of government. It is plain, too, that, unless the language of the amendment and the decisions of this Court are to be ignored, the liberty which the amendment protects is not freedom from restraint of all law or of any law which reasonable men may think an appropriate means for dealing with any of those matters of public concern with which it is the business of government to deal. There is a grim irony in speaking of the freedom of contract of those who, because of their economic necessities, give their service for less than is needful to keep body and soul together. But if this is freedom of contract no one has ever denied that it is freedom which may be restrained, notwithstanding the Fourteenth Amendment, by a statute passed in the public interest.

In many cases this Court has sustained the power of legislatures to prohibit or restrict the terms of a contract, including the price term, in order to accomplish what the legislative body may reasonably consider a public purpose. They include cases, which have neither been overruled nor discredited, in which the sole basis of regulation was the fact that circumstances, beyond the control of the parties, had so seriously curtailed the regulative power of competition as to place buyers or sellers at a disadvantage in the bargaining struggle, such that a legislature might reasonably have contemplated serious consequences to the community as a whole and have sought to avoid them by regulation of the terms of the contract. . . .

No one doubts that the presence in the community of a large number of those compelled by economic necessity to accept a wage less than is needful for subsistence is a matter of grave public concern, the more so when, as has been demonstrated here, it tends to produce ill health, immorality and deterioration of the race. The fact that at one time or another Congress and the legislatures of seventeen states, and the legislative bodies of twenty-one foreign countries, including Great Britain and its four commonwealths, have found that wage regulation is an appropriate corrective for serious social and economic maladjustments growing out of inequality in bargaining power, precludes, for me, any assumption that it is a remedy beyond the bounds of reason. It is difficult to imagine any grounds, other than our own personal economic predilections, for saying that the contract of employment is any the less an appropriate subject of legislation than are scores of others, in dealing with which this Court has held that legislatures may curtail individual freedom in the public interest.

If it is a subject upon which there is power to legislate at all, the Fourteenth Amendment makes no distinction between the methods by which legislatures may deal with it, any more than it proscribes the regulation of one term of a bargain more than another if it is properly the subject of regulation. No one has yet attempted to say upon what basis of history, principles of government, law or logic, it is within due process to regulate the hours and conditions of labor of women . . . and of men . . . and the time and manner of payment of the wage . . . , but that regulation of the amount of the wage passes beyond the constitutional limitation; or to say upon what theory the amount of a wage is any the less the subject of regulation in the public interest than that of insurance premiums . . . , or of the commissions of insurance brokers . . . , or of the charges of grain elevators . . . , or of the price which the farmer receives for his milk, or which the wage earner pays for it.

These considerations were developed at length in *Tyson* v. *Banton* and in *Ribnik* v. *McBride* [pp. 197, 202, this volume] and need not be further elaborated now. It is true that the Court rejected them there, but it later accepted and applied them as the basis of decision in *Nebbia* v. *New York,* 291 U. S. 502 [and other cases cited]. Both precedent and, what is more important, reason, require their acceptance now. See *Burnet* v. *Coronado Oil and Gas Co.* [page 176, this volume]. In upholding state minimum-price regulation in the milk industry [in the *Nebbia* case] the Court declared:

> "So far as the requirement of due process is concerned, and in the absence of other constitutional restriction, a state is free to adopt whatever economic policy may reasonably be deemed to promote public welfare, and to enforce that policy by legislation adapted to its purpose. The courts are without authority either to declare such policy, or, when it is declared by the legislature, to override it. If the laws passed are seen to have a reasonable relation to a proper legislative purpose, and are neither arbitrary nor discriminatory, the requirements of due process are satisfied, and judicial determination to that effect renders a court *functus officio.*"

That declaration and decision should control the present case. They are irreconcilable with the decision and most that was said in the *Adkins* case. They have left the Court free of its restriction as a precedent, and free to declare that the choice of the particular form of regulation by which grave economic maladjustments are to be remedied is for legislatures and not for the courts.

In the years which have intervened since the *Adkins* case we have had opportunity to learn that a wage is not always the resultant of free bargaining between employers and employees; that it may be one forced upon employees by their economic necessities and upon the employers by the most ruthless of their competitors. We have had opportunity to perceive more clearly that a wage insufficient to support the worker does not visit its consequences upon him alone; that it may affect profoundly the entire economic structure of society and, in any case, that it casts on every taxpayer, and on government itself, the burden of solving the problems of poverty, subsistence, health and morals of large numbers in the community. Because of their nature and extent these are public problems. A generation ago they were for the individual to solve; today they are the burden of the nation. I can perceive no more objection, on constitutional grounds, to their solution by requiring an industry to bear the subsistence cost of the labor which it employs, than to the imposition upon it of the cost of industrial accidents. . . .

It is not for the courts to resolve doubts whether the remedy by wage regulation is as efficacious as many believe, or is better than some other, or is better even than the blind operation of uncontrolled economic forces. The legislature must be free to choose unless government is to be rendered impotent. The Fourteenth Amendment has no more embedded in the Constitution our preference for some particular set of economic beliefs than it has adopted, in the name of liberty, the system of theology which we may happen to approve.

I know of no rule or practice by which the arguments advanced in support of an application for *certiorari* restrict our choice between conflicting precedents in deciding a question of constitutional law which the petition, if granted, requires us to answer. Here the question which the petition specifically presents is whether the New York statute contravenes the Fourteenth Amendment. In addition, the petition assigns as a reason for granting it that "the construction and application of the Constitution of the United States and a prior decision" of this Court "are necessarily involved", and again, that "the circumstances prevailing under which the New York law was enacted call for a reconsideration of the *Adkins* case in the light of the New York act and conditions aimed to be remedied thereby". Unless we are now to construe and apply the Fourteenth Amendment without regard to our decisions since the *Adkins* case, we could not rightly avoid its reconsideration even if it were not asked. We should follow our decision in the *Nebbia* case and leave the selection and the method of the solution of the problems to which the statute is addressed where it seems to me the Constitution has left them, to the legislative branch of the government.

Morehead v. *New York ex rel. Tipaldo*
298 U. S. 587, 631 Decided June 1, 1936

[In 1937 the dissenting view prevailed. The minimum-wage law of the State of Washington was validated in *West Coast Hotel* v. *Parrish,* 300 U. S. 379, and the *Adkins* case was expressly overruled.]

USING A COMPANY UNION

SHOP CRAFT workers of an interstate rail carrier formed a union which was certified by the National Mediation Board, under the Railway Labor Act, as the duly accredited representative of the railroad's mechanical department employees. The railroad refused to treat with this union; instead it sought to induce its workers against affiliating with any labor group other than the association of workers which the railroad itself maintained.

The railroad contended that it was not legally bound to negotiate with the certified representative; that its "back shop" employees were engaged solely in intrastate commerce, and that the trial court's decree restraining it from making an agreement with any other labor organization was a denial of due process.

Justice Stone spoke for a unanimous Court. After giving the background of the controversy he took up the petitioning railroad's contentions, told how Congress tried to avoid labor strife, and demonstrated why the provisions of the Railway Labor Act were valid and applicable. He added:

FIRST. *The Obligation Imposed by the Statute.* By Title III of the Transportation Act of February 28, 1920, . . . Congress set up the Railroad Labor Board as a means for the peaceful settlement, by agreement or by arbitration, of labor controversies between interstate carriers and their employees. It sought "to encourage settlement without strikes, first by conference between the parties; failing that, by reference to adjustment boards of the parties' own choosing, and if this is ineffective, by a full hearing before a National Board * * *". . . The decisions of the Board were supported by no legal sanctions. The disputants were not "in any way to be forced into compliance with the statute or with the judgments pronounced by the Labor

Board except through the effect of adverse public opinion". . . .

In 1926 Congress, aware of the impotence of the Board, and of the fact that its authority was generally not recognized or respected by the railroads or their employees, made a fresh start toward the peaceful settlement of labor disputes affecting railroads, by the repeal of the 1920 Act and the adoption of the Railway Labor Act. . . . By the new measure Congress continued its policy of encouraging the amiable adjustment of labor disputes by their voluntary submission to arbitration before an impartial board, but it supported that policy by the imposition of legal obligations. It provided means for enforcing the award obtained by arbitration between the parties to labor disputes. (§ 9.) In certain circumstances it prohibited any change in conditions, by the parties to an unadjusted labor dispute, for a period of thirty days, except by agreement. (§ 10.) It recognized their right to designate representatives for the purpose of the Act "without interference, influence or coercion exercised by either party over the self-organization or designation of representatives by the other." (§ 2, Third.)

Under the last-mentioned provision this Court held, in *Texas & N. O. R. Co.* v. *Brotherhood of Railway & S. S. Clerks,* 281 U. S. 548, that employees were free to organize and to make choice of their representatives without the "coercive interference" and "pressure" of a company union organized and maintained by the employer; and that the statute protected the freedom of choice of representatives, which was an essential of the statutory scheme, with a legal sanction which it was the duty of courts to enforce by appropriate decree.

The prohibition against such interference was continued and made more explicit by the amendment of 1934. Petitioner does not challenge that part of the decree which enjoins any interference by it with the free choice of representatives by its employees, and the fostering, in the circumstances of this case, of the company union. That contention is not open to it in view of our decision in the *Railway Clerks* case, *supra,* and of the unambiguous language of § 2, Third, and Fourth, of the Act, as amended.

But petitioner insists that the statute affords no legal sanction for so much of the decree as directs petitioner to "treat with" respondent Federation "and exert every reasonable effort to make and maintain agreements concerning rates of pay, rules and working conditions, and to settle all disputes whether arising out of the application of such agreements or otherwise". It points out that the requirement for reasonable effort to reach an agreement is couched in the very words of § 2, First, which were taken from § 301 of the Transportation Act, and which were held to be without legal sanction in that Act. . . . It is argued that they cannot now be given greater force as reënacted in the Railway Labor Act of 1926, and continued in the 1934 amendment. But these words no longer stand alone and unaided by mandatory provision of the statute as they did when first enacted. The amendment of the Railway Labor Act added new provisions in § 2, Ninth, which make it the duty of the Mediation Board, when any dispute arises among the carrier's employees, "as to who are the representatives of such employees," to investigate the dispute and to certify, as was done in this case, the name of the organization authorized to represent the employees. It commands that "Upon receipt of such certification the carrier shall treat with the representative so certified as the representative of the craft or class for the purposes of this Act."

It is, we think, not open to doubt that Congress intended that this requirement be mandatory upon the railroad employer, and that its command, in a proper case, be enforced by the courts. The policy of the Transportation Act of encouraging voluntary adjustment of labor disputes, made manifest by those provisions of the Act which clearly contemplated the moral force of public opinion as affording its ultimate sanction, was, as we have seen, abandoned by the enactment of the Railway Labor Act. Neither the purposes of the later Act, as amended, nor its provisions when read, as they must be, in the light of our decision in the *Railway Clerks* case, lend support to the contention that its enactments, which are mandatory in form and capable of enforcement by judicial process, were intended to be without legal sanction.

Experience had shown, before the amendment of 1934, that when there was no dispute as to the organizations authorized to represent the employees, and when there was willingness of the employer to meet such representative for a discussion of their grievances, amicable adjustment of differences had generally followed and strikes had been avoided. On the other hand, a prolific source of dispute had been the maintenance by the railroads of company unions and the denial by railway management of the authority of representatives chosen by their employees. . . . Section 2, Ninth, of the amended Act, was specifically aimed at this practice. It provided a means for ascertaining who are the authorized representatives of the employees through intervention and certification by the Mediation Board, and commanded the carrier to treat with the representative so certified. That the command was limited in its application to the case of intervention and certification by the Mediation Board indicates not that its words are precatory, but only that Congress hit at the evil "where experience shows it to be most felt". . . .

Petitioner argues that the phrase "treat with" must be taken as the equivalent of "treat" in its intransitive sense, as meaning "regard" or "act towards", so that compliance with its mandate requires the employer to meet the authorized representative of the employees only if and when he shall elect to negotiate with them. This suggestion disregards the words of the section, and ignores the plain purpose made manifest throughout the numerous provisions of the Act. Its major objective is the avoidance of industrial strife, by conference between the authorized representatives of employer and employee. The command to the employer to "treat with" the authorized representative of the employees adds nothing to the 1926 Act, unless it requires some affirmative act on the part of the employer. . . . As we cannot assume that its addition to the statute was purposeless, we must take its meaning to be that which the words suggest, which alone would add something to the statute as it was before amendment, and which alone would tend to effect the purpose of the legislation. The statute does not undertake to compel agreement between the employer and employees, but it does command those preliminary steps without which no agreement can be reached. It at least requires the employer to meet and confer with the authorized representative of its employees, to listen to their complaints, to make reasonable effort to compose differences—in short, to enter into a negotiation for the settlement of labor disputes such as is contemplated by § 2, First.

Petitioner's insistence that the statute does not warrant so much of the decree as forbids it to enter into contracts of employment with its individual employees is based upon a misconstruction of the decree. Both the statute and the decree are aimed at securing settlement of labor disputes by inducing collective bargaining with the true representative of the employees and by preventing such bargaining with any who do not represent them. The obligation imposed on the employer by § 2, Ninth, to treat with the true representative of the employees as designated by the Mediation Board, when read in the light of the declared purposes of the Act, and of the provisions of § 2, Third and Fourth, giving to the employees the right to organize and bargain collectively through the representative of their own selection, is exclusive. It imposes the affirmative duty to treat only with the true representative, and hence the negative duty to treat with no other.

We think, as the Government concedes in its brief, that the injunction against the petitioner's entering into any contract concerning rules, rates of pay and working conditions, except with respondent, is designed only to prevent collective bargaining with anyone purporting to represent employees, other than respondent, who has been ascertained to be their true representative. When read in its context it must be taken to prohibit the negotiation of labor contracts, generally applicable to employees in the mechanical department, with any representative other than respondent, but not as precluding such individual contracts as petitioner may elect to make directly with individual employees. The decree, thus construed, conforms, in both its affirmative and negative aspects, to the requirements of § 2.

Propriety of Relief in Equity. Petitioner contends that if the statute is interpreted as requiring the employer to negotiate with the representative of his employees, its obligation is not the appropriate subject of a decree in equity; that negotiation depends on desires and mental attitudes which are beyond judicial control, and that since equity cannot compel the parties to agree, it will not compel them to take the preliminary steps which may result in agreement.

There is no want of capacity in the court to direct complete performance of the entire obligation: both the negative duties not to maintain a company union and not to negotiate with any representative of the employees other than respondent and the affirmative duty to treat with respondent. Full performance of both is commanded by the decree in terms which leave in no uncertainty the requisites of performance. In compelling compliance with either duty it does far less than has been done in compelling the discharge of a contractual or statutory obligation calling for a construction or engineering enterprise . . . or in granting specific performance of a contract for the joint use of a railroad bridge and terminals. . . . Whether an obligation has been discharged, and whether action taken or omitted is in good faith or reasonable, are everyday subjects of inquiry by courts in framing and enforcing their decrees.

It is true that a court of equity may refuse to give any relief when it is apparent that that which it can give will not be effective or of benefit to the plaintiff. Equity will not decree the execution of a partnership agreement since it cannot compel the parties to remain partners . . . or compel one to enter into performance of a contract of personal service which it cannot adequately control. . . . But the extent to which equity will go to give relief where there is no adequate remedy at law is not a matter of fixed rule.

It rests rather in the sound discretion of the court. . . . Whether the decree will prove so useless as to lead a court to refuse to give it, is a matter of judgment to be exercised with reference to the special circumstances of each case rather than to general rules which at most are but guides to the exercise of discretion. It is a familiar rule that a court may exercise its equity powers, or equivalent *mandamus* powers . . . to compel courts, boards, or officers to act in a matter with respect to which they may have jurisdiction or authority, although the court will not assume to control or guide the exercise of their authority. . . .

In considering the propriety of the equitable relief granted here, we cannot ignore the judgment of Congress, deliberately expressed in legislation, that where the obstruction of the company union is removed, the meeting of employers and employees at the conference table is a powerful aid to industrial peace. Moreover, the resources of the Railway Labor Act are not exhausted if negotiation fails in the first instance to result in agreement. If disputes concerning changes in rates of pay, rules or working conditions, are "not adjusted by the parties in conference," either party may invoke the mediation services of the Mediation Board (§ 5, First) or the parties may agree to seek the benefits of the arbitration provision of § 7. With the coercive influence of the company union ended, and in view of the interest of both parties in avoiding a strike, we cannot assume that negotiation, as required by the decree, will not result in agreement, or lead to successful mediation or arbitration, or that the attempt to secure one or another through the relief which the district court gave is not worth the effort.

More is involved than the settlement of a private controversy without appreciable consequences to the public. The peaceable settlement of labor controversies, especially where they may seriously impair the ability of an interstate rail carrier to perform its service to the public, is a matter of public concern. That is testified to by the history of the legislation now before us, the reports of committees of Congress having the proposed legislation in charge, and by our common knowledge. Courts of equity may, and frequently do, go much farther both to give and withhold relief in furtherance of the public interest than they are accustomed to go when only private interests are involved. . . . The fact that Congress has indicated its purpose to make negotiation obligatory is in itself a declaration of public interest and policy which should be persuasive in inducing courts to give relief. It is for similar reasons that courts, which traditionally have refused to compel performance of a contract to arbitration, . . . enforce statutes commanding performance of arbitration agreements. . . .

The decree is authorized by the statute and was granted in an appropriate exercise of the equity powers of the court.

SECOND. *Constitutionality of § 2 of the Railway Labor Act. (A) Validity Under the Commerce Clause.* The power of Congress over interstate commerce extends to such regulations of the relations of rail carriers to their employers as are reasonably calculated to prevent the interruption of interstate commerce by strikes and their attendant disorders. . . . The Railway Labor Act (§ 2) declares that its purposes, among others, are "To avoid any interruption to commerce or to the operation of any carrier engaged therein," and "to provide for the prompt and orderly settlement of all disputes concerning rates of pay, rules or working conditions". The provisions of the Act and its history, to which reference has been made, establish that such are its purposes, and that the latter is in aid of the former. What has been said indicates clearly that its provisions are aimed at the settlement of industrial disputes by the promotion of collective bargaining between employers and the authorized representative of their employees, and by mediation and arbitration when such bargaining does not result in agreement. It was for Congress to make the choice of the means by which its objective of securing the uninterrupted service of interstate railroads was to be secured, and its judgment, supported as it is by our long experience with industrial disputes, and the history of railroad labor relations, to which we have referred, is not open to review here. The means chosen are appropriate to the end sought and hence are within the congressional power. . . .

But petitioner insists that the Act as applied to its "back shop" employees is not within the commerce power since their duties have no direct relationship to interstate transportation. Of the 824 employees in the six shop crafts eligible to vote for a choice of representatives, 322 work in petitioner's "back shops" at Princeton, West Virginia. They are there engaged in making classified repairs, which consist of heavy repairs on locomotives and cars withdrawn from service for that purpose for long periods (an average of 105 days for locomotives and 109 days for cars). The repair work is upon the equipment used by petitioner in its transportation service, 97% of which is interstate. At times a continuous stream of engines and cars passes through the "back shops" for such repairs. When not engaged in repair work, the back shop employees perform "store order work", the manufacture of material such as rivets and repair parts, to be placed in railroad stores for use at the Princeton shop and other points on the line.

The activities in which these employees are engaged have such a relation to the other confessedly interstate activities of the petitioner that they are to be regarded as a part of them. All taken together fall within the power of Congress over interstate commerce. . . . Both courts below have found that interruption by strikes of the back shop employees, if more than temporary, would seriously cripple petitioner's interstate transportation. The relation of the back shop to transportation is such that a strike of petitioner's employees there, quite apart from the likelihood of its spreading to the operating department, would subject petitioner to the danger, substantial, though possibly indefinable in its extent, of interruption of the transportation service. The cause is not remote from the effect. The relation between them is not tenuous. The effect on commerce cannot be regarded as negligible. See [case cited], holding participation of back shop employees in the nation-wide railroad shopmen's strike of 1922 to constitute an interference with interstate commerce. As the regulation here in question is shown to be an appropriate means of avoiding that danger, it is within the power of Congress.

It is no answer, as petitioner suggests, that it could close its back shops and turn over the repair work to independent contractors. Whether the railroad should do its repair work in its own shops, or in those of another, is a question of railroad management. It is petitioner's determination to make its own repairs which has brought its relations with shop employees within the purview of the Railway Labor Act. It is the nature of the work done and its relation to interstate transportation which afford adequate basis for the exercise of the regulatory power of Congress.

The *Employers' Liability Cases,* 207 U. S. 463, 498, which mentioned railroad repair shops as a subject beyond the power to regulate commerce, are not controlling here. Whatever else may be said of that pronouncement, it is obvious that the commerce power is as much dependent upon the type of regulation as its subject matter. It is enough for present purposes that experience has shown that the failure to settle, by peaceful means, the grievances of railroad employees with respect to rates of pay, rules or working conditions, is far more likely to hinder interstate commerce than the failure to compensate workers who have suffered injury in the course of their employment.

(B) Validity of § 2 of the Railway Labor Act Under the Fifth Amendment. The provisions of the Railway Labor Act applied in this case, as construed by the court below, and as we construe them, do not require petitioner to enter into any agreement with its employees, and they do not prohibit its entering into such contract of employment as it chooses, with its individual employees. They prohibit only such use of the company union as, despite the objections repeated here, was enjoined in the *Railway Clerks* case, and they impose on petitioner only the affirmative duty of "treating with" the authorized representatives of its employees for the purpose of negotiating a labor dispute.

Even though Congress, in the choice of means to effect a permissible regulation of commerce, must conform to due process

. . . , it is evident that where, as here, the means chosen are appropriate to the permissible end, there is little scope for the operation of the due process clause. The railroad can complain only of the infringement of its own constitutional immunity, not that of its employees. . . . And the Fifth Amendment, like the Fourteenth—see *West Coast Hotel Co.* v. *Parrish,* 300 U. S. 379, decided this day [sustaining state minimum-wage legislation]—is not a guaranty of untrammeled freedom of action and of contract. In the exercise of its power to regulate commerce, Congress can subject both to restraints not shown to be unreasonable. Such are the restraints of the safety appliance act . . . , of the act imposing a wage scale on rail carriers . . . , of the Railroad Employers' Liability Act . . . , of the act fixing maximum hours of service for railroad employees whose duties control or affect the movement of trains . . . , of the act prohibiting the prepayment of seamen's wages. . . .

Each of the limited duties imposed upon petitioner by the statute and the decree do not differ in their purpose and nature from those imposed under the earlier statute and enforced in the *Railway Clerks* case. The quality of the action compelled, its reasonableness, and therefore the lawfulness of the compulsion, must be judged in the light of the conditions which have occasioned the exercise of governmental power. If the compulsory settlement of some differences, by arbitration, may be within the limits of due process . . . , it seems plain that the command of the statute to negotiate for the settlement of labor disputes, given in the appropriate exercise of the commerce power, cannot be said to be so arbitrary or unreasonable as to infringe due process.

Adair v. *United States,* 208 U. S. 161, and *Coppage* v. *Kansas,* 236 U. S. 1, have no present application. The provisions of the Railway Labor Act invoked here neither compel the employer to enter into any agreement, nor preclude it from entering into any contract with individual employees. They do not "interfere with the normal exercise of the right of the carrier to select its employees or to discharge them". . . .

There remain to be considered petitioner's contentions that

the certificate of the National Mediation Board is invalid and that the injunction granted is prohibited by the provisions of the Norris-LaGuardia Act, of March 23, 1932. . . .

Validity of the Certificate of the National Mediation Board. In each craft of petitioner's mechanical department a majority of those voting cast ballots for the Federation. In the case of the blacksmiths the Federation failed to receive a majority of the ballots of those eligible to vote, although a majority of the craft participated in the election. In the case of the carmen and coach cleaners, a majority of the employees eligible to vote did not participate in the election. There has been no appeal from the ruling of the district court that the designation of the Federation as the representative of the carmen and coach cleaners was invalid. Petitioner assails the certifications of the Federation as the representative of the blacksmiths because less than a majority of that craft, although a majority of those voting, voted for the Federation.

Section 2, Fourth, of the Railway Labor Act provides: "The majority of any craft or class of employees shall have the right to determine who shall be the representative of the craft or class for the purposes of this Act." Petitioner construes this section as requiring that a representative be selected by the votes of a majority of eligible voters. It is to be noted that the words of the section confer the right of determination upon a majority of those eligible to vote, but is silent as to the manner in which that right shall be exercised. Election laws providing for approval of a proposal by a specified majority of an electorate have been generally construed as requiring only the consent of the specified majority of those participating in the election. . . . Those who do not participate "are presumed to assent to the expressed will of the majority of those voting". . . .

We see no reason for supposing that § 2, Fourth, was intended to adopt a different rule. If, in addition to participation by a majority of a craft, a vote of the majority of those eligible is necessary for a choice, an indifferent minority could prevent the resolution of a contest, and thwart the purpose of the Act, which is dependent for its operation upon the selection of representatives. There is the added danger that the absence of eligible voters may be due less to their indifference than to coercion by the employer. The opinion of the trial court discloses that the Mediation Board scheduled an election to be determined by a majority of the eligible voters, but that the Federation's subsequent protest that the Railway was influencing the men not to vote caused the Board to hold a new election to be decided by the ballots of a majority of those voting.

It is significant of the congressional intent that the language of § 2, Fourth, was taken from a rule announced by the United States Railroad Labor Board, acting under the labor provisions of the Transportation Act of 1920. . . . Prior to the adoption of the Railway Labor Act, this rule was interpreted by the Board . . . , where it appeared that a majority of the craft participated in the election. The Board ruled that a majority of the votes cast was sufficient to designate a representative. A like interpretation of § 2, Fourth, was sustained in [case cited].

The petitioner also challenges the validity of the certificate of the National Mediation Board in this case because it fails to state the number of eligible voters in each craft or class. The certificate states that respondent "has been duly designated and authorized to represent the mechanical department employees" of petitioner. It also shows on its face the total number of votes cast in each craft in favor of each candidate, but omits to state the total number of eligible voters in each craft. Petitioner insists that this is a fatal defect in the certificate, upon the basis of those cases which hold that where a finding of fact of an administrative officer or tribunal is prerequisite to the making of a rule or order, the finding must be explicitly set out. . . .

The practice contended for is undoubtedly desirable, but it is not required by the present statute or by the authorities upon which petitioner relies. The National Mediation Board makes no order. The command which the decree of the court enforces is that of the statute, not of the Board. Its certificate that the Federation is the authorized representative of the employees is the ultimate finding of fact prerequisite to enforcement by the courts of the command of the statute. There is no contention that this finding is conclusive in the absence of a finding of the basic facts on which it rests—that is to say, the number of eligible voters, the number participating in the election and the choice of the majority of those who participate. Whether the certification, if made as to those facts, is conclusive, it is unnecessary now to determine. But we think it plain that if the Board omits to certify any of them, the omitted fact is open to inquiry by the court asked to enforce the command of the statute. . . . Such inquiry was made by the trial court which found the number of eligible voters and thus established the correctness of the Board's ultimate conclusion. The certificate, which conformed to the statutory requirement, was *prima facie* sufficient, and was not shown to be invalid for want of the requisite supporting facts.

Validity of the Injunction Under the Norris-LaGuardia Act. Petitioner assails the decree for its failure to conform to the requirements of § 9 of the Norris-LaGuardia Act, which provides: "every restraining order or injunction granted in a case involving or growing out of a labor dispute shall include only a prohibition of such specific act or actions as may be expressly complained of in the bill of complaint or petition filed in such case and as shall be expressly included in . . . findings of fact made and filed by the court". The evident purpose of this section, as its history and context show, was not to preclude mandatory injunctions, but to forbid blanket injunctions against labor unions, which are usually prohibitory in form, and to confine the injunction to the particular acts complained of and found by the court. We deem it unnecessary to comment on other similar objections, except to say that they are based on strained and unnatural constructions of the words of the Norris-LaGuardia Act, and conflict with its declared purpose (§ 2) that the employee "shall be free from interference, restraint, or coercion of employers of labor, or their agents, in the designation of such representatives or in self-organization or in other concerted activities for the purpose of collective bargaining or other mutual aid or protection".

It suffices to say that the Norris-LaGuardia Act can affect the present decree only so far as its provisions are found to conflict with those of § 2, Ninth, of the Railway Labor Act, authorizing the relief which has been granted. Such provisions cannot be rendered nugatory by the earlier and more general provisions of the Norris-LaGuardia Act. . . .

The Virginian Railway Co. v. *System Federation No. 40, Railway Employees Department of American Federation of Labor, 300 U. S. 515* *Decided March 29, 1937*

STATE SOCIAL SECURITY

THE SAME day that the Court upheld the constitutionality of the Federal Social Security Act it sustained the Alabama Unemployment Compensation Act, passed in conformity with the federal statute. Justice Sutherland voiced the dissenters' objection that the Alabama law was "so arbitrary as to result in a denial both of due process and equal protection of the laws". They particularly found fault with the method of pooling employer-contributions in a common fund from which unemployment benefits were paid. For the majority Justice Stone declared it was the legislature's function to choose the means to the legitimate objective of relief, and he showed that the means which it selected was reasonable and valid.

First, Justice Stone described the Alabama law, which required employers of eight or more employees for twenty or more weeks in the year to pay a certain percentage of their total monthly payrolls into the state Unemployment Compensation Fund. The fund was to be deposited in the Unemployment Trust Fund of the United States Government and requisitioned by the state to pay prescribed benefits. The Alabama law was approved by the Federal Social Security Board, and contributors to the state fund were entitled to 90 percent credit on contributions imposed by the federal statute.

The state law was attacked on various grounds: as an infringement of the due process and equal protection clauses of the Fourteenth Amendment, as an unconstitutional surrender to the national government of the sovereign power of the state, and as a measure owing its passage to the coercive action of Congress in the enactment of the Social Security Act. Justice Stone continued:

TAXES, which are but the means of distributing the burden of the cost of government, are commonly levied on property or its use, but may likewise be laid on the exercise of personal rights and privileges. As has been pointed out by the opinion in the *Chas. C. Steward Machine Co.* case [upholding the federal statute], such levies including taxes on the exercise of the right to employ or to be employed, were known in England and the Colonies before the adoption of the Constitution, and must be taken to be embraced within the wide range of choice of subjects of taxation, which was an attribute of the sovereign power of the states at the time of the adoption of the Constitution, and which was reserved to them by that instrument. As the present levy has all the indicia of a tax, and is of a type traditional in the history of Anglo-American legislation, it is within the state taxing power, and it is immaterial whether it is called an excise or by another name. . . . Its validity under the federal Constitution is to be determined in the light of constitutional principles applicable to state taxation.

Validity of the Tax Under the Fourteenth Amendment

FIRST. *Validity of the Tax* Qua *Tax.* It is inherent in the exercise of the power to tax that a state be free to select the subjects of taxation and to grant exemptions. Neither due process nor equal protection imposes upon a state any rigid rule of equality of taxation. . . . This Court has repeatedly held that inequalities which result from a singling out of one particular class for taxation or exemption, infringe no constitutional limitation. . . .

Like considerations govern exemptions from the operation of a tax imposed on the members of a class. A legislature is not bound to tax every member of a class or none. It may make distinctions of degree having a rational basis, and when subjected to judicial scrutiny they must be presumed to rest on that basis if there is any conceivable state of facts which would support it. . . .

This restriction upon the judicial function, in passing on the constitutionality of statutes, is not artificial or irrational. A state legislature, in the enactment of laws, has the widest possible latitude within the limits of the Constitution. In the nature of the case it cannot record a complete catalogue of the considerations which move its members to enact laws. In the absence of such a record courts cannot assume that its action is capricious, or that with its informed acquaintance with local conditions to which the legislation is to be applied, it was not aware of facts which afford reasonable basis for its action. Only by faithful adherence to this guiding principle of judicial review of legislation is it possible to preserve to the legislative branch its rightful independence and its ability to function.

(a) Exclusion of Employers of Less Than Eight. Distinctions in degree, stated in terms of difference in number, have often been the target of attack. . . . It is argued here, and it was ruled by the court below, that there can be no reason for a distinction, for purposes of taxation, between those who have only seven employees and those who have eight. Yet, this is the type of distinction which the law is often called upon to make. [Cases cited.] It is only a difference in numbers which marks the moment when day ends and night begins, when the disabilities of infancy terminate and the status of legal competency is assumed. It separates large incomes which are taxed from the smaller ones which are exempt, as it marks the difference between the proprietors of larger businesses who are taxed and the proprietors of smaller businesses who are not.

Administrative convenience and expense in the collection or measurement of the tax are alone a sufficient justification for the difference between the treatment of small incomes or small taxpayers and that meted out to others. . . . We cannot say that the expense and inconvenience of collecting the tax from smaller employers would not be disproportionate to the revenue obtained. For it cannot be assumed that the legislature could not rightly have concluded that generally the number of employees bears a relationship to the size of the payroll and therefore to the amount of the tax, and that the large number of small employers and the paucity of their records of employment would entail greater inconvenience in the collection and verification of the tax than in the case of larger employers.

It would hardly be contended that the state, in order to tax payrolls, is bound to assume the administrative cost and burden of taxing all employers having a single employee. But if for that or any other reason it may exempt some, whether it should draw the line at one, three, or seven, is peculiarly a question for legislative decision. The decision cannot be said to be arbitrary because it falls in the twilight zone between those members of the class which plainly can and those which plainly cannot expediently be taxed.

(b) Exemption of Particular Classes of Employers. It is arbitrary, appellees contend, to exempt those who employ agricultural laborers, domestic servants, seamen, insurance agents, or close relatives, or to exclude charitable institutions, interstate railways, or the government of the United States or of any state or political subdivision. A sufficient answer is an appeal to the principle of taxation already stated, that the state is free to select a particular class as a subject for taxation. The character of the exemptions suggests simply that the state has chosen, as the subject of its tax, those who employ labor in the processes of industrial production and distribution.

Reasons for the selections, if desired, readily suggest themselves. Where the public interest is served one business may be left untaxed and another taxed, in order to promote the one . . . , or to restrict or suppress the other. . . . The legislature may withhold the burden of the tax in order to foster what it conceives to be a benevolent enterprise. This Court has often sustained the exemption of charitable institutions . . . , and exemption for the encouragement of agriculture. . . . Similarly, the legislature is free to aid a depressed industry such as shipping. The exemption of business operating for less than twenty weeks in the year may rest upon similar reasons, or upon the desire to encourage seasonal or unstable industries.

Administrative considerations may explain several exemptions. Relatively great expense and inconvenience of collection may justify the exemption from taxation of domestic employers, farmers, and family businesses, not likely to maintain adequate employment records, which are an important aid in the collection and verification of the tax. The state may reasonably waive the formality of taxing itself or its political subdivisions. Fear of constitutional restrictions, and a wholesome respect for the proper policy of another sovereign, would explain exemption of the United States, and of the interstate railways. . . . In no case do appellees sustain the burden which rests upon them of showing that there are no differences, between the exempt employers and the industrial employers who are taxed, sufficient to justify differences in taxation.

(c) Tax on Employees. Appellees extend their attack on the statute from the tax imposed on them as employers to the tax imposed on employees. But they cannot object to a tax which they are not asked to pay, at least if it is separable, as we think it is, from the tax they must pay. The statute contains the usual separability clause. . . . The taxation of employees is not prerequisite to enjoyment of the benefits of the Social Security Act. The collection and expenditure of the tax on employers do not depend upon taxing the employees, and we find nothing in the language of the statute or its application to suggest that the tax on employees is so essential to the operation of the statute as to restrict the effect of the separability clause. Distinct taxes imposed by a single statute are not to be deemed inseparable unless that conclusion is unavoidable. . . .

From what has been said, it is plain that the tax *qua* tax conforms to constitutional requirements, and that our inquiry as to its validity would end at this point if the proceeds of the tax were to be covered into the state treasury, and thus made subject to appropriation by the legislature.

SECOND. *Validity of the Tax as Determined by Its Purposes.* The devotion of the tax to the purposes specified by the Act requires our consideration of the objections pressed upon us that the tax is invalid because the purposes are invalid, and because the methods chosen for their execution transgress constitutional limitations. It is not denied that since the adoption of the Fourteenth Amendment state taxing power can be exerted only to effect a public purpose and does not embrace the raising of revenue for private purposes. . . . The states, by their constitutions and laws, may set their own limits upon their spending power . . . , but the requirements of due process leave free scope for the exercise of a wide legislative discretion in determining what expenditures will serve the public interest.

This Court has long and consistently recognized that the public purposes of a state, for which it may raise funds by taxation, embrace expenditures for its general welfare. . . . The existence of local conditions which, because of their nature and extent, are of concern to the public as a whole, the modes of advancing the public interest by correcting them or avoiding their consequences, are peculiarly within the knowledge of the legislature, and to it, and not to the courts, is committed the duty and responsibility of making choice of the possible methods. . . . As with expenditures for the general welfare of the United States . . . , whether the present expenditure serves a public purpose is a practical question addressed to the law-making department, and it would require a plain case of departure from every public purpose which could reasonably be conceived to justify the intervention of a court. . . . The present case exhibits no such departure.

(a) Relief of Unemployment as a Public Purpose. Support of the poor has long been recognized as a public purpose. . . . We need not labor the point that expenditures for the relief of the unemployed, conditioned on unemployment alone, without proof of indigence of recipients of the benefits, is a permissible use of state funds. For the last six years the nation, unhappily, has been placed in a position to learn at first hand the nature and extent of the problem of unemployment, and to appreciate its profound influence upon the public welfare. Detailed accounts of the problem and its social and economic consequences, to be found in public reports of the expenditures of relief funds, and in the studies of many observers, afford a basis for the legislative judgment. It suffices to say that they show that unemployment has apparently become a permanent incident of our industrial system; that it varies, in extent and intensity, with fluctuations in the volume of seasonal businesses and with the business cycle. It is dependent with special and unpredictable manifestations, upon technological changes and advances in methods of manufacture, upon changing demands for manufactured products—dictated by changes in fashion or the creation of desirable substitutes, and upon the establishment of new sources of competition.

The evils of the attendant social and economic wastage permeate the entire social structure. Apart from poverty, or a less extreme impairment of the savings which afford the chief protection to the working class against old age and the hazards of illness, a matter of inestimable consequence to society as a whole, and apart from the loss of purchasing power, the legislature could have concluded that unemployment brings in its wake increase in vagrancy and crimes against property, reduction in the number of marriages, deterioration of family life, decline in the birth rate, increase in illegitimate births, impairment of the health of the unemployed and their families and malnutrition of their children.

Although employment in Alabama is predominantly in agriculture, and the court below found that agricultural unemployment is not an acute problem, the census reports disclose the steadily increasing percentage of those employed in industrial pursuits in Alabama. The total amount spent for emergency relief in Alabama, in the years 1933 to 1935 inclusive, exceeded $47,000,000, of which $312,000 came from state funds, $2,243,000 from local sources, and the balance from relief funds of the federal government. These figures bear eloquent witness to the inability of local agencies to cope with the problem without state action and resort to new taxing legislation. Expenditure of public funds under the present statute, for relief and unemployment, will afford some protection to a substantial group of employees, and we cannot say that it is not for a public purpose.

The end being legitimate, the means is for the legislature to choose. When public evils ensue from individual misfortunes or needs, the legislature may strike at the evil at its source. If the purpose is legitimate because public, it will not be defeated because the execution of it involves payments to individuals. . . . "Individual interests are aided only as the common interest is safeguarded." . . .

(b) Extension of Benefits. The present scheme of unemployment relief is not subject to any constitutional infirmity, as respondents argue, because it is not limited to the indigent or because it is extended to some less deserving than others, such as those discharged for misconduct. While we may assume that the state could have limited its award of unemployment benefits to the indigent and to those who had not been rightfully discharged from their employment, it was not bound to do so. Poverty is one, but not the only evil consequence of unemployment. Among the benefits sought by relief is the avoidance of destitution, and of the gathering cloud of evils which beset the worker, his family and the community after wages cease and before destitution begins. We are not unaware that industrial workers are not an affluent class, and we cannot say that a scheme for the award of unemployment benefits, to be made only after a substantial "waiting period" of unemployment, and then only to the extent of half wages and not more than $15 a week for at most sixteen weeks a year, does not effect a public purpose, because it does not also set up an elaborate machinery for excluding those from its benefits who are not indigent. Moreover, the state could rightfully decide not to discourage thrift. . . . And as the injurious effects of unemployment are not limited to the unemployed worker, there is scope for legislation to mitigate those effects, even though unemployment results from his discharge for cause.

(c) Restriction of Benefits. Appellees again challenge the tax by attacking as arbitrary the classification adopted by the legislature for the distribution of unemployment benefits. Only the employees of those subject to the tax share in the benefits. Appellees complain that the relief is withheld from many as deserving as those who receive benefits. The choice of beneficiaries, like the selection of the subjects of the tax, is thus said to be so arbitrary and discriminatory as to infringe the Fourteenth Amendment and deprive the statute of any public purpose.

What we have said as to the validity of the choice of the subjects of the tax is applicable in large measure to the choice of beneficiaries of relief. In establishing a system of unemployment benefits the legislature is not bound to occupy the whole field. It may strike at the evil where it is most felt . . . , or where it is most practicable to deal with it. . . . It may exclude others whose need is less . . . , or whose effective aid is attended by inconvenience which is greater. . . .

As we cannot say that these considerations did not lead to the selection of the classes of employees entitled to unemployment benefits, and as a state of facts may reasonably be conceived which would support the selection, its constitutionality must be sustained. There is a basis, on grounds of administrative convenience and expense, for adopting a classification which would permit the use of records, kept by the taxpayer and open to the tax gatherer, as an aid to the administration of benefit awards, as is the case here, where the recipients of benefits are selected from the employees of those who pay the tax. Special complaint is made of the discrimination against those with only six co-workers, as contrasted with those who have more. We have already shown that a distinction in terms of the number of employees is not on its face invalid. Here the legislative choice finds support in the consideration reached by students of the problem, that unemployment is less likely to occur in businesses having a small number of employees.

THIRD. *Want of Relationship Between the Subjects and the Benefits of the Tax.* It is not a valid objection to the present tax, conforming in other respects to the Fourteenth Amendment, and devoted to a public purpose, that the benefits paid and the persons to whom they are paid are unrelated to the persons taxed and the amount of the tax which they pay—in short, that those who pay the tax may not have contributed to the unemployment and may not be benefited by the expenditure. Appellees' contention that the statute is arbitrary, in so far as it fails to distinguish between the employer with a low unemployment experience and the employer with a high unemployment experience, rests upon the misconception that there must be such a relationship between the subject of the tax (the exercise of the right to employ) and the evil to be met by the appropriation of the proceeds (unemployment). We have recently stated the applicable doctrine. "But if the tax, *qua* tax, be good, as we hold it is, and the purpose specified be one which would sustain a subsequent and separate appropriation made out of the general funds of the Treasury, neither is made invalid by being bound to the other in the same act of legislation." . . . Nothing is more familiar in taxation than the imposition of a tax upon a class or upon individuals who enjoy no direct benefit from its expenditure, and who are not responsible for the condition to be remedied.

A tax is not an assessment of benefits. It is, as we have said, a means of distributing the burden of the cost of government. The only benefit to which the taxpayer is constitutionally entitled is that derived from his enjoyment of the privileges of living in an organized society, established and safeguarded by the devotion of taxes to public purposes. . . . Any other view would preclude the levying of taxes except as they are used to compensate for the burden on those who pay them, and would involve the abandonment of the most fundamental principle of government—that it exists primarily to provide for the common good. A corporation cannot object to the use of the taxes which it pays for the maintenance of schools because it has no children. . . . This Court has repudiated the suggestion, whenever made, that the Constitution requires the benefits derived from the expenditure of public moneys to be apportioned to the burdens of the taxpayer, or that he can resist the payment of the tax because it is not expended for purposes which are peculiarly beneficial to him. . . .

Even if a legislature should undertake, what the Constitution does not require, to place the burden of a tax for unemployment benefits upon those who cause or contribute to unemployment, it might conclude that the burden cannot justly be apportioned among employers according to their unemployment experience. Unemployment in the plant of one employer may be due to competition with another, within or without the state, whose factory is running to capacity; or to tariffs, inventions, changes in fashions or in market or business conditions, for which no employer is responsible, but which may stimulate the business of one or impair or even destroy that of another. Many believe that the responsibility for the business cycle, the chief cause of unemployment, cannot be apportioned to individual employers in accordance with their employment experience; that a business may be least responsible for the depression from which it suffers most.

The Alabama legislature may have proceeded upon the view, for which there is abundant authority, that the causes of unemployment are too complex to admit of a meticulous appraisal of employer responsibility. It may have concluded that unemployment is an inseparable incident of modern industry, with its most serious manifestations in industrial production; that employees will be best protected, and that the cost of the remedy, at least until more accurate and more complete data are available, may best be distributed, by imposing the tax evenly upon all industrial production, and in such form that it will be added to labor costs which are ultimately absorbed by the public in the prices which it pays for consumable goods.

If the question were ours to decide, we could not say that the legislature, in adopting the present scheme rather than another, had no basis for its choice, or was arbitrary and unreasonable in its action. But, as the state is free to distribute the burden of a tax without regard to the particular purpose for which it is to be used, there is no warrant in the Constitution for setting the tax aside because a court thinks it could have drawn a better statute or could have distributed the burden more wisely. Those are functions reserved for the legislature.

Since the appellees may not complain if the expenditure has no relation to the taxed class of which they are members, they obviously may not complain because the expenditure has *some* relation to that class, that those benefited are employees of those taxed; or because the legislature has adopted the expedient of spreading the burden of the tax to the consuming public by imposing it upon those who make and sell commodities. It is irrelevant to the permissible exercise of the power to tax that some pay the tax who have not occasioned its expenditure, or that in the course of the use of its proceeds for a public purpose the legislature has benefited individuals, who may or may not be related to those who are taxed.

Relationship of the State and Federal Statutes

There remain for consideration the contentions that the state act is invalid because its enactment was coerced by the adoption of the Social Security Act, and that it involves an unconstitutional surrender of state power. Even though it be assumed that the exercise of a sovereign power by a state, in other respects valid, may be rendered invalid because of the coercive effect of a federal statute enacted in the exercise of a power granted to the national government, such coercion is lacking here. It is unnecessary to repeat now those considerations which have led to our decision in the *Chas. C. Steward Machine Co.* case, that the Social Security Act has no such coercive effect. As the Social Security Act is not coercive in its operation the Unemployment Compensation Act cannot be set aside as an unconstitutional product of coercion. The United States and the State of Alabama are not alien governments. They coexist within the same territory. Unemployment within it is their common concern. Together the two statutes now before us embody a coöperative legislative effort by state and national governments for carrying out a public purpose common to both, which neither could fully achieve without the coöperation of the other. The Constitution does not prohibit such coöperation.

As the state legislation is not the product of a prohibited coercion, there is little else to which appellees can point as indicating a surrender of state sovereignty. As the opinion in the *Chas. C. Steward Machine Co.* case points out, full liberty of action is secured to the state by both statutes. The unemployment compensation fund is administered in accordance with state law by the state commission. The statute may be repealed at the will of the legislature, and in that case the state will be free to withdraw at any time its unexpended share of the Unemployment Trust Fund from the Treasury of the United States, and to use it for any public purpose. And, for the reasons stated in the opinion in the *Chas. C. Steward Machine Co.* case, we conclude that the deposit by the state of its compensation fund in the Unemployment Trust Fund involves no more of a surrender of sovereignty than does the choice of any other depository for state funds. The power to contract and the power to select appropriate agencies and instrumentalities for the execution of state policy are attributes of state sovereignty. They are not lost by their exercise.

Many other arguments are pressed upon us. They require no discussion save as their answer is implicit in what we have said. The state compensation act, on its face, and as applied to appellees, is subject to no constitutional infirmity.

Carmichael v. *Southern Coal & Coke Co.*
301 U. S. 495   Decided May 24, 1937

EMPLOYER-DOMINATION OF A UNION

The National Labor Relations Act, drawing from the experience of the Railway Labor Act, declared the domination of an employee organization by the employer an unfair labor practice interfering with the workers' right to bargain collectively through representatives of their own choosing. In a situation where the setup of a company union completely obstructed this right, the National Labor Relations Board ordered the employer to withdraw all recognition from the company union although no election had been held by the employees.

Justice Stone showed that the Board acted within the authority conferred on it. After stating the pertinent facts concerning the Pennsylvania Greyhound Lines, the employer in question, and the Employees Association, which it formed and dominated, the Justice quoted sections of the Act: § 7 giving employees the right to self-organization, § 8 declaring employer-interference with this right and employer-domination or interference with any labor organization to be unfair labor practices, and § 10 giving the Board authority to hear complaints of unfair labor practices and directing the Board when to issue cease-and-desist orders and "to take such affirmative action * * * as will effectuate the policies of this Act".

NOTWITHSTANDING the mandatory form of § 10(c), its provisions in substance leave to the Board some scope for the exercise of judgment and discretion in determining, upon the basis of the findings, whether the case is one requiring an affirmative order, and in choosing the particular affirmative relief to be ordered. Hence, upon the challenge of the affirmative part of an order of the Board, we look to the Act itself, read in the light of its history, to ascertain its policy, and to the facts which the Board has found, to see whether they afford a basis for its judgment that the action ordered is an appropriate means of carrying out that policy.

The history of the Act and its language show that its ruling purpose was to protect interstate commerce by securing to employees the rights established by § 7 to organize, to bargain collectively through representatives of their own choosing, and to engage in concerted activities for that and other purposes. . . . This appears both from the formal declaration of policy in § 1 of the Act . . . and from § 7, in itself a declaration of policy which, in conjunction with § 10(c), it adopts as the controlling guide to administrative action.

Before enactment of the National Labor Relations Act this Court had recognized that the maintenance of a "company union," dominated by the employer, may be a ready and effective means of obstructing self-organization of employees and their choice of their own representatives for the purpose of collective bargaining. Section 2 (3) of the Railway Labor Act of 1926 had provided that representatives, for the purposes of the Act, should be designated by employer and employees "without interference, influence, or coercion exercised by either party over the self-organization or designation of representatives by the other." We had held that in enforcing this provision, employer recognition of a company union might be enjoined and the "disestablished," as an appropriate means of preventing interference with the rights secured to employees by the statute. . . . [See *Virginian Railway* case, page 52, this volume.]

Congress, in enacting the National Labor Relations Act, had in mind the experience in the administration of the Railway Labor Act, and declared that the former was "an amplification and further clarification of the principles" of the latter. . . . It had before it the *Railway Clerks* case [281 U. S. 548] which had emphasized the importance of union recognition in securing collective bargaining . . . , and there were then available data showing that once an employer has conferred recognition on a particular organization it has a marked advantage over any other in securing the adherence of employees, and hence in preventing the recognition of any other. The National Labor Relations Act continued and amplified the policy of the Railway Labor Act by its declaration in § 7, and by providing generally in § 8 that any interferences in the exercise of the rights guaranteed by § 7 and specifically the domination or interference with the formation or administration of any labor organization were unfair labor practices. To secure to employees the benefits of self-organization and collective bargaining through representatives of the employees' own choosing, the Board was authorized by § 10(c) to order the abandonment of unfair labor practices and to take affirmative action which would carry out the policy of the Act.

In recommending the adoption of this latter provision the Senate Committee [on Education and Labor] called attention to the decree which, in the *Railway Clerks* case, had compelled the employer to "disestablish its company union as representative of its employees". . . . The report of the House Committee on Labor on this feature of the Act, after pointing out that collective bargaining is "a sham when the employer sits on both sides of the table by supporting a particular organization with which he deals," declared:

"The orders will of course be adapted to the need of the individual case; they may include such matters as refraining from collective bargaining with a minority group, recognition of the agency chosen by the majority for the purposes of collective bargaining, posting of appropriate bulletins, refraining from bargaining with an organization corrupted by unfair labor practices." . . .

It is plain that the challenged provisions of the present order are of a kind contemplated by Congress in the enactment of § 10(c) and are within its terms. There remains the question whether the findings adequately support them.

The Board's subsidiary findings of fact fully sustain its conclusion that respondents had engaged in unfair labor practices, by active participation in the organization and administration of the Employees Association, which they dominated throughout its history, and to whose financial support they had contributed; and that they had interfered with, restrained and coerced their employees in the exercise of the rights confirmed by § 7 to form for themselves a labor organization and to bargain collectively through representatives of their own choosing.

It is unnecessary to repeat in full detail the facts disclosed by the findings. They show that before the enactment of the National Labor Relations Act, respondents, whose employees were unorganized, initiated a project for their organization under company domination. In the course of its execution officers or other representatives of respondent were active in promoting the plan, in urging other employees to join, in the preparation of the details of organization, including the by-laws, in presiding over organization meetings, and in selecting employee representatives of the organization.

The by-laws and regulations provided that all motorbus operators, maintenance men and clerical employees, after three months service, automatically became members of the Association, and that only employees were eligible to act as employee representatives. No provisions were made for meetings of members, nor was a procedure established whereby employees might instruct their representatives, or whereby those representatives might disseminate information or reports. Grievances were to be taken up with regional committees with final review by a Joint Reviewing Committee made up of an equal number of regional chairmen and of management representatives, but review in those cases could not be secured unless there was a joint submission of the controversy by employee and management representatives.

Change of the by-laws without employer consent was precluded by a provision that amendment should be only on a two-thirds vote of the Joint Reviewing Committee, composed of an equal number of employer and employee representatives. Employees paid no dues, all the Association expenses being borne by the management.

Although the Association was in terms created as a bargaining agency for the purpose of "providing adequate representation" for respondents' employees by "securing for them satisfactory adjustment of all controversial matters", it has functioned only to settle individual grievances. On the one recorded occasion when the employees sought a wage increase the company representatives prevented its consideration by refusing to join in the submission to the Joint Reviewing Committee.

In May, 1935, shortly before the passage of the Act, certain of respondents' Pittsburgh employees organized a local union, Local Division No. 1063 of the Amalgamated Association of Street, Electric Railway & Motor Coach Employees of America, affiliated with the American Federation of Labor, and continued to hold meetings of the organization after the passage of the Act on July 5, 1935. Before and after that date, respondents' officers were active in warning employees against joining the union and in threatening them with discharge if they should join, and in keeping the union meetings under surveillance.

Section 10(c) declares that the Board's findings of fact "if supported by evidence, shall be conclusive". Whether the continued recognition of the Employees Association by respondents would in itself be a continuing obstacle to the exercise of the employees' right of self-organization and to bargain collectively through representatives of their own choosing, is an inference of fact to be drawn by the Board from the evidence reviewed in its subsidiary findings. . . .

We may assume that there are situations in which the Board would not be warranted in concluding that there was any occasion for withdrawal of employer recognition of an existing union before an election by employees under § 9(c), even though it had ordered the employer to cease unfair labor practices. But here respondents, by unfair labor practices, have succeeded in establishing a company union so organized that it is incapable of functioning as a bargaining representative of employees. With no procedure for meetings of members or for instructing employee representatives, and with no power to bring grievances before the Joint Reviewing Committee without employer consent, the Association could not without amendment of its by-laws be used as a means of collective bargaining contemplated by § 7; and amendment could not be had without the employer's approval.

In view of all the circumstances the Board could have thought that continued recognition of the Association would serve as a means of thwarting the policy of collective bargaining by enabling the employer to induce adherence of employees to the Association in the mistaken belief that it was truly representative and afforded an agency for collective bargaining, and thus to prevent self-organization. The inferences to be drawn were for the Board and not the courts. . . . There was ample basis for its conclusion that withdrawal of recognition of the Association by respondents, accompanied by suitable publicity, was an appropriate way to give effect to the policy of the Act.

As the order did not run against the Association it is not entitled to notice and hearing. Its presence was not necessary in order to enable the Board to determine whether respondents had violated the statute or to make an appropriate order against them. . . .

Respondents suggest that the case had become moot by reason of the fact that since the Board made its order it has certified the Brotherhood of Railroad Trainmen as representative of the motorbus drivers of the Pennsylvania company for purposes of collective bargaining and that in a pending proceeding under § 9(c) for the certification of a representative of the other Pittsburgh employees, to which the Employees Association is not a party, the Pennsylvania company and Local Division No. 1063, who are parties, have made no objection to the proposed certification. But an order of the character made by the Board, lawful when made, does not become moot because it is obeyed or because changing circumstances indicate that the need for it may be less than when made.

We have considered but find it unnecessary to comment upon other objections to the order, of less moment.

National Labor Relations Board v. *Pennsylvania Greyhound Lines et al., 303 U. S. 261* *Decided February 28, 1938*

JURISDICTION OVER CONTRACT SHOPS

IN LINE with the power of Congress, under the commerce clause of the Constitution, to protect interstate commerce from interference due to intrastate activities, the Supreme Court held that a "contract shop" in New Jersey manufacturing for a firm in New York was within the National Labor Relations Board's jurisdiction, regardless of the volume of business involved. Justices McReynolds and Butler criticized this decision as "such attenuated reasoning," destructive of the federal system. The majority opinion by Justice Stone answered the objections.

The question before the Court, as stated by Justice Stone, was whether the National Labor Relations Act was applicable to employers, not themselves engaged in interstate commerce, who processed materials supplied to them by the owners from outside the state. The finished garments were shipped out of the state. After a strike in this "contract shop" the Board found that the employers' unfair labor practices had led and tended to lead to "labor disputes burdening and obstructing commerce and the free flow of commerce", and the Board ordered the employers to desist from these practices.

It has been settled by repeated decisions of this Court that an employer may be subject to the National Labor Relations Act although not himself engaged in commerce. The end sought in the enactment of the statute was the prevention of the disturbance to interstate commerce consequent upon strikes and labor disputes induced or likely to be induced because of unfair labor practices named in the Act. That those consequences may ensue from strikes of the employees of manufacturers who are not engaged in interstate commerce where the cessation of manufacture necessarily results in the cessation of the movement of the manufactured product in interstate commerce, has been repeatedly pointed out by this Court. . . . Long before the enactment of the National Labor Relations Act it had been many times held by this Court that the power of Congress extends to the protection of interstate commerce from interference or injury due to activities which are wholly intrastate.

Here interstate commerce was involved in the transportation of the materials to be processed across state lines to the factory of respondents and in the transportation of the finished product to points outside the state for distribution to purchasers and ultimate consumers. Whether shipments were made directly to respondents [Somerset Manufacturing Co., at Somerville, N. J.], as the Board found, or to a representative of Lee Sportswear Company [the shippers, a New York firm] at the factory, as respondents contend, is immaterial. It was not any the less interstate commerce because the transportation did not begin or end with the transfer of title of the merchandise transported. . . . Transportation alone across state lines is commerce within the constitutional control of the national government and subject to the regulatory power of Congress. . . .

Nor do we think it important, as respondents seem to argue, that the volume of commerce here involved, though substantial, was relatively small as compared with that in the cases arising under the National Labor Relations Act which have hitherto engaged our attention. The power of Congress to regulate interstate commerce is plenary and extends to all such commerce be it great or small. . . . The exercise of congressional power under the Sherman Act, the Clayton Act, the Federal Trade Commission Act, or the National Motor Vehicle Theft Act, has never been thought to be constitutionally restricted because in any particular case the volume of the commerce affected may be small. The amount of commerce regulated is of special significance only to the extent that Congress may be taken to have excluded commerce of small volume from the operation of its regulatory measure by express provision or fair implication.

The language of the National Labor Relations Act seems to make it plain that Congress has set no restrictions upon the jurisdiction of the Board to be determined or fixed exclusively by reference to the volume of interstate commerce involved. Section 2(6) defines commerce as "trade, traffic, commerce, transportation, or communication among the several States", without reference to its volume, and declares in subsection (7) that "The term 'affecting commerce' means in commerce, or burdening or obstructing commerce or the free flow of commerce, or having led or tending to lead to a labor dispute burdening or obstructing commerce or the free flow of commerce." Section 10(a) confers on the Board authority "to prevent any person from engaging in any unfair labor practice (listed in § 8) affecting commerce."

The Act on its face thus evidences the intention of Congress to exercise whatever power is constitutionally given to it to regulate commerce by the adoption of measures for the prevention or control of certain specified acts—unfair labor practices—which provoke or tend to provoke strikes or labor disturbances affecting interstate commerce. Given the other needful conditions, commerce may be affected in the same manner and to the same extent in proportion to its volume, whether it be great or small. Examining the Act in the light of its purpose and of the circumstances in which it must be applied we can perceive no basis for inferring any intention of Congress to make the operation of the Act depend on any particular volume of commerce affected more than to which courts would apply the maxim *de minimis.* [The maxim that the law takes no account of trifles.]

There are not a few industries in the United States which, though conducted by relatively small units, contribute in the aggregate a vast volume of interstate commerce. Some, like the clothing industry, are extensively unionized and have had a long and tragic history of industrial strife. It is not to be supposed that Congress, in its attempted nationwide regulation of interstate commerce through the removal of the causes of industrial strife affecting it, intended to exclude such industries from the sweep of the Act. In this, as in every other case, the test of the Board's jurisdiction is not the volume of the interstate commerce which may be affected but the existence of a relationship of the employer and his employees to the commerce such that, to paraphrase § 10(a) in the light of constitutional limitations, unfair labor practices have led or tended to lead "to a labor dispute burdening or obstructing commerce."

It is no longer open to question that the manufacturer who regularly ships his product in interstate commerce is subject to the authority conferred on the Board with respect to unfair labor practices whenever such practices on his part have led or tend to lead to labor disputes which threaten to obstruct his shipments. . . . We cannot say, other things being equal, that the tendency differs in kind, quantity or effect merely because the merchandise which the manufacturer ships instead of being his own, is that of the consignee or his customers in other states. In either case commerce is in danger of being obstructed in the same way and to the same extent.

Here, although respondents' manufacturing business is small, employing from sixty to 200 employees, its product is regularly shipped in interstate commerce. The Board's finding that respondents' unfair labor practices have led and tend to lead to labor disputes burdening interstate commerce and interfering with its free flow is supported by the evidence. Moreover, the Board has found specifically that respondents' unfair labor practices in attempting to prevent the unionization of their factory did in fact lead to a strike in respondents' tailoring establishment, with a consequent reduction of about 50 percent in respondents' output. These findings are not challenged.

The threatened consequences to interstate commerce are as immediate and as certain to flow from respondents' unfair labor practices as were those which were held to result from unfair labor practices in [N. L. R. B. cases cited]. That the volume of commerce affected is smaller than in other cases in which the jurisdiction of the Board has been upheld, for reasons already stated, is in itself without significance.

National Labor Relations Board v. *Fainblatt*
306 U. S. 601 *Decided April 17, 1939*

CERTIFYING A BARGAINING UNIT

An American Federation of Labor union of longshoremen disputed the National Labor Relations Board's certification of a C. I. O. affiliate as the collective bargaining unit for virtually all longshoremen on the Pacific Coast. The contention was that the Wagner Act did not contemplate or authorize "the designation by the Board of an employee unit constituting all the employees of different employers in different and distant geographical districts of the United States". Also, that the Act did afford a right to review an order of the Board.

For a unanimous Court, Justice Stone granted that the Act provided for review but he showed, by the language of the statute and its legislative history, that Congress deliberately chose to distinguish between an "order" restraining an unfair labor practice and a "certification" in representation proceedings. If hardship ensued from exclusion of the latter action from review, this argument should be "addressed to Congress and not to the courts," he said. The single issue here was whether the certification was an "order" reviewable under the provisions of the statute.

By the provisions of the Wagner Act the Board is given two principal functions to perform. One, defined by § 9, which as enacted, is headed "Representatives and Elections", is the certification, after appropriate investigation and hearing, of the name or names of representatives, for collective bargaining, of an appropriate unit of employees. The other, defined by § 10, which as enacted, is headed "Prevention of Unfair Labor Practices", is the prevention by the Board's order, after hearing and by a further appropriate proceeding in court, of the unfair labor practices enumerated in § 8. One of the outlawed practices is the refusal of an employer to bargain with the representative of his employees, § 8, Fifth.

Certification involves, under § 9(b), decision by the Board whether "the unit appropriate for the purposes of collective bargaining shall be the employer unit, craft unit, plant unit, or subdivision thereof", and the ascertainment by the Board under § 9(c) of the bargaining representative who, under § 9(a), must be "designated or selected * * * by the majority of the employees in the unit appropriate for such (bargaining) purposes".

The Board is authorized by § 9(c) "whenever a question affecting commerce arises concerning the representation of employees" to investigate "such controversy" and to certify the names of the appropriate bargaining representatives. In conducting the investigation it is required to provide for appropriate hearing upon due notice "and may take a secret ballot of employees, or utilize any other suitable method" of ascertaining such representatives.

By § 9(d) whenever an order of the Board is made pursuant

to § 10(c) directing any person to cease an unfair labor practice and there is a petition for enforcement or review of the order by a court, the Board's "certification and the record of such investigation" is to be included in the transcript of the entire record required to be filed under § 10(e) or (f), and the decree of the court enforcing, modifying, or setting aside the order of the Board is to be made and entered upon the pleadings, testimony and proceedings set forth in the transcript.

It is to be noted that § 9, which is complete in itself, makes no provision, in terms, for review of a certification by the Board and authorizes no use of the certification or of the record in a certification proceeding, except in the single case where there is a petition for enforcement or review of an order restraining an unfair labor practice as authorized by § 10(c). In that event the record in the certification proceeding is included in the record brought up on review of the Board's order restraining an unfair labor practice. It then becomes a part of the record upon which the decree of the reviewing court is to be based.

All other provisions for review of any action of the Board are found in § 10, which, as its heading indicates, relates to the prevention of unfair labor practices. Nowhere in this section is there mention of investigations or certifications authorized and defined by § 9.

Section 10(a) authorizes the Board "to prevent any person from engaging in any unfair labor practice (listed in § 8) affecting commerce". Section 10(b) prescribes the procedure of the Board when any person is charged with engaging in any unfair labor practice, and requires that the persons so charged shall be served with a complaint and notice of hearing by the Board with opportunity to file an answer and be heard. Section 10(c) directs the Board, if it is of opinion, as the result of the proceedings before it, that any person named in the complaint has engaged in an unfair labor practice "to issue" "an order" directing that person to cease the practice and commanding appropriate affirmative action. If the Board is of opinion that there has been no unfair labor practice it is directed "to issue" "an order" dismissing the complaint. Section 10(e) authorizes a petition to the appropriate federal Court of Appeals by the Board for the enforcement of its order prohibiting an unfair labor practice.

This brings us to the provisions for review of action taken by the Board in § 10(f) which is controlling in the present proceeding. That subdivision appears as an integral part of § 10. All the other subdivisions relate exclusively to proceedings for the prevention of unfair labor practices. Both they and subdivision (f) are silent as to the proceedings or certifications authorized by § 9.

Section 10(f), providing for review, speaks only of a "final order of the Board". It gives a right to review to persons aggrieved by a final order upon petition to a Court of Appeals in the circuit "wherein the unfair labor practice in question was alleged to have been engaged in or wherein such person resides or transacts business, or in the Court of Appeals of the District of Columbia."

It directs that the order shall be reviewed on the entire record before the Board, "including the pleadings and testimony" upon which the order complained of was entered, although no complaint or other pleading is mentioned by § 9 relating to representation proceedings and certificates.

Subdivision (f) provides that upon petition for review by an aggrieved person "the court shall proceed in the same manner as in the case of an application by the Board under subdivision (e)," and it is given the same jurisdiction "to grant to the Board such temporary relief or restraining order as it deems just and proper, and in like manner to make and enter a decree enforcing, modifying and enforcing as so modified, or setting aside in whole or in part the order of the Board". . . .

In analyzing the provisions of the statute in order to ascertain its true meaning, we attribute little importance to the fact that the certification does not itself command action. Administrative determinations which are not commands may for all practical purposes determine rights as effectively as the judgment of a court, and may be reëxamined by courts under particular statutes providing for the review of "order". . . .

We must look rather to the language of the statute, read in the light of its purpose and its legislative history, to ascertain whether the "order" for which the review in court is provided is contrasted with forms of administrative action differently described as a purposeful means of excluding them from the review provisions.

Here it is evident that the entire structure of the Act emphasizes, for purposes of review, the distinction between an "order" of the Board restraining an unfair labor practice and a certification in representation proceedings. The one authorized by § 10 may be reviewed by the court on petition of the Board for enforcement of the order, or of a person aggrieved, in conformity to the procedure laid down in § 10, which says nothing of certifications.

The other, authorized by § 9, is nowhere spoken of as an order, and no procedure is prescribed for its review apart from an order prohibiting an unfair labor practice. The exclusion of representation proceedings from the review secured by the provision of § 10(f) is emphasized by the clauses of § 9(d), which provide for certification by the Board of a record of a representation proceeding only in the case when there is a petition for review of an order of the Board restraining an unfair labor practice. The statute on its face thus indicates a purpose to limit the review afforded by § 10 to orders of the Board prohibiting unfair labor practices, a purpose and a construction which its legislative history confirms.

Upon the introduction of the bill which was enacted as the Wagner Act, Congress had pointedly brought to its attention the experience under Public Resolution 44 of June 19, 1934. . . That resolution authorized the National Labor Relations Board, predecessor of respondent, "to order and conduct elections" by employees of any employer to determine who were their representatives for bargaining purposes.

Section 2 provided that any order of the Board should be reviewed in the same manner as orders of the Federal Trade Commission under the Federal Trade Commission Act. The reports of the congressional committees upon the bill which became the Wagner Act refer to the long delays in the procedure prescribed by Resolution 44, resulting from applications to the federal appellate courts for review of orders for elections. And in considering the provisions of § 9(d) the committee reports were emphatic in their declaration that the provisions of the bill for court review did not extend to proceedings under § 9 except as incidental to review of an order restraining an unfair labor practice under § 10. The bill was similarly explained on the Senate floor by the committee chairman, who declared:

"It provides for review in the courts only after the election has been held and the Board has ordered the employer to do something predicated upon the results of an election." . . .

The conclusion is unavoidable that Congress, as the result of a deliberate choice of conflicting policies, has excluded representation certifications of the Board from the review by federal appellate courts authorized by the Wagner Act except in the circumstances specified in § 9(d).

An argument much pressed upon us is, in effect, that Congress was mistaken in its judgment that the hearings before the Board in proceedings under § 9(c), with review only when an order is made under § 10(c) directing the employer to do something, "provides an appropriate safeguard and opportunity to be heard" . . . and that "this provides a complete guarantee against arbitrary action by the Board." . . .

It seems to be thought that this failure to provide for a court review is productive of peculiar hardships, which were perhaps not foreseen in cases where the interests of rival unions are affected. But these are arguments to be addressed to Congress and not the courts.

The argument, too, that Congress has infringed due process by withholding from federal appellate courts a jurisdiction which they never possessed is similarly without force. . . .

The Board argues that the provisions of the Wagner Act, particularly § 9(d), have foreclosed review of its challenged action by independent suit in the district court, such as was allowed under other acts providing for a limited court review in [cases cited].

But that question is not presented for decision by the record before us. Its answer involves a determination whether the Wagner Act, in so far as it has given legally enforcible rights, has deprived the district courts of some portion of their original jurisdiction conferred by § 24 of the Judicial Code.

It can be appropriately answered only upon a showing in such a suit that unlawful action of the Board has inflicted an injury on the petitioners for which the law, apart from the review provisions of the Wagner Act, affords a remedy. This question can be properly and adequately considered only when it is brought to us for review upon a suitable record.

International Longshoremen's Ass'n v. *National Labor Relations Board* — *Decided January 2, 1940*

FREEDOM OF ASSEMBLY

UNDER city ordinances regulating public meetings and the distribution of literature, officials of Jersey City obstructed an attempted membership drive by the Committee for Industrial Organization and meetings to discuss the National Labor Relations Act. The mayor, Frank Hague, insisted that the ordinances were valid. He found support in Justices Butler and McReynolds, who declared against interference with the municipality. But the majority of the Court held the regulations void. Justice Roberts asserted the right of citizens of the United States under the privileges and immunities clause of the Fourteenth Amendment to discuss national legislation and discountenanced denial of such a citizen's privilege to use the streets and parks "for communication of views on national questions." Justice Stone took a broader view: freedom of speech and assembly for a lawful purpose was a right "secured to all persons" by the due process clause of the Fourteenth Amendment. He wrote:

IT HAS BEEN explicitly and repeatedly affirmed by this Court, without a dissenting voice, that freedom of speech and of assembly for any lawful purpose are rights of personal liberty secured to all persons, without regard to citizenship, by the due process clause of the Fourteenth Amendment. . . . It has never been held that either is a privilege or immunity peculiar to citizenship of the United States, to which alone the privileges and immunities clause refers . . . and neither can be brought within the protection of that clause without enlarging the category of privileges and immunities of United States citizenship as it has hitherto been defined.

As will presently appear, the right to maintain a suit in equity to restrain state officers, acting under a state law, from infringing the rights of freedom of speech and of assembly guaranteed by the due process clause, is given by Act of Congress to every person within the jurisdiction of the United States whether a citizen or not, and such a suit may be maintained in the district court without allegation or proof that the jurisdictional amount required by § 24(1) of the Judicial Code is involved. Hence there is no occasion, for jurisdictional purposes or any other, to consider whether freedom of speech and of assembly are immunities secured by the privileges and immunities clause of the Fourteenth Amendment to citizens of the United States, or to revive the contention, rejected by this Court in the *Slaughter-House Cases,* 16 Wall. 36, that the privileges and immunities of United States citizenship, protected by that clause, extend beyond those which arise or grow out of the relationship of United States citizens to the national government. [See *Colgate* v. *Harvey,* p. 259, this volume.]

That such is the limited application of the privileges and immunities clause seems now to be conceded by my brethren. But it is said that the freedom of respondents [the C.I.O. et al.] with which the petitioners [Mayor Hague et al.] have interfered is the "freedom to disseminate information concerning the provisions of the National Labor Relations Act, to assemble peaceably for discussion of the Act, and of the opportunities and advantages offered by it", and that these are privileges and immunities of citizens of the United States secured against state abridgment by the privileges and immunities clause of the Fourteenth Amendment. It has been said that the right of citizens to assemble for the purpose of petitioning Congress for the redress of grievances is a privilege of United States citizenship protected by the privileges and immunities clause. . . . We may assume for present purposes, although the step is a long and by no means certain one . . . that the right to assemble to discuss the advantages of the National Labor Relations Act is likewise a privilege secured by the privileges and immunities clause to citizens of the United States, but not to others, while freedom to assemble for the purpose of discussing a similar state statute would not be within the privileges and immunities clause. But the difficulty with this assumption is, as the record and briefs show, that it is an afterthought first emerging in this case after it was submitted to us for decision, and like most afterthoughts in litigated matters it is without adequate support in the record.

The respondents in their bill of complaint specifically named and quoted Article IV, § 2, now conceded to be inapplicable, and the due process and equal protection clauses of the Fourteenth Amendment as the provisions of the Constitution which secure to them the rights of free speech and assembly. They omitted the privileges and immunities clause of the Fourteenth Amendment from their quotation. They made no specific allegation that any of those whose freedom had been interfered with by petitioners was a citizen of the United States. The general allegation that the acts of petitioners complained of violate the rights of "citizens of the United States, including the individual plaintiffs here," and other allegations of like tenor, were denied by petitioners' answer. There is no finding by either court below that any of the respondents or any of those whose freedom of speech and assembly has been infringed are citizens of the United States, and we are referred to no part of the evidence in which their citizenship is mentioned or from which it can be inferred.

Both courts below found, and the evidence supports the findings, that the purpose of respondents, other than the Civil Liberties Union, in holding meetings in Jersey City, was to organize labor unions in various industries in order to secure to workers the benefits of collective bargaining with respect to betterment of wages, hours of work and other terms and conditions of employment. Whether the proposed unions were to be organized in industries which might be subject to the National Labor Relations Act or to the jurisdiction of the National Labor Relations Board does not appear. Neither court below has made any finding that the meetings were called to discuss, or that they ever did in fact discuss, the National Labor Relations Act.

The findings do not support the conclusion that the proposed meetings involved any such relationship between the national government and respondents or any of them, assuming they are citizens of the United States, as to show that the asserted right or privilege was that of a citizen of the United States, and I cannot say that an adequate basis has been laid for supporting a theory—which respondents themselves evidently did not entertain—that any of their privileges as citizens of the United States, guaranteed by the Fourteenth Amendment, were abridged, as distinguished from the privileges guaranteed to all persons by the due process clause.

True, the findings refer to the suppression by petitioners of exhibits, one of which turns out to be a handbill advising workers they have the legal right, under the Wagner Act, to choose their own labor union to represent them in collective bargaining. But the injunction, which the Court now rightly sustains, is not restricted to the protection of the right, said to pertain to United States citizens, to disseminate information about the Wagner Act. On the contrary, it extends and applies in the broadest terms to interferences with respondents in holding any lawful meeting and disseminating any lawful information by circular, leaflet, handbill and placard.

If, as my brethren think, respondents are entitled to maintain in this suit only the rights secured to them by the privileges and immunities clause of the Fourteenth Amendment—here the right to disseminate information about the National Labor Relations Act—it is plain that the decree is too broad. Instead of enjoining, as it does, interferences with all meetings for all purposes and the lawful dissemination of all information, it should have confined its restraint to interferences with the dissemination of information about the National Labor Relations Act, through meetings or otherwise. The court below rightly omitted any such limitation from the decree, evidently because, as it declared, petitioner's acts infringed the due process clause, which guarantees to all persons freedom of speech and of assembly for any lawful purpose.

No more grave and important issue can be brought to this Court than that of freedom of speech and assembly, which the due process clause guarantees to all persons regardless of their citizenship, but which the privileges and immunities clause secures only to citizens, and then only to the limited extent that their relationship to the national government is affected. I am unable to rest decision here on the assertion, which I think the record fails to support, that respondents must depend upon their limited privileges as citizens of the United States in order to sustain their cause, or upon so palpable an avoidance of the real issue in the case, which respondents have raised by their pleadings and sustained by their proof.

That issue is whether the present proceeding can be maintained under § 24(14) of the Judicial Code as a suit for the protection of rights and privileges guaranteed by the due process clause. I think respondents' right to maintain it does not depend on their citizenship and cannot rightly be made to turn on the existence or nonexistence of a purpose to disseminate information about the National Labor Relations Act. It is enough that petitioners have prevented respondents from holding meetings and disseminating information whether for the organization of a labor union or for any other lawful purpose.

If it be the part of wisdom to avoid unnecessary decision of constitutional questions, it would seem to be equally so to avoid the unnecessary creation of novel constitutional doctrine, inadequately supported by the record, in order to attain an end easily and certainly reached by following the beaten paths of constitutional decision.

The right to maintain the present suit is conferred upon the individual respondents by the due process clause and acts of Congress, regardless of their citizenship and of the amount in controversy. Section 1 of the Civil Rights Act of April 20, 1871, . . . provided that "any person who, under color of any law, statute, ordinance * * * of any state, shall subject, or cause to be subjected, any person within the jurisdiction of the United States to the deprivation of any rights, privileges, or immunities secured by the Constitution of the United States shall * * * be liable to the party injured in any action at law, suit in equity, or other proper proceeding for redress". And it directed that such proceedings should be prosecuted in the several district or circuit courts of the United States. The right of action given by this section was later specifically limited to "any citizen of the United States or other person within the jurisdiction thereof", and was extended to include rights, privileges and immunities secured by the laws of the United States as well as by the Constitution.

As thus modified the provision was continued as § 1979 of the Revised Statutes and now constitutes § 43 of Title 8 of the United States Code. It will be observed that the cause of action, given by the section in its original as well as its final form, extends broadly to deprivation by state action of the rights, privileges and immunities secured to persons by the Constitution. It thus includes the Fourteenth Amendment and such privileges and immunities as are secured by the due process and equal protection clauses, as well as by the privileges and immunities clause of that amendment. It will also be observed that they are those rights secured to persons, whether citizens of the United States or not, to whom the amendment in terms extends the benefit of the due process and equal protection clauses.

Following the decision of the *Slaughter-House Cases* and before the later expansion by judicial decision of the content of the due process and equal protection clauses, there was little scope for the operation of this statute under the Fourteenth Amendment. The observation of the Court in *United States* v. *Cruikshank,* 92 U. S. 542, 551, that the right of assembly was not secured against state action by the Constitution, must be attributed to the decision in the *Slaughter-House Cases* that only privileges and immunities peculiar to United States citizenship were secured by the privileges and immunities clause, and to the further fact that at that time it had not been decided that the right was one protected by the due process clause.

The argument that the phrase in the statute "secured by the Constitution" refers to rights "created", rather than "protected" by it, is not persuasive. The preamble of the Constitution, proclaiming the establishment of the Constitution in order to "secure the Blessings of Liberty", uses the word "secure" in the sense of "protect" or "make certain". That the phrase was used in this sense in the statute now under consideration was recognized in *Carter* v. *Greenhow,* 114 U. S. 317, 322, where it was held as a matter of pleading that the particular cause of action set up in the plaintiff's pleading was in contract and was not to redress deprivation of the "right secured to him by that clause of the Constitution" (the contract clause), to which he had "chosen not to resort". See, as to other rights protected by the Constitution and hence secured by it, brought within the provisions of Revised Statutes § 5508 [cases cited].

Since freedom of speech and freedom of assembly are rights secured to persons by the due process clause, all of the individual respondents are plainly authorized by § 1, of the Civil Rights Act of 1871 to maintain the present suit in equity to restrain infringement of their rights. As to the American Civil Liberties Union, which is a corporation, it cannot be said to be deprived of the civil rights of freedom of speech and of assembly, for the liberty guaranteed by the due process clause is the liberty of natural, not artificial, persons. . . .

The question remains whether there was jurisdiction in the district court to entertain the suit, although the matter in controversy cannot be shown to exceed $3,000 in value because the asserted rights, freedom of speech and freedom of assembly, are of such a nature as not to be susceptible of valuation in money. The question is the same whether the right or privilege asserted is secured by the privileges and immunities clause or any other.

[An analysis of the question of jurisdiction is here omitted.]

The conclusion seems inescapable that the right conferred by the Act of 1871 to maintain a suit in equity in the federal courts to protect the suitor against a deprivation of rights or immunities secured by the Constitution has been preserved, and that whenever the right or immunity is one of personal liberty, not dependent for its existence upon the infringement of property rights, there is jurisdiction in the district court under § 24(14) of the Judicial Code to entertain it without proof that the amount in controversy exceeds $3,000. As the right is secured to "any person" by the due process clause, and as the statute permits the suit to be brought by "any person" as well as by a citizen, it is certain that resort to the privileges and immunities clause would not support the decree which we now sustain and would involve constitutional experimentation as gratuitous as it is unwarranted. We cannot be sure that its consequences would not be unfortunate.

Hague, Mayor, et al. v. *Committee for Industrial Organization, et al., 307 U.S. 496, 518* *Decided June 5, 1939*

Corporate Practices

REORGANIZERS COMPENSATING THEMSELVES

The bankers of a railroad, which went into receivership, formed stockholders' protective committees, became reorganization managers, and effected a plan for a new company. Their plan included a fund of $4 for each share of stock exchanged, intended to cover costs, and of each $4 the sum of $1.50 was to be set aside for their own compensation. The Interstate Commerce Commission approved a securities issue of the new company on the express condition that the $4 fund be impounded and not paid out unless authorized by the Commission.

In the district court the reorganizers presented the I.C.C. order and accomplished a transfer of the railroad property. Later they sought to have the condition invalidated; and obtained a decree enjoining enforcement of that part of the order which prohibited disbursement out of the $1.50 fund, aggregating $1,044,000.

The Supreme Court, Justice Sutherland speaking for the majority, affirmed the decree, holding that the $1.50 fund was created by private agreement between the reorganizers and stockholders under the plan; that this was a contract beyond the Commission's statutory and constitutional power. The government contended that if the railroad exercised the authority granted by a conditional order, it perforce accepted the condition. But Justice Sutherland said acceptance of the valid part of an order did not ratify an unlawful proviso.

The dissenting justices thought the decree should be reversed and the I.C.C. order upheld. In the view of Justices Stone, Holmes and Brandeis, the Court should not permit the order to stand as an unqualified approval of the securities issue after striking down the condition upon which the I.C.C. gave that order. Justice Stone examined the entire reorganization scheme and the conduct of the managers. He objected also to judicial invasion of the Commission's province.

THE OBVIOUS PURPOSE of subsection (2) of § 20(a) of the Interstate Commerce Act as added by § 439 of the Transportation Act is the prevention of any issue of securities by a rail carrier unless the Interstate Commerce Commission, "after investigation * * * of the purposes and uses of the proposed issue and the proceeds thereof, * * * finds that such issue * * * is * * * compatible with the public interest * * * and * * * reasonably necessary and appropriate" for the corporate purposes of the carrier. I suppose no one would doubt, and the opinion of the Court seems to concede, that if the assessments which, under the reorganization plan, were to be levied upon the stockholders of the old company, were all to be paid into the new one in exchange for the new securities, it would have been the duty of the Commission to investigate the purposes and uses of the new issue and its proceeds; and if it found that the issue to raise a fund for the payment of extravagant reorganization expenses was not compatible with the public interest, or reasonably necessary and appropriate for the corporate purposes of the new company, the Commission could have refused to approve it. Under subsection (3) the Commission could have provided against improper expenditures by annexing to its order the very condition which it added in the present case.

But it is said that, because no part of the $1.50 fund provided by the stockholders to pay for the reorganization would necessarily ever come into the possession or control of the new company, and since its disposition was a mere matter of private contract between the stockholders and the reorganization managers, the condition was beyond the power of the Commission. The question is thus presented, whether the salutary provisions of § 20(a) can be avoided, and an issue of securities, so far as it is made to raise a fund to defray excessive reorganization expenses, withdrawn from the control of the Commission, by the simple expedient of so arranging the reorganization plan that reorganization managers may retain and disburse, from the moneys paid in by the old stockholders to procure stock in the reorganized company, such amounts as may be required for reorganization expenses.

The history of the receivership resulting in the present reorganization will be found in the report of the Commission in the *Chicago, Milwaukee & St. Paul Ry. Co. Investigation,* 131 I.C.C. 615, issued the same day as its report in the present case. The old company having reached the end of its financial rope, and protective committees representing respectively the bondholders, the preferred, and the common stockholders having been organized, its bankers, the present reorganization managers, were active in bringing about the receivership and have since dominated the reorganization. The Commission said:

> "For months prior to the receivership they [the railroad's directors] were impotent. It was an ideal situation for the bankers to control. This they promptly did, arranged all the details, framed up the committees favorably to themselves, put themselves on the bondholders' protective committee and constituted themselves reorganization managers."

As managers they formulated the reorganization plan, and incorporated it in an agreement between themselves and the committees. In every practical sense, the reorganization managers controlled the foreclosure proceedings resulting in the sale of the property of the old company. Their representatives were the purchasers at the foreclosure sale. They created and controlled the new company, which is the appellee here. The reorganization plan gave them full power to modify it as a whole or in detail, with the approval of the committee representing the securities affected. They were authorized to carry out the plan; and in doing so they were empowered to act for, and as intermediaries between, the committees, the stockholders, and the new company. Both preferred and common stockholders of the old company were required by the plan to surrender their stock in that company, and to pay $32 for each share of their common stock, and $28 for each of their preferred, in order to procure the securities of the new company. The alternative was loss of their rights as stockholders, which were still of substantial value. The plan called for the use of these sums to pay certain obligations of the old company, and such miscellaneous fiscal requirements of the new as were not supplied by the proceeds of its funded debt, and to create the $1.50 fund, from which were to be paid, in the uncontrolled discretion of the managers, the reorganization expenses incurred in launching the new company and securing the transfer to it of the business and property of the old.

It would seem that technical distinctions between possible methods of procuring payment of the last from funds raised by a security issue of the new company ought not to affect the authority of the Commission. I should have thought that, under our decisions, the Commission, where its order controls only the action of the appellee, might look through legal forms and, disregarding the corporate entity of appellee, treat the action of the reorganization managers, in dealing with the sums paid by the stockholders for the new stock of appellee, as that of their creature and *alter ego,* the appellee. . . .

But even if we disregard this identity of interest, and whatever the form of the transaction, whether the reorganization expenses were to be paid out by the new company directly, or merely for its account by the reorganization managers, its creators, in order to enable it to acquire the railroad property for the benefit of its stockholders, the source of the expense fund was the assessments paid by the old stockholders, in reality and legal effect part consideration for, and proceeds of, the issue of the new stock. To say that so much of the reorganization agreement as related to the creation and expenditure of the $1.50 fund for the payment of these expenses was a mere private agreement, unrelated to the issue of securities, with which the Commission is vitally concerned, is to ignore its plain terms and disregard its practical operation.

The first installment of the assessments was not to be paid in by the stockholders until the plan under which the new securities were to be issued was declared operative by the managers. Stockholders who failed to pay the installments in full could acquire no rights to securities in the new company. It cannot be supposed that one dollar of the $1.50 fund would ever have been contributed by stockholders, had not the reorganization agreement definitely undertaken to issue the securities under the plan to those stockholders who deposited their stock and made the required payments. The creation of this fund for the payment of the reorganization and other expenses was a part of the necessary price exacted for the new securities. It was an important purpose for which the new stock was issued, and one of the purposes which the Commission was directed by the statute to investigate in determining, as it was bound to do, whether the issue was in the public interest and reasonably necessary and appropriate for the corporate purposes of appellee. The considerations affecting the judgment of the Commission in passing upon the reasonable necessity for the issue, its effect upon the public interest and upon the carrier's performance of its public service, are the same whether the expense fund was to be paid directly to the new company for disbursement by it, or short circuited, through the managers, from stockholders of the old to the various claimants for services rendered in creating the new.

Neither the public interest nor the duty imposed on the Interstate Commerce Commission is limited to insuring the payment of debts by any particular railroad, or procuring for it an adequate amount of money or property for the securities which it issues. An important purpose of the Transportation Act of 1920 was to preserve for the nation the transportation system as a whole, and, to that end, to secure a fair return on capital devoted to the transportation service. . . . The preservation of the transportation system and the stability of its credit essential to its preservation depend not alone upon the ability of individual carriers to meet their obligations, but upon the ability of all to attract the investment of funds in their securities. If such investments are impaired by receiverships of the carriers, followed by reorganization of excessive cost, and if railroad shareholders, compelled by the necessities of their situation, must contribute to the rehabilitation of their properties excessive amounts upon which the reorganized carrier may not earn an adequate return, railroad credit in a broad sense is affected, the permanency and stability of the transportation system as a whole is impaired, and the public interest suffers.

No one familiar with the financial and corporate history of this country could say, I think, that railroad credit and the marketability of railroad securities have not been profoundly affected, for long periods of time, if not continuously, by the numerous railroad reorganizations, in the course of which junior security holders have found it impossible to save more than a remnant of their investment, and that only by the assumption of a heavy burden of expense, too often the result of wasteful and extravagant methods of reorganization.

The public likewise has an interest in the costs of reorganization insofar as they may affect rates and the application of the recapture provision of the Transportation Act. Such costs may play an important part in the going-concern value of the new company, which is an element of value for rate-making purposes. . . . In *United Railways* v. *West* [page 148, this volume] a substantial amount was included in the rate base to cover "Cost of Financing". The mere fact that going-concern value is supplied from sources other than the treasury of the carrier, here the stockholders of the old company who became stockholders of the new, is not material. . . . The Commission is specially charged with public duties with respect to rates, valuation, and the administration of the recapture provisions. In all these respects the public interest may be adversely affected if railroad securities may be issued to effect, either directly or indirectly, the payment of excessive costs of reorganization.

If example were needed of the nature and extent of the public interest which may be involved, it is afforded by the present case. In passing upon the present issue of securities, the Commission had before it the results of its elaborate *Investigation* of the Chicago, Milwaukee & St. Paul Ry. Co., entered into after the receivership, in the course of which it commented on the excessive fees and commissions paid in the past by the railway company to its bankers, the present reorganization managers. It had before it tentative estimates of the total cost of reorganization running as high as $6,494,900. The $4 fund set apart for expenses approximated $9,330,000, of which the $1.50 fund was a part aggregating about $3,500,000, out of which were to be paid the reorganization managers, various protective committees, counsel, and depositaries. The estimated expenses to be paid from this fund ranged from $2,636,000 to $3,381,000, of which the compensation to be paid to the reorganization managers was $1,044,000.

These estimates were eighteen months old at the time the Commission made its report. The Commission concluded that the record was insufficient to enable it to arrive at an opinion as to the reasonableness of these expenses. It reserved jurisdiction to take testimony and to make further inquiry as to the expenses of reorganization, and the nature and scope of the services performed for the compensation fees claimed; but in order that the reorganization might proceed and the railroad property be released from the receivership, the authority for the issue of the new securities was granted upon the condition that the appellee impound the entire $4 fund, which was to be paid out only upon order of court or the Commission.

Since the Commission had concluded that the expenses might be excessive and that there was no adequate safeguard against improper payments, it could, under the express terms of the statute, have rejected the application. But it is said that even though the Commission might rightly have refused its permission to issue the securities, still, having granted permission, it could not annex this condition to the order; and that, as it could not compel the reorganization managers to impound the expense fund paid over to them, or to submit the reasonableness of the expenses which they had incurred to the Commission or the court, it was an arbitrary and unwarranted exercise of power to make the Commission's approval of the stock issue conditional upon such action.

If that were a valid argument, it would follow that the Commission, notwithstanding the authority given it by subsection (3), could never attach any condition to its approval of an issue of securities, when compliance with the condition would involve the performance of acts which the Commission could not command. But the only purpose of subsection (3) would seem to be to enable the Commission to induce, not compel, action, by annexing to its order, as the statute authorizes, "such terms and conditions as the Commission may deem necessary or appropriate". Notwithstanding this broad language, it may be assumed that only those conditions which, like the present, are germane to the purposes of subsection (2) are intended; and that, consequently, only such terms and conditions may be annexed to the order as tend in some measure to remove objections to the issue, which legitimately might be the basis of withholding favorable action.

If the Commission, as I think it might, could have refused to approve the present issue of securities on the ground that they were to be issued to procure payment of reorganization expenses which were or might be excessive, then, plainly, under the provisions of subsection (3) and within the purview of subsection (2), it could have made its consent to the issue conditional upon the modification of the plan, in such manner as to preclude the payment of unreasonable expenses. Appellee was not obliged to comply with the condition, since it was not compelled to proceed with the plan, although compliance with it, through the exercise of the power of the managers to modify the plan, would not, so far as appears, have been impossible or even difficult. But as the condition was one which the Commission had power to impose, appellee, having accepted the plan, cannot repudiate the condition.

Even if it be held that the condition which the Commission attached to its order was beyond its authority, I should still have thought the present case not a proper one for a court of equity to lend its aid to the appellee, and in any event that the decree below should have been so framed as to leave no doubt that the Commission was free to treat the whole order as though it had not been made.

So far as appears, not until appellee filed the present petition did it disclose any purpose to disregard the condition upon which the order depended. In the meantime it had taken full advantage of the benefits of the order. After it was granted, appellee presented to the Commission two supplemental petitions for orders authorizing payments from the expense fund, of specific amounts for corporate purposes, not including any item payable out of the $1.50 fund. The first of these was granted. Appellee stated in its first petition:

> "The applicant will make such further application or applications, if any, with respect to matters dealt with in the Commission's order and not covered hereby as from time to time may be necessary or proper."

The order of the district court having jurisdiction of the foreclosure directed that deeds of the property should not pass to the appellee until it should have been authorized by the Commission to issue the securities. The appellee, without disclosing any purpose not to comply with the Commission's order, petitioned the district court for an order directing the delivery of the deeds, exhibiting, the court below found, the order and certificate of the Commission. Upon consideration of this application, the court ordered the delivery of the deeds; and appellee then issued the new securities. Only after the reorganization had thus become an accomplished fact by appellee taking the benefit of so much of the order as suited its purposes, did it elect to repudiate the condition upon which the order was founded. Of the appellee's application to the district court, the court below rightly said, "The petition was a representation to the court that plaintiff [appellee here] had accepted the order and expected to comply with the condition. * * * "

If appellee were unable or unwilling to comply with the order as made, equity and good conscience required, at least, either disclosure of that fact to the district court before securing the transfer of the railroad property to it; application, upon full statement of the facts, to the Commission to exercise the jurisdiction, which it had reserved, to approve a modified plan; or prompt initiation of the present proceedings to test the validity of the order before a situation had been created prejudicial to the public interest and to the Commission's performance of its duties. Instead, appellee adopted a course of conduct consistent throughout only with its apparent purpose to comply with the order; and now, without tendering any excuse for the belated disclosure of its real purpose, it asks relief from the condition only after it has enjoyed benefits which it cannot be said would have been granted without the condition. Neither this Court nor the court below is acting any the less as a court of equity because its powers are invoked to deal with an order of the Interstate Commerce Commission. The failure to conform to those elementary standards of fairness and good conscience which equity may always demand as a condition of its relief to those who seek its aid, seems to require that such aid be withheld from this appellee. . . .

By the opinion of the Court, the order of the Commission, so far as it approves the issue of the securities, is treated as effective without the condition. But even if we assume that the condition which the Commission attached to the order is beyond its power, we should not attempt to substitute our judgment for that of the Commission, since the statute requires its consent, not ours; and we should not allow the order to stand without the condition, since that is not the order which the Commission made. By the Transportation Act, the giving or withholding of consent to the issue of securities is an administrative power, conferred, not upon the courts, but upon the Interstate Commerce Commission. Courts may determine whether the Commission lacks the power to impose a particular condition; but they may not strike from an order the condition upon which it was granted, and thus declare that it shall stand although the condition is not complied with. . . .

Whether or not the Commission has in fact consented does not turn on whether the condition is good or bad, but on whether it can fairly be said that the Commission would have given its unqualified consent independently of the condition. As the report of the Commission discloses, consent to the issue was given only with reluctance, to release the properties from the receivership at the earliest possible moment, but with the undoubted assumption on its part as a moving cause for its consent, that by annexing the condition it would exercise control over the reorganization expenses, with respect to the amount of which it had expressed grave concern. With four of the Commissioners voting unconditionally against the issue, I see no sufficient warrant for assuming that any would have voted for it without the condition and without the further investigation which it thought necessary, and which it was authorized to make before unconditionally approving the issue. Both the report and the order of the Commission state that the authority granted was upon the "express condition" which is now the subject of this controversy. If in the face of this language there can be any doubt as to the intention of the Commission, we need not speculate upon what it might have done, had it thought it was without power to impose the condition, since it is able to speak for itself if this Court permits it to do so by setting aside the entire order without prejudice to further action by the Commission, under the statute, upon the application for approval of the issue of the securities.

The judgment below, as interpreted by this Court, not only

makes effective an order different from any the Commission has granted, but precludes any future action by the Commission in the performance of its statutory duty. In this respect the case differs from those in which this Court has set aside an unconstitutional condition imposed by state legislation on a foreign corporation seeking to do business within a state. In those cases the judgment of this Court in no way restricts the further exercise of the legislative power of the state in any constitutional manner. Here the Commission is ousted from the exercise of power which Congress has given it, and an order is sanctioned authorizing an issue of securities which it cannot be said the Commission has approved, and which this Court does not purport to say is appropriate under the statute.

United States v. *Chicago, Milwaukee, St. Paul & Pacific Ry. Co.*
282 U.S. 311, 331 *Decided January 5, 1931*

"UNCONSCIONABLE CONDUCT" OF DIRECTORS

A STOCKHOLDER of the American Tobacco Company, a New Jersey corporation with principal place of business in New York, sued in a New York state court for the return of stock to the company's treasury by directors who had allotted it to themselves. Defendants removed the case to the federal court, which dismissed the complaint because the allotments were made pursuant to a New Jersey statute and that state's courts had made no decisions to serve as a guide; plaintiff should seek enforcement of his rights, if any, in the courts of New Jersey.

Justice Butler, delivering the opinion of the Supreme Court, observed that a stockholders' meeting had approved the directors' plan of allotting shares to employees, whereby directors were not to be ineligible. Although plaintiff charged that the statute had been used "as a cover for a raid upon the corporate treasury," Justice Butler declared this was a controversy over the company's internal affairs, and all questions relating to the plan's validity might be determined conveniently in the New Jersey courts.

Justices Stone, Brandeis and Cardozo believed that the directors had violated their duty as fiduciaries and the case should not be dismissed but decided on its merits in favor of the petitioner. Justice Stone said the stockholders were deceived by directors who were "the chief beneficiaries of their own munificence" by presenting a so-called plan which did not comply with the plain language of the statute. The "integrity of the conduct of large business concerns" was increasingly a matter of national concern.

The American Tobacco Company, organized under the laws of New Jersey, is a large and prosperous corporation, engaged in the manufacture and distribution of cigarettes and other forms of tobacco. It has upwards of 40,000 stockholders. At the commencement of this suit it had a board of sixteen directors, including a president, five vice-presidents, a secretary and a treasurer, all actively engaged in its management. For many years these officers have received large annual fixed salaries, as well as large annual cash profit-sharing bonuses paid under a by-law of the company, adopted in 1912. . . .

In the year 1930, the profit-sharing bonus of the president, added to his fixed salary of $168,000, gave him a total compensation of over $1,010,000, which was further augmented by a special "credit" of $273,470. In the same year, four of the five vice-presidents received an aggregate annual salary and bonus of more than $2,077,000. In addition, a number of stock subscription plans have from time to time been put into operation by the directors, without authority of the charter or by-laws of the corporation, or the knowledge or approval of its stockholders, by which they largely benefited. In that of 1926, the respondent Hill, the president and also a director of the company, acquired 8,000 shares of common stock, and other directors, who are respondents here, received substantial amounts. In that of 1929, one year before the transactions now complained of, 46,500 of 51,750 shares of common stock, purchased by the corporation and set aside for the purpose, were sold to the corporate directors at $47 per share less than market value. Convenient arrangements were made for postponed payment of the purchase price. Respondents received 23,050 shares, of which the president received 15,050.

On January 28, 1931, a new allotment of stock was made, which is the subject of this litigation. On that day, the Board of Directors (the president and officers constituting a majority of those in attendance) considered and passed upon the adequacy of the compensation which its members were then receiving for their services to the corporation, and the necessity of conferring further benefits on themselves in order to insure the continuance of those services. Having resolved these questions in their own favor, they proceeded to award additional benefits in the form of the privilege to subscribe to unissued common stock B of the corporation, at a small fraction of its market value.

By resolution of that date, they put into effect a stock subscription plan by which 56,712 shares of unissued common stock B of the corporation were distributed in accordance with recommendations made by the president. Of this number 32,370, more than half, were allotted to the directors, of which 13,440 were allotted to the president. The remaining 24,342 shares were allotted in relatively small amounts to 525 employees. None of the recipients was of lower rank than factory subassistant. Four hundred and seventy-three received allotments of less than 100 shares each, the greater majority receiving from 15 to 50 shares. The stated consideration for issue of the stock was a subscription price of $25 per share, the par value, and the services of the allottee, not specifically described, to be rendered to the American Tobacco Company for the remainder of the year.

The certificates of stock were to be delivered to the respondents, the Guaranty Trust Company of New York and an individual, as trustees. They were authorized to borrow money upon them to the extent of $25 per share, in order to effect immediate payment of the subscription price to the tobacco company, to apply dividends received on account of the purchase price to be paid by the allottees and to deliver the certificates to them after the close of the year, upon payment in full of their subscriptions.

They were given discretion to waive performance of the stipulated service by any allottee and in the event that the subscriber was discharged or resigned from the employ of the company within the year, to cancel the subscription agreement or not, as they pleased.

On the day of the resolution allotting the stock, its market price was $112 per share, more than four times the subscription price. It was then paying, and has ever since paid, dividends at the rate of $5 per year, sufficient to pay the subscription price in five years. Valuing the subscription privilege by the difference between the subscription price and the market value of the shares, the president received by the allotment the equivalent of $1,169,280, in addition to his annual compensation of more than $1,000,000. The stock subscription rights awarded the five vice-presidents, similarly valued, amounted to $1,451,595. That the subscription privilege, accorded for the avowed purpose of assuring the continuance of these executives in the company's employ, was then and has been ever since of great value, upon any theory of valuation, is not questioned.

Conceiving himself aggrieved by this transaction, petitioner, a non-assenting stockholder, brought two suits in the Supreme Court of New York, the state in which he resides, joining as defendants the American Tobacco Company, the trustees of the allotted stock, and certain of the directors, including the president, secretary, treasurer and five vice-presidents, one of whom has since died and two of whom were not served with process. Included in the relief sought was a decree that the corporation, its officers and directors be enjoined from carrying out the stock allotments and that the stock allotted to the directors be surrendered to the company. On motion of defendants, the tobacco company and a nonresident director, the causes were removed to the District Court for Southern New York, on grounds of diversity of citizenship of the parties to a separable controversy, and there consolidated.

Thus called upon in this suit to account for their stewardship and to justify their action, the defendants, the respondents here, place their whole reliance upon a statute of New Jersey in conformity with which, they contend, they secured, in advance, the authorization of the stockholders to make the challenged allotments of stock.

Section 1, c. 175, of the New Jersey Laws for 1920 . . . authorizes any New Jersey corporation to provide and carry out a plan for "(a) the issue or the purchase and sale of its capital stock to any or all of its employees and those actively engaged in the conduct of its business or to trustees on their behalf * * * and for aiding any such employees and said other persons in paying for such stock by contributions, compensation for services, otherwise. * * * " Section 2(b) . . . provides that, where, as in this case, the corporation has been formed without charter or by-law provisions authorizing the issuance or the purchase and sale of stock for such purposes, "the board of directors shall first formulate such plan or plans and pass a resolution declaring that in its opinion the adoption thereof is advisable, and shall call a meeting of the stockholders to take action thereon. * * * " It requires an affirmative vote of two-thirds in interest of each class of stockholders, present at the meeting, for the adoption of the plan.

In June, 1930, the directors, purporting to act under this statute, presented to the stockholders, by notice of a special meeting, a so-called "plan" under which the employees of the corporation and those actively engaged in its business were to be permitted to subscribe to unissued shares of its common stock B. The notice of the meeting was accompanied by a document designated "Employees' Stock Subscription Plan," and by a copy of resolutions of the board of directors authorizing the submission of the plan to the stockholders, proposing a reduction in the par value of the common stock and the nonvoting common stock B from $50 to $25 per share, and an increase of the authorized common stock from 1,000,000 to 2,000,000 shares, and of the authorized common stock B from 2,000,0000 to 4,000,000 shares, each stockholder to receive two shares of the new stock for one of the old. By thus increasing the authorized, unissued shares of common B, stock was to be made available for subscription by employees.

The Employees' Stock Subscription Plan proposed

"to allot for subscription * * * by way of additional compensation for services to be rendered, shares of unissued common stock B * * * to such employees of the corporation and/or its subsidiaries and those actively engaged in the conduct of its or their business as may be selected. * * * "

The prescribed method of execution of the plan was that

"the Board of Directors may, at such time or times as it may determine * * * offer and allot such stock for subscription * * * in such amounts and proportions, to such persons, at such prices, not less than the par value of the shares allotted, payable in full or in such installments, and upon such other terms and conditions, all as shall be determined with respect to each offering of stock to each individual pursuant to authority to be granted by the Board of Directors to the President for such purpose."

Accompanying the notice of the meeting was a circular letter by the president to stockholders in which they were told of the prosperous condition of the company, that the purpose of the stock allotment plan was to encourage those who had made the company's success possible to continue in its employ, and that it was the expectation of the Board of Directors, if the program set forth in the notice of the meeting and accompanying documents should be approved by stockholders, to declare an extra dividend of $4 per share on the common stock and common stock B, and to initiate regular quarterly dividends on the newly authorized shares of common stock and common stock B at the increased annual rate of $5 per share. The letter closed with a request to sign and return the enclosed proxy, thereby indicating "your approval of the proposed steps and your support of your Company's management".

Moved, perhaps, by these inducements, the proposal was approved at the meeting by vote of the requisite number of shares of each class.

No disclosure was made to the stockholders by the officers and directors of the stock subscription plans previously put into operation by them, without authority of the charter or by-laws or the knowledge and approval of the stockholders. No disclosure was made of the number or amounts of the annual cash bonuses which had been paid to the president and vice-presidents of the company, under the by-law adopted in 1912, and never, so far as appears, subsequently mentioned to the stockholders until after the stock allotments here involved. The only hint of the intention of the management to participate in the proposed Employees' Stock Subscription Plan was contained in a single sentence appearing in the Plan:

"No employee, or person actively engaged in the conduct of the business of the Corporation, or its subsidiaries, shall be deemed ineligible to the benefits of the Plan by reason of being also a director of the Corporation or of any of its subsidiaries or of holding any office therein."

With all these facts presented by the pleadings, the District Court, acknowledging its jurisdiction both as a federal court and a court of equity to decide the case on its merits, nevertheless, held that as the suit concerns the internal affairs of a New Jersey corporation, discretion should be exercised to dismiss it without prejudice to its maintenance in the courts of New Jersey. On appeal, the Circuit Court of Appeals for the Second Circuit, Judge Swan dissenting, considered the merits and upheld the legality of the stock allotments. The decree of dismissal was affirmed on the merits and the trial court has entered a final decree accordingly. This Court now reverses that judgment, reëstablishing the original decree of the trial court, on the ground that a proper exercise of judicial discretion requires that the case should not be heard. Thus after approximately two years of litigation in state and federal courts, all of which could, and I think should, have decided the case on the merits, the plaintiff must now start the litigation afresh in the courts of New Jersey.

In determining whether the federal courts should decline to exercise the jurisdiction conferred on them by removal, the nature of this controversy and its merits cannot be ignored. I do not stop to consider numerous objections to the stock allotments, urged by petitioner, which are not without weight. It suffices for present purposes that no plan of sufficient definiteness to comply with the New Jersey statute was ever submitted to the stockholders for their approval; and that even if it be conceded that a "plan" was approved, the action of the directors in allotting the stock to themselves, in violation of their duty as fiduciaries, exceeded the authority conferred upon them by the stockholders, and was, therefore, *ultra vires.*

The statute directs that the board of directors shall "first formulate such plan", declare it "advisable", and call a meeting of stockholders to act on it. Without presenting for the consideration of the stockholders any workable plan of stock allotment, the directors, in effect, asked the stockholders to confer plenary authority on them to formulate a plan and to carry it into execution without any disclosure of its provisions. After the meeting, as before, no stockholder, not in the confidence of the directors, knew in what the plan consisted, who were the persons to participate in it, what principle was to control their selection or determine the amount of stock they were to receive, or the price they were to pay.

It is a misuse of words of plain meaning to speak of such a proposal as a "plan", much less a formulated plan for stock allotment to employees, or as one which, in the form presented to the stockholders, the directors could have pronounced advisable or have carried into operation. It was no more than an invitation to stockholders to abrogate the discretion which the statute vested in them to approve a formulated plan, having at least some aspects of definiteness, and vest in the directors powers which could be conferred on them only by charter amendment in the manner prescribed by the statute. The invitation was accompanied by a skillfully phrased suggestion that it was necessary to accept it in order to hold the services of the employees, and that, if accepted, the directors would cause new benefits to flow into the pockets of stockholders in the form of extra and increased dividends. Such a maneuver cannot rightly be regarded as a compliance with the plain language of the statute, which requires the directors first to formulate a plan for stock allotment and declare it advisable, and then to submit it to the stockholders for their approval. If it were, it would be difficult to suggest any conceivable purpose of the statute which could not be thwarted by a similar procedure.

The respondents stand in no better position, even if we assume that the proposal submitted to the stockholders was a formulated plan, within the meaning of the New Jersey statute. For in that case, authority for the directors' action must be found in the stockholders' approval of the proposal which they submitted, and we must interpret the proposal and the action taken by the stockholders in terms of their legitimate expectation that the directors were complying with their duty as fiduciaries and not dealing with them at arm's length. They were entitled to read the proposal in the light of the fundamental duty of directors to derive no profit from their own official action, without the consent of the stockholders, obtained after full and fair revelation of every circumstance which might reasonably influence them to withhold their consent. . . . They were entitled to assume that the proposal involved nothing which did not fairly appear on its face and above all that it was not a cloak for a scheme by which the directors were to enrich themselves in great amounts at the expense of the corporation, of whose interest they were the legal guardians.

The respondents must, therefore, rest their case on the bare statement in their proposal to the stockholders that no employee or person actively engaged in the business of the company "shall be deemed ineligible to the benefits of the Plan" because a director or officer. But it would be extravagant to say that these words, addressed by men in the position of trustees to their beneficiaries gave warning of wholesale gratuities which the directors subsequently bestowed upon themselves. No more extensive authority could be derived from this language than the disclosure which it made. By consenting that the directors should be "eligible" to share in a plan avowedly for the benefit of employees, the stockholders did not consent that they should be the chief beneficiaries of their own unrestrained munificence, or that they should add any new bounties to the unrevealed stock allotments and bonuses which the directors had previously enjoyed in secrecy. Even if the stockholders consented that some of the directors should be eligible to benefit from action taken by other disinterested directors, they certainly did not consent that the allotments should be made by a group of directors who, because of the magnitude of the benefits they anticipated for themselves, were obviously incapable of passing an independent and unbiased judgment upon the propriety of the distribution which they coöperated in making to each other. Respondents' contention that if the directors were unable to vote on each other's participation no plan could be put into effect under which a majority of the directors were to participate, is without weight, for it obviously could be if the statute were followed and the plan revealed in its entirety to the stockholders.

To surmount these difficulties, respondents point to the fact that a representative of petitioner stated at the stockholders' meeting that favorable action on the proposal might result in the issuance of a large amount of stock to employees, including officers and directors, without adequate consideration, and that this did not induce the stockholders to express their disapproval. It is unnecessary to speculate whether this outcome is to be attributed to the fact that those present, being without the aid of prevision, regarded the prediction as too improbable to be credited, or to the fact that those who attended the meeeting were not, for the most part, the stockholders, but the recipients of their proxies selected by the management of the corporation for the occasion. A statement made to them would, as a New Jersey court has said, fall "upon ears not allowed to hear and minds not permitted to judge; upon automatons, whose principals are uninformed of their own injury". . . . In any event it is enough that neither in the notice of meeting and accompanying documents, which the stockholders saw and on which they relied, nor at the meeting itself, did the officers and directors disclose that such was their purpose.

We need not conjecture whether, if the directors had had the hardihood to disclose in advance the benefits which they were to award to themselves, the stockholders would nevertheless have given their approval. Nor is it important that these directors have successfully managed the corporation and that under their direction it has earned large profits for its stockholders. Their business competence did not confer on them the privilege of making concealed or unauthorized profits or relieve them of the elementary obligation which the law imposes on all corporate directors to deal frankly and openly with stockholders in seeking their consent to benefit personally by reason of their relationship to the corporation.

The directors, having failed to comply with petitioner's reasonable demand that they exercise their authority to bring this suit in the name of the corporation, petitioner was not required by general equitable principles or by Equity Rule 27 to appeal to the stockholders before bringing it, as the action complained of here was not one which the stockholders could ratify. . . . Authority of the directors to bestow gratuities upon themselves in the form of subscription rights must be found in a plan approved in advance as the statute provides, by two-thirds of each class of stockholders. If no plan was presented to stockholders, as I think was the case, the entire stock issue was *ultra vires* and cannot be ratified any more than any other unauthorized disposition of corporate assets. If the proposal to the stockholders is regarded as a plan, so far as ordinary employees are concerned, as it plainly does not embrace authority to the directors to confer such extravagant benefits upon themselves, the result is the same, as to the stock allotted to the directors.

I cannot agree that a proper exercise of discretion requires us to deny to the petitioner the relief to which he is so clearly entitled. This is the first time that this Court has held that a federal court should decline to hear a case on the ground that it concerns the internal affairs of a corporation foreign to the state in which it sits. We may assume, without deciding, that neither a federal nor a state court of equity will, as a general rule, undertake to administer the internal affairs of a foreign corporation. But the case before us is, in this respect, unlike a suit to dissolve the corporation and wind up its affairs . . . , or compel the declaration of a dividend . . . , or interfere with the election of officers or the meetings of shareholders or directors. . . .

We are presented with no problem of administration. The only relief which the petitioner merits on the record before us or which he asks here is a decree that certain directors, now before the Court, restore to the treasury of the corporation, also before the Court, certain shares of stock alleged to have been illegally issued to them, and that certificates for the stock now in possession of the trustees, who are likewise before the Court, be surrendered. There are no more obstacles to the rendition of an effective decree than in any other case in which a stockholder seeks reparation for depredations upon the corporate property committed by directors, some of whom only are before the Court. . . . The decree will be completely satisfied by delivery of the certificates, properly endorsed, to the corporation. There is and can be no suggestion that such a decree cannot be pronounced and enforced as effectively by the courts in New York as it could be by those in New Jersey. . . .

The opinion of the Court concedes, as, indeed, the authorities which it cites show, that the decision does not rest upon any definite rule of general application. It is said that jurisdiction will be declined whenever considerations of convenience, efficiency and justice point to the courts of the state of the corporate domicil as appropriate tribunals for the determination of the particular case. Such considerations are said to require that this suit be dismissed though the petitioner is thereby subjected to all the hazards of starting his action anew, in the courts of New Jersey.

To support this conclusion, only two objections to the maintenance of the suit are suggested in the opinion of this Court or in that of the district court below. One is that numerous beneficiaries of the stock allotment, most of whom are not officers or directors of the corporation, are not made parties to this suit and presumably can be reached as a group only by suit in New Jersey. Hence, the intimation is, if we decide this case and other suits should subsequently be brought in other jurisdictions, different results may be reached on the same questions, a possibility which can be avoided by forcing the petitioner to bring a single suit in New Jersey. The other objection is that the Court would be called upon to decide a novel question of New Jersey law.

As petitioner has chosen to assert demands necessarily restricted to the stock issued by the directors to themselves, he had no occasion to join as parties the several hundred lesser employees, the great preponderance of whom received allotments of less than fifty shares of stock. Indeed, as the unconscionable conduct of the participating directors, a major factor in this case, would afford no basis for proceeding against the other allottees, it is by no means certain that the suit would be cast in any different form if brought in New Jersey.

The somewhat speculative possibility that those of the participating directors who have not been served with process in this suit may be called to answer in some other court and exonerated is of slight importance compared to the considerations favoring the exercise of jurisdiction. Petitioner has chosen to bring his suit in New York. He and all but one of the individual defendants reside there. The principal office of the American Tobacco Company is in New York City and it is there that its books and records are found, its board of directors meets and the acts complained of took place. There the respondent, Guaranty Trust Company, is located, and its co-trustee resides. Before the decree can be enforced it must be obtained and the litigation must be brought to a successful conclusion. That involves the production in court of the necessary evidence. Of the parties to this case none but the American Tobacco Company is amenable to process in New Jersey; all are amenable in the Southern District of New York. In New York, petitioner can compel them and others connected with the corporation to attend as witnesses; all can be ordered to make complete discovery; and petitioner can compel the production at the trial of the records of both corporate defendants. We cannot assume that compulsion will not be necessary. The tobacco company carried to the highest court of the state its resistance to petitioner's preliminary application to inspect its books. . . . In New York also the individual defendants and the trust company can be reached by injunction *pendente lite,* restraining the transfer to innocent purchasers of the stock, certificates for which are already issued and in the hands of the trust company. Under the circumstances of this case, only considerations of more compelling force than the possibility of inconsistent decree should lead a forum, convenient in so many respects, to decline jurisdiction.

I come then to the only ground which can plausibly be urged for declining the jurisdiction—that in one, but not necessarily a conclusive aspect of the case, the Court may be called on to decide questions of New Jersey law which, although novel, can hardly be said to be complicated or difficult. If there were any principle of federal jurisprudence, generally applicable, that in cases between private parties federal courts of equity may, in their discretion, decline jurisdiction because called upon to decide an unsettled question of state law, I would willingly acquiesce in declining it here. But this Court has not declared such a principle and does not recognize it now. On the contrary, whether jurisdiction rests on diversity of citizenship or on a substantial constitutional question, this Court has consistently ruled that it is the duty of a federal court of original jurisdiction, and of this Court on appeal from its decree, to pass on any state question necessarily involved, however novel, and that the decision may be rested on that ground alone. . . .

Unless we are now to abandon that long settled practice, I can see much more reason for passing on this question than upon many others which this Court has decided. Our judgment would conflict with no local decisions . . . , nor apply an alien policy to matters which are the subject of delicate feeling in the state. . . . Indeed, we may not even avoid deciding the question of state law by sending the case to New Jersey, for it is not suggested that if petitioner should elect to sue in the federal court for New Jersey, or if the suit should be properly brought there by removal from the state court, either that court or this may decline jurisdiction. Thus we should do no more in deciding the question of New Jersey law now than if the case were brought to us from the federal courts in New Jersey.

Even if decision of the question of New Jersey law were more embarrassing than it appears to be here, a proper exercise of discretion would seem to require that the bill be retained, and that an interlocutory injunction restraining any disposition of the stock by respondents be granted as prayed, pending the diligent prosecution by petitioner of a suit in New Jersey. . . .

If federal courts are to continue the general practice of deciding novel questions of state law whenever there are necessary or convenient grounds for the disposition of cases pending before them, there are peculiarly cogent reasons why there should be no departure from the practice in cases like the present. While a corporation in legal theory has only one domicil, in practice its activities are often nationwide and the legal domicil of the corporation, as in this case, is neither the place of its real corporate life nor the home of its officers and directors. Hence, if stockholders' suits, such as the present, are to be maintained with any hope of success, the practical necessities of making parties, securing evidence, obtaining the production of documents and relief by injunction against individual wrongdoers, justify, if they do not compel, their prosecution in the particular jurisdiction where necessary parties and witnesses may be found, rather than in the place of the technical corporate domicil.

Extension of corporate activities, distribution of corporate personnel, stockholders and directors through many states, and the diffusion of corporate ownership, separated from corporate management, make the integrity of the conduct of large business corporations increasingly a matter of national rather than local concern (cf. A. A. Berle, Jr., and Gardiner C. Means, *The Modern Corporation and Private Property*), to which the federal courts should be quick to respond when their jurisdiction is rightly invoked. We should be slow, indeed, to make a reluctance to decide questions of state law, not exhibited in other classes of cases, the ground for declining to decide this one.

Rogers v. *Guaranty Trust Co. of New York et al.*
288 U. S. 123, 133 Decided January 23, 1933

DOMINATION BY A HOLDING COMPANY

UNDER the "commodities clause" of the Interstate Commerce Act railroad carriers are forbidden to transport articles in which they have a direct or indirect interest. The government alleged violation by a railroad which was wholly owned by the United States Steel Corporation, a holding company whose producing subsidiaries furnished 60 percent of the road's tonnage.

Justice McReynolds, for the majority, which decided against the government, cited a case where common ownership of stock of a railroad and a shipper was held not necessarily unlawful; as Congress had not amended the commodities clause since that decision, it must be concluded that the interpretation had Congress' approval. Although the government rested on a later case involving domination by a holding company, Justice McReynolds said it must be rejected as a declaration of abstract principle. Here the railroad functioned as an independent carrier, and the evidence showed no such control.

Three dissenting justices, Stone, Brandeis and Cardozo, read the evidence differently. They looked "through the forms to the realities of the relation" and found a record of "complete subservience" to the Steel Corporation. "Those familiar with present-day methods of corporate control," Justice Stone wrote, "will not be so naïve. . . ."

The language of the commodities clause, read in the light of its legislative history, can leave no doubt that its purpose was to withhold from every interstate rail carrier the inducement and facility for favoritism and abuse of its powers as a common carrier, which experience had shown are likely to occur when a single business interest occupies the inconsistent position of carrier and shipper. See *United States* v. *Reading Co.*, 253 U. S. 26. Before the enactment of the commodities clause, Congress, by sweeping prohibitions, had made unlawful every form of rebate to shippers and every form of discrimination in carrier rates, service, and facilities, injurious to shippers or the public. By the Sherman Anti-Trust Act it had forbidden combinations in restraint of interstate commerce. But it did not stop there. The commodities clause was aimed, not at the practices of railroads already penalized, but at the suppression of the power and the favorable opportunity, inseparable from actual control of both shipper and carrier by the same interest, to engage in practices already forbidden and others inimical to the performance of carrier duties to the public. . . .

It is not denied that the "indirect" interest of the carrier in the commodity transported, at which the statute strikes, may be effected through the instrumentality of a holding company which owns the stock both of the carrier and the company which manufactures and ships the commodity. This was definitely established by the decision in *United States* v. *Reading Co.*, *supra,* where it was held that the power of control through holding company ownership of all the capital stock both of an interstate rail carrier and a shipper producing the commodity carried, plus an active exercise of that control, are enough to make the transportation unlawful.

While it was recognized, as had been held [in a case cited by the majority], that mere ownership, by a carrier or a shipper, of the stock of the other, does not call the statute into operation, the Court was careful to point out that, "where such ownership of stock is resorted to, not for the purpose of participating in the affairs of the corporation in which it is held in a manner normal and usual with stockholders, but for the purpose of making it a mere agent, or instrumentality or department of another company, the courts will look through the forms to the realities of the relation between the companies as if the corporate agency did not exist and will deal with them as the justice of the case may require". Domination in fact by a holding company both of the rail carrier and the producing shipper of commodities, in addition to its legal power to dominate them, is enough to bring the carrier within the prohibition of the commodities clause.

The only question for our decision is whether the complete power of the United States Steel Corporation, through stock ownership, to dominate both appellee and certain shippers over its lines, has been exercised sufficiently to exemplify the evil which the commodities clause was intended to prevent, and so to bring appellee within its condemnation. It is of no consequence that complaints of rebates by appellee to United States Steel Corporation subsidiaries have not been sustained . . . , or that the Steel Corporation and its subsidiaries have been held not to infringe the Sherman Anti-Trust Act. . . . The commodities clause does not forbid rebating or attempts to monopolize interstate commerce, which are dealt with by other statutes. It is concerned with transportation of commodities by a rail carrier where the carrier and the producer and shipper are so dominated by the same interest, through the exercise of power secured by stock ownership, as to make rebates, discriminations, attempts to monopolize, and other abuses of carrier power easy, and their detection and punishment difficult.

It is not important, as the court below thought, that in the relations between the Steel Corporation and its subsidiaries "there was a scrupulous recognition of the separate entities", or that all transactions between them were "in the form of transactions and communications between two separate and distinct corporations", or that the business and accounts of each subsidiary "were kept separate and distinct" from those of others. Nor is it of any moment, as this Court seems to imply, that the affiliates do not have the same officers and directors, and that some years ago they abandoned the practice of maintaining interlocking directorates.

Those familiar with present-day methods of corporate control will not be so naïve as to suppose that the complete domination in fact of its subsidiaries by a holding company owning all their stock is in any way inconsistent with scrupulous recognition of their separate corporate entities, or with the maintenance of separate accounts and distinct personnels of officers and directors. Every holding company presupposes a relationship between it and a distinct corporate entity and its power to control the latter. Where the issue is whether that power has been exercised, "courts will look through the forms to the realities of the relation between the companies as if the corporate agencies did not exist". Hence we are presently concerned with what is in fact done in the Steel Corporation's exercise of its power to control, not with the particular legal forms or methods under cover of which control may in fact be effected. And, since we must look to its acts of control, in addition to its power acquired by stock ownership, as the decisive test, we must scrutinize what has occurred in the past as the best indication of the manner and extent of the use which may be made of the power in the future.

In appraising the Steel Corporation's acts of control over the appellee, it is of significance that the dominant interest in the intercompany relationship, unlike that in the earlier cases brought before the Court, is that of production and not of transportation. Appellee, although a common carrier, subject to public duties and responsibilities, is, in its relation to the Steel Corporation and its subsidiaries, but an appanage to their vast steel-producing business. While the commodities clause makes no distinction between the one type of domination and the other, such control of a railroad is far more menacing to the public and to rival producers than is domination of producer interests by a carrier. When the carrier interest predominates, extension of its transportation facilities beyond the demands of its producing affiliates, and even to their competitors, with resulting benefit to the public, may well ensue. But, where the producing interest is dominant, and the carrier is chiefly engaged in transporting the commodities of producing affiliates, restricted or indifferent service to competing producers and to the public, tardy or inadequate extension of facilities, discrimination in furnishing service and facilities, are dangers especially to be anticipated.

In such a relationship, control of carrier capital accumulation, expansion, and expenditure, is a peculiarly convenient and effective means of subordinating carrier public service to the interests of production, by restriction of carrier expansion which would benefit the public and competing producers, or by allowing it only under discriminatory conditions. It is with these general considerations in mind, especially pertinent to the present case, that its facts should be examined.

Since its formation in 1901, the Steel Corporation has owned all the capital stock of the appellee railroad and of the Illinois Steel Company, a manufacturing company which appellee serves. Through lease, in 1909, of the Chicago, Lake Shore & Eastern Railway line, and the acquisition of appurtenant trackage rights over another line, appellee secured and maintains direct transportation facilities between the Illinois Steel Company and mines and quarries, all subsidiaries of the Steel Corporation. Sixty percent of appellee's tonnage is furnished by Steel Corporation subsidiaries.

Although the Steel Corporation is exclusively a holding and not an operating company, its by-laws defining the president's duties provide that he "shall have general charge of the business of the corporation relating to manufacturing, mining and transportation". The record shows that this authority is exercised by close and constant supervision over the business and affairs of Steel Corporation subsidiaries, not through the formal proceedings of stockholders' and directors' meetings, but through conferences and correspondence taking place directly between the officers of the Steel Corporation and those of its subsidiaries.

From 1901 to 1920 there were on appellee's board of directors never less than four officers or directors of the Steel Corporation, selected from its most important officers. Since 1920 the appellee's board of directors has been selected by appellee's president and elected by him acting as proxy for the Steel Corporation. He has likewise selected the officers, who have been elected by the board at his suggestion. The record is replete with evidence, chiefly correspondence, showing the complete subservience of appellee's president to the officers of the Steel Corporation in matters of corporate policy. The subservience of appellee's board of directors to its president, and through him in turn to the Steel Corporation, is exemplified by appellee's settled practice from 1910 until the time of suit of entering into contracts without any previous approval by its board of directors. At its annual meeting of directors the contracts which have been previously entered into, and often have already been performed, are ratified and confirmed. This procedure was followed with respect to all contracts, some 2,313 in number, executed on behalf of appellee between 1910 and 1933.

Appellee's fiscal policy has for many years been dominated and rigidly controlled by the Steel Corporation. Dividends have been habitually declared and the amount of them fixed only after securing, by correspondence, the consent and approval of the officers of the Steel Corporation. The Steel Corporation draws to itself the surplus funds of its subsidiaries, including appellee, which are deposited with it, for its own use, often upon its specific request or demand, and at a rate of interest which it fixes. These funds are withdrawn by draft of the subsidiary, payable only upon acceptance by the Steel Corporation, and customarily upon notice given in advance. From 1920 to 1933 appellee's aggregate deposits with the Steel Corporation were $79,000,000, of which $32,000,000 were made at the request or demand of the Steel Corporation.

Since its formation the Steel Corporation has maintained under its direction and control a clearance account, by which monthly settlement is made of intercompany accounts among its various subsidiaries. All of appellee's settlements of such accounts, except freight charges and traffic claims, are cleared through this account. The account is managed by the controller of the Steel Corporation. Interest is charged or allowed on balances due in the account at a rate of interest fixed by the treasurer of the Steel Corporation. Terms of settlement are controlled by it and not by free bargaining of debtor and creditor.

By direction of the finance committee of the Steel Corporation, its subsidiaries, including appellee, are required to obtain in advance the approval of the committee of all expenditures for capital account and improvements in excess of a specified amount. From 1920 to 1932 the limit was $10,000, since which it has been $5,000. Since 1908 the officers of the Steel Corporation have issued from time to time, to all its subsidiaries, instructions outlining in detail the rules and procedure governing their application to the Steel Corporation for its approval of their expenditures for improvements. This requirement was not perfunctory. Failure to secure from the officers of the Steel Corporation, in advance, the approval of capital expenditures, brought from them by letter or telegram swift reminder of the neglect. Requests for approval of proposed expenditures have been the occasion for careful inquiry by the officers of the Steel Corporation as to their necessity and propriety. In recent years approximately 70 percent of appellee's total capital expenditures have been of the class requiring consent by the Steel Corporation. Included were items directly affecting appellee's transportation service, such as the cost of rolling stock, procuring an adequate water supply for its engines, improvement of its right of way, and additional yard facilities.

With such minute and continuous control of capital outlays of appellee by an organization primarily interested in production rather than common carrier service, it is not surprising that the only expansion of appellee during the period of control has been its lease of the line of the Chicago, Lake Shore & Eastern Railway, a subsidiary of a Steel Corporation producing affiliate, the Illinois Steel Company, which it served almost exclusively, and the acquisition through this lease of a trackage privilege over the Chicago & Eastern Illinois Railroad, restricted to the hauling of products of producing subsidiaries of the Steel Corporation—an arrangement by which appellee raised its tonnage from subsidiaries of the Steel Corporation from 25 percent to 60 percent.

It was the chairman of the board of the Steel Corporation, not the officers of appellee, who had the deciding voice in determining whether the lease should be taken and who assumed active control of the negotiations for its acquisition. Again, in 1920, when the trackage agreement was subject to cancellation by reason of the receivership of the Chicago & Eastern Illinois, it was the chairman of the board of the Steel Corporation who actively controlled the successful negotiation for a continuance of the agreement.

The record discloses many other forms of actual control of the business and affairs of appellee by the Steel Corporation which it is unnecessary to detail. It is enough that those mentioned, when examined in their setting, show with convincing force that the appellee railroad is in fact obedient to the dominating control of producers of commodities which it transports. In every instance when the Steel Corporation has conceived that it had any interest to subserve, appellee has willingly done its bidding. In none has there been any indication of a disposition to pursue any policy not at least tacitly approved by the Steel Corporation. The active and continuous control over appellee's finances and expenditures is alone sufficient to create a continuing danger of neglect and abuse of appellee's carrier duties in favor of the dominating production and shipping interest, a temptation and an opportunity which it was the purpose of the commodities clause to forestall. In addition, the Steel Corporation has exerted that power, in the acquisition of the Lake Shore lease and its appurtenant trackage rights, to secure special advantages for its producing subsidiaries. The trackage rights extend only to hauling their own product, not that of their rivals.

This relationship passes far beyond that which is normal between a railroad and its stockholders and establishes a control over appellee's policy as complete as though it were but a department of the Steel Corporation. If the commodities clause permits control such as is exhibited here, one is at a loss to say what scope remains for the operation of the statute. Whatever views may be entertained of the soundness and wisdom of the decision in [case cited by the majority], it neither requires nor excuses our reduction of the commodities clause to a cipher in the calculations of those who control the railroads of the country.

United States v. *Elgin, Joliet & Eastern Ry. Co.*
298 U. S. 492, 504 *Decided May 25, 1936*

Public Utility Rate-Making

COST OF REPRODUCTION NEW

A "RECAPTURE ORDER" of the Interstate Commerce Commission, under the Interstate Commerce Act (Transportation Act of 1920), directed the St. Louis & O'Fallon Railway Company to pay the I.C.C. one-half of its earnings in excess of six percent of the value of the property. The road denied excess, disputing the Commission's valuation.

The Supreme Court's decision pointed out that the statute commanded the Commission to give due consideration to all elements of value recognized by the law of the land. One of these elements, approved in a series of Court decisions, was "the present cost of construction or reproduction". Justice McReynolds declared for the majority that the Commission had failed to consider this rule and was therefore in error.

Justice Brandeis dissented in an exhaustive opinion joined by Justices Holmes and Stone. True, Congress directed consideration "to all elements", but neither Congress nor the Court required the I.C.C. to give evidence of reproduction cost mechanical effect. The Commissioners were divided on whether Congress intended to let them determine what weight to give that evidence; their own majority reported that railroad value "approaches more nearly the reasonable and necessary investment in property than the cost of reproducing it at a particular time". Justice Stone wrote a separate opinion, supported by Holmes and Brandeis:

I AGREE with what Mr. Justice Brandeis has said, and add a word only by way of emphasis of those aspects of the case which appear to me sufficient, apart from all other considerations, to sustain the finding of the Commission.

The report of the Interstate Commerce Commission is rejected and its order set aside on the sole ground that, in a recapture proceeding under § 15a of the Interstate Commerce Act, it has failed to consider present reproduction cost or value of appellant's property and so to "give due consideration to all the elements of value recognized by the law of the land for rate making purposes." No constitutional question is involved.

The Commission was called upon to value a railroad, with less than nine miles of main line track, which had been constructed prior to 1900. Much of its equipment was purchased before 1908; a considerable part being acquired secondhand. Its traffic was very largely dependent on the output of a few coal mines which it served.

In performing its task, the Commission had before it the cost of reproduction new of appellant's structural property, estimated on the basis of 1914 unit prices, "with the knowledge that the costs of reproduction so arrived at were not greatly different from the original costs". It had evidence of the actual cost of later additions and replacements, of the physical condition of the railroad and equipment, of the character, volume, and sources of its traffic, of its working capital and revenues and expenses. It possessed, through its valuation department, special knowledge of the property of this carrier. Through its own experience it had the benefit of an expert knowledge of all the factors affecting value of railway property growing out of changes in methods of transportation, of improvement in transportation appliances, and the consequent obsolescence of existing equipment, of improvement in methods of railroad construction and consequent reductions in cost. Although it had estimates of present construction costs in the form of index figures based on the comparative general price levels of labor and materials for 1914 and each of the recapture years, which it considered and discussed in its report, there was no evidence before it of the actual present cost of construction of this or any other railroad or any affirmative showing that, if appellant's road was to be built and equipped anew, competent railroad engineers would deem the present structure and equipment suitable for or adaptable to the economical and efficient management contemplated by the statute.

After stating that it had before it the evidence above outlined, including that of reproduction cost, and such other matters as the carrier desired to bring to its attention, the Commission added, "From this accumulated information we have formed our judgment as to the fair basic single sum values, not by the use of any formula, but after consideration of all relevant facts". That the Commission gave consideration to present reproduction costs appears not only from its own statement, but from the fact that it gave full effect to increased current market values in determining the value of land and to additions and betterments since June 30, 1914, taken at their cost less depreciation. In the light of those considerations which affect the present value of appellant's structural property which Mr. Justice Brandeis has mentioned, I cannot say that the Commission did not have before it the requisite data for forming a trustworthy judgment of the value of appellant's road or that it failed to give to proof of reproduction cost all the weight to which it was entitled on its merits. Had the Commission not turned aside to point out in its report the economic fallacies of the use of reproduction cost as a standard of value for rate-making purposes, which it nevertheless considered and to some extent applied, I suppose it would not have occurred to any one to question the validity of its order.

I cannot avoid the conclusion that, in substance, the objection, now upheld, to the order of the Commission, is not that it failed to consider or give appropriate weight to evidence of present reproduction cost of appellant's road, but that it attached less weight to present construction costs than to other factors before it affecting adversely the present value of the structural property. That this was the real nature of the objection voiced by the dissenting Commissioners seems to me apparent from their opinion. They seem to assume that, as a result of *Southwestern Tel. Co.* v. *Public Service Commission,* 262 U. S. 276, and other cases in this Court, the Commission as a matter of law may never, under any circumstances, find that the value of the structural part of a railroad does not exceed its fair value of an earlier date, if the Commission has before it evidence of later increased construction costs. They say, "under the law of the land", in valuing a railroad under § 15a, "we must accord weight in the legal sense to the greatly enhanced cost of material, labor and supplies" during the recapture periods. Weight in the legal sense is evidently taken to be not that accorded by an informed judgment but imposed by some positive rule of law.

Without discussion of the evidence and other data which received the consideration of the Commission, the opinion of this Court seems to proceed on the broad assumption that the evidence relied on, mere synthetic estimates of costs of reproduction, must so certainly and necessarily outweigh all other considerations affecting values as to require the order of the Commission to be set aside. In effect the Commission is required to give to such index figures an evidential value to which it points out they are not entitled when applied to railroad properties in general or to this one in particular, and this, so far as appears, without investigation of the soundness of the reasons of the Commission for rejecting them.

This Court has said that present reproduction costs must be considered in ascertaining value for rate-making purposes. But it has not said that such evidence, when fairly considered, may not be outweighed by other considerations affecting value, or that any evidence of present reproduction costs, when compared with all the other factors affecting value, must be given a weight to which it is not entitled in the judgment of the tribunal "informed by experience" and "appointed by law" to deal with the very problem now presented. . . . But, if "weight in the legal sense" must be given to evidence of present construction costs, by the judgment now given we do not lay down any legal rule which will inform the Commission how much weight, short of its full effect, to the exclusion of all other considerations, is to be given to the evidence of synthetic costs of construction in valuing a railroad property. If full effect were to be given to it in all cases, then, as the Commission points out in its report, the railroads of the country, valued by the Commission in 1920 at nineteen billion dollars, would have had in that year a reproduction value of forty billion dollars, and we would arrive at the economic paradox that the value of the railroads may be far in excess of any amount on which they could earn a return. If less than full effect may be given, it is difficult for me to see how, without departure from established principles, the Commission could be asked to do more than it has already done—to weigh the evidence guided by all the proper considerations—or how, if there is evidence upon which its findings may rest, we can substitute our judgment for that of the Commission. Such, I believe, is the "due consideration" which the statute requires of "all the elements of value recognized by the law of the land for rate-making purposes".

As I cannot say *a priori* that increased construction costs may not be more than offset by other elements affecting adversely the present value of appellant's property, and as there was evidence before the Commission to support its findings, I can only conclude that the judgment below should be affirmed. In any case, in view of the statement of the Commission that it considered all relevant facts, including the elements of value brought to its attention by the carrier, I should not have supposed that we could rightly set aside the present order without some consideration of the probative value of the evidence of present reproduction costs which the Commission discussed at length in its report.

St. Louis & O'Fallon Ry. Co. v. *United States*
279 U. S. 461, 548 Decided May 20, 1929

DEPRECIATION ACCOUNT FOR REPLACEMENT

THE Public Service Commission of Maryland fixed the fares of a Baltimore street railway company so as to permit a return of 6.26 percent on the valuation of its property. The valuation was not disputed, but the Commission based the allowance for depreciation upon the cost of the company's property. The state Court of Appeals held that this was wrong: depreciation charges should be based on present value. Justice Sutherland, for the Supreme Court majority, declared the latter view was "plainly right" and the company should be granted the rate of fares it sought, which would bring 7.44 percent.

Justice Brandeis' dissent included a long discourse on the nature and purpose of depreciation charges, Justice Holmes concurring. Briefly, Justice Stone made additional observations.

I AGREE with what Mr. Justice Brandeis has said, both as to the propriety of excluding from the rate base the value of the franchise or easement donated to the railway company and with respect to the method of ascertaining depreciation. But of this I would say a further word.

I will assume, for present purposes, that as a result of *Smyth* v. *Ames,* 169 U. S. 466, the function of a depreciation account for rate-making purposes must be taken to be the establishment of a fund for the replacement of plant rather than the restoration of cost or value of the original plant investment. But what amount annually carried to reserve will be sufficient to replace all the elements of a composite property purchased at various times, at varying price levels, as they wear out or become obsolete, is a question, not of law but of fact. It is a question which must be answered on the basis of a prediction of the salvage value of the obsolete elements, the character of the articles which will be selected to replace them when replacement is necessary, and their cost at the time of replacement.

Obviously, that question cannot be answered by *a priori* reasoning. Experience is our only guide, tempered by the consideration of such special or unusual facts and circumstances as would tend to modify the results of experience. Experience, which embraces the past fifteen years of high price levels, and the studies of experts, resulting in the universally accepted practice of accountants and business economists, as recounted in detail by Mr. Justice Brandeis, have demonstrated that depreciation reserve, calculated on the basis of cost, has proven to be the most trustworthy guide in determining the amount required to replace, at the end of their useful life, the constantly shifting elements of a property such as the present. Costs of renewals made during the present prolonged period of high prices and diminishing replacement costs tend to offset the higher cost of replacing articles purchased in periods of lower prices. I think that we should be guided by that experience and practice in the absence of proof of any special circumstances showing that they are inapplicable to the particular situation with which we are now concerned.

Such proof, in the present case, is wanting. The only circumstance relied on for a different basis of depreciation, and one which is embraced in that experience, is the current high price level, which has raised the present reproduction value of the carrier's property, as a whole, above its cost. That, of course, might be a controlling consideration if we were dealing with present replacements or their present cost, instead of replacements to be made at various uncertain dates in the future, of articles purchased at different times in the past, at varying price levels. But I cannot say that since such prices at the present moment are high, as a result of post-war inflation, a rate of return which is sufficient to yield 7.78 percent on present reproduction value, after adequate depreciation based on cost of the carrier's property, is confiscatory because logic requires the prediction that the elements of petitioner's property cannot, in years to come, be renewed or replaced with adequate substitutes, at less than the present average reproduction cost of the entire property—and this in the face of the facts that the cost of replacements in the past fifteen years has been for the most part at higher price levels than at present, that the amount allowed by the Commission for depreciation has been in practice more than sufficient for all replacement requirements throughout the period of higher price levels, and that the company has declared and paid dividends which were earned only if this depreciation reserve was adequate.

To say that the present price level is necessarily the true measure of future replacement cost is to substitute for a relevant fact which I should have thought ought to be established as are other facts, a rule of law which seems not to follow from *Smyth* v. *Ames* and to be founded neither upon experience nor expert opinion and to be unworkable in practice. In the present case it can be applied only by disregarding evidence which would seem persuasively to establish the very fact to be ascertained.

United Rys. & Electric Co. of Baltimore v. *West*
280 U. S. 234, 289 *Decided January 6, 1930*

"ERRONEOUS METHOD OF VALUATION"

UPON determining the value of a telephone company's property, the Maryland Public Service Commission ordered rate reductions. The company insisted on a higher valuation and rates which would yield a 7½ percent return. The district court, using a valuation method of its own, found the commission's order confiscatory (as yielding only 4½ percent) and enjoined enforcement.

The Supreme Court, through Justice Roberts, called the lower court's method just as arbitrary, but held that the commission's adoption of price-trend indices was fundamentally erroneous procedure violating due process. The decree was affirmed.

Justice Stone regarded it as a novel proposition that the rate order should be set aside when confiscation was not proven. He followed the Roberts opinion step by step to its startling conclusion, and on the way showed that the skill and thoroughness of the Commission had not been impugned. Justices Brandeis and Cardozo concurred in this dissent:

THE SOLE ISSUE . . . is whether there is confiscation of appellee's property by reduction of its rates. It is not within the province of the federal courts to prescribe rates or to revise rates fixed by state authority, unless property is taken without due process in violation of the Fourteenth Amendment. . . . This Court, in setting aside the order of the commission and leaving the old rates in force, does not pass upon that issue. It does not hold that the rate fixed by the commission will confiscate appellee's property, nor does it agree with the determination of the district court below that it will. For it is declared that the district court has not followed the rules sanctioned by this Court for determining the fair value of the property of a public service company and, in consequence, its conclusion that there has been confiscation must be rejected. But, notwithstanding the errors of the district court, this Court upholds its decree. The order of the commission is thus set aside, upon a ground not raised upon the record or considered by the court below. This is done not because the rate is confiscatory, but because the method by which the commission arrived at its conclusion, which is now pronounced "inapt" and "erroneous", is declared to be unconstitutional.

The Fourteenth Amendment is thus said to be infringed, not because the appellee has been deprived of any substantive right, but because the commission's action is deemed a denial of due process in the procedural sense. But not even the procedure is condemned because it lacks those essential qualities of fairness and justice which are all the Fourteenth Amendment has hitherto been supposed to exact of bodies exercising judicial or quasi-judicial functions. The commission has punctiliously adhered to a procedure which acts only after notice and hears before it condemns. . . . The sole transgression, for which its painstaking work is set at naught, is that, in the exercise of the administrative judgment of this body "informed by experience" and "appointed by law" to deal with the very problem now presented . . . it has relied upon a study of the historical cost and ascertained value of appellee's plant in the light of price indices, showing declines in prices, in arriving at the present fair value of the property, a procedure on which this Court has hitherto set the seal of its approval. . . .

In this state of the record it is unnecessary to consider whether the appellee has sustained the burden placed upon it of establishing confiscation, or to demonstrate, as I think may be done, that the facts found by the court below, and on which it acted, fall far short of showing that appellee's property is in any danger of confiscation. It is enough to point out that this Court has rejected the conclusions of the district court because it used book value as a measure of present fair value in times of falling prices, and that even with its findings of fair value, probable earnings and rate of depreciation, the district court found that the rate of return would be approximately 4½ percent on the property of one of the most stable of public utilities. If adjustment be made for a plainly excessive depreciation allowance, the rate of return on the court's figures would be raised to 5.10 percent.

The company supported its claim of confiscation by no evidence of the current yields of comparable investments and by no evidence of the rate of return generally obtaining in the money market. The general conditions of the money market and the rate of return on invested capital may have a controlling influence in determining the issue of confiscation. . . . There is at least grave doubt whether a return of 4½ percent is so out of line with the current yield on invested capital as to be deemed confiscatory. This doubt, if accepted principles be applied, must be resolved against the company, which has offered no evidence by which the doubt could be removed. Twenty-five years ago, in times far more prosperous than these, this Court unanimously declined to take judicial notice that an estimated net return of 4 percent would be confiscatory. . . .

In determining whether the procedure of the commission involves any denial of federal right, open to review by collateral attack in the federal courts, it is important to consider a little more closely the nature of its "error". In 1925 the fair value of respondent's property as of 1923 was judicially determined by a federal district court of three judges, in a suit brought to set aside the commission's determination. . . . The commission had found the fair value of the property to be $24,350,000, about $1,500,000 more than net historical cost. The court found the fair value to be $29,500,000, an increase of 21 percent over the commission's valuation and of 29 percent over cost. The court arrived at the increase by precisely the same basic method which the commission employed in the present case, except that the commission has applied it here with far greater care and thoroughness.

With this history before it the commission, in its report in the present case, states:

"Both the Company and the Commission realized that to attempt to find the present day fair value of the Company's property by the usual method of taking an inventory of all items of property owned by the Company and pricing out those items at present day prices would not only take at least two years of constant work but would cost the Company not less than $300,000 and cost the State a very substantial sum. It was agreed that index numbers should be used in arriving at present day costs."

It is of no importance that the "agreement" to which the commission refers was not formally spread upon the record, for the record itself shows that no objection was made to the introduction in evidence of the price indices offered both by the commission and by appellee, and that no effort was made by either party to prove the value of appellee's property by engineers' appraisals of the whole property, or by estimates of present value based on expert observation or knowledge of the entire property. By common consent the case was tried before the commission on the theory that present fair value for rate making purposes could be arrived at with substantial accuracy by the application of price indices to the 1923 value as it had been judicially ascertained, and to the cost of subsequent annual additions to the property after deducting accrued depreciation.

The commission did not adopt any single index. It prepared its own index for translating book value into present fair value, on the basis of an elaborate study of price indices of recognized merit. The result of this study it adopted and applied as more trustworthy than the index prepared by appellee, the salient features of which will presently be considered.

The commission did not refuse to receive or to consider any of the evidence presented. Its decision and order were based upon an examination, commendable for thoroughness and skill, of all the evidence. Its error, if error there was, did not consist in receiving and considering the evidence submitted of indices showing changes in commodity and other prices. It would have been error for the commission not to have considered it. In *St. Louis & O'Fallon R. Co.* v. *United States* [page 143, this volume], this Court set aside a recapture order of the Interstate Commerce Commission on the sole ground that the Commission had failed to consider evidence before it tending to show that the reproduction cost of the structural property of the railroad was greater than original cost. The only evidence of this character disclosed by the record consisted of index figures showing the comparative price levels of labor and materials for 1914 and each of the subsequent recapture years. The valuation of the property by the Commission was set aside by this Court on the ground that the Commission had failed to consider the evidence of increased value over cost.

In [another case] this Court held that the Supreme Court of Pennsylvania, in sustaining the action of a state commission, rightly rejected engineers' appraisals and estimates of value in favor of a lower valuation by the commission based on cost and a study of charts showing the price trends of labor and materials from 1924 to 1930 inclusive. In affirming the judgment of the state court, this Court expressly approved this method of arriving at fair value, although it was less meticulously and carefully applied than by the commission in this case, and held that the evidence of cost and of price trends, of the same character as those on which the commission acted here, outweighed engineering appraisals of the whole property, which the appellee here did not choose to offer.

The extent of the commission's error thus appears to be that in considering all the evidence before it, in the manner approved by [the decision in the Pennsylvania case], it thought that the 1923 value of the appellee's plant and equipment, and actual cost of subsequent additions, reasonably adjusted so as to conform to generally recognized changes in the prices of labor and materials, as shown by reliable price indices, would afford a better guide to present fair value than the evidence offered by the company. The results thus obtained were checked against current wage scales in construction industries in Baltimore and vicinity, and against the prices of specific commodities entering into the construction of telephone equipment.

The company's evidence consisted of its own price index, derived by appraising samples of its property, ranging from 1 percent to 20 percent of the total property of each type, and assuming similar appraisals for each intervening year since 1923. Its index was based in substantial part on monopoly prices charged appellee for equipment purchased from its affiliate, the Western Electric Company, which is subject to the same corporate control as appellee, and on its own labor costs for construction work as shown by its books at a time when it was engaged in no important construction. The Western Electric Company is shown to have increased its prices of equipment 10.2 percent in November, 1930, at the very time when prices of commodities and similar manufactures were declining. This increase is reflected in the index used by the company.

Upon all the evidence, the commission concluded that appellee did not sustain the burden resting on it . . . of showing the reasonableness of the prices paid by it to its affiliate. The labor costs of the small amount of construction work carried on by the company were shown to be materially higher than those prevailing in the construction trades in Baltimore and vicinity. In 1930 (the date chosen by the company) they were about 147 percent of their 1923 level, while in December, 1932 (the valuation date), Baltimore wages generally were about 87 percent of that level. It is unnecessary to discuss other defects of appellee's proof so extreme as to discredit it. Its reliance here upon its own proof is at most perfunctory. It seeks only to sustain the conclusions of the court below, which this Court rejects.

Public utility commissions, like other quasi-judicial and judicial bodies, must try cases on the evidence before them. No basis has been suggested for declaring that the work of the commission must be rejected because of its reliance upon evidence which it was bound to consider, unless we are also prepared to say that its result was wrong. If we are unable on any ground to find that confiscation will occur, I cannot say that actual cost or ascertained value of the structural equipment of the telephone company, trended in accordance with reliable price indices, is any less trustworthy evidence of present fair value than the more customary engineers' appraisals and estimates, which appellee did not think it worth while to offer, or that, in any case, such a determination infringes any constitutional immunity.

In assuming the task of determining judicially the present fair replacement value of the vast properties of public utilities, courts have been projected into the most speculative undertaking imposed upon them in the entire history of English jurisprudence. Precluded from consideration of the unregulated earning capacity of the utility, they must find the present theoretical value of a complex property, built up by gradual accretions through long periods of years. Such a property has no market value, because there is no market in which it is bought and sold. Market value would not be acceptable, in any event, because it would plainly be determined by estimates of future regulated earnings. Estimates of its value, including the items of "overheads" and "going concern value", cannot be tested by any actual sale or by the actual present cost of constructing and assembling the property under competitive conditions. Public utility properties are not thus created full fledged at a single stroke. If it were to be presently rebuilt in its entirety, in all probability it would not be constructed in its present form.

When we arrive at a theoretical value based upon such uncertain and fugitive data we gain at best only an illusory certainty. No court can evolve from its inner consciousness the answer to the question whether the illusion of certainty will invariably be better supported by a study of the actual cost of the property adjusted to price trends, or by a study of the estimates of engineers based upon data which never have existed and never will. The value of such a study is a question of fact in each case, to be ascertained like any other in the light of the record, and with some regard to the expert knowledge and experience of the commission which, in the present case, are obviously great.

It is said that the price indices "were not prepared as an aid to the appraisal of property", that "they were intended merely to indicate price trends", a suggestion that seems to assume that known price trends are irrelevant to the determination of the present fair value of property whose cost is known. It is also said that the "wide variation of results of the employment of different indices * * * impugns their accuracy as implements of appraisal". The use of a single price index to the exclusion of all others, it is true, might well produce as inaccurate a result as if a single engineer's estimate were used to the exclusion of all others, and without test of its verity. But the record affords striking evidence of the accuracy of the composite index translators prepared and used by the commission, quite apart from the relatively close agreement in the results obtained by the individual indices.

From 1923 until 1930, when the Western Electric raised its prices, the commission's index translator accurately reflected the changes in price actually paid by appellee for its purchased equipment, and the commission and company indices were in close conformity. Eliminating these price changes and the excessive labor costs appearing in the company's own index, the resulting present fair value of appellee's equipment did not differ substantially from the commission's valuation of it. So far as the results of the use of standard price indices are impugned by their variation, an examination of the present record will disclose that the results obtained by the application of price indices to the historical cost of plant are far less variable than engineers' valuations and in general are probably more trustworthy.

To speak of either class of evidence as so accurate as to require a commission as a matter of law to accept it, or so inaccurate as to require the rejection of a valuation based upon it, is to attribute to the valuation process a possibility of accuracy and certainty wholly fictitious. Present fair value at best is but an estimate. Historical cost appropriately adjusted by reasonable recognition of price trends appears to be quite as common sense a method of arrival at a present theoretical value as any other. For a period of twenty years or more of rising prices, commissions and courts, including this one, have regarded price variations as persuasive evidence that present fair value was more than cost. I see no reason for concluding that they are of less weight in times of declining prices.

If I am mistaken in this view, it does not follow that a like error of judgment by a state commission is a violation of the Constitution, and that a federal court can rightly set aside its order, even though there is no confiscation. It is true that in [a case cited by the majority] this Court, in holding invalid an order arbitrarily lowering rates which the only evidence of probative value showed were already confiscatory, criticized the method adopted by the commission and characterized its action as a denial of due process. But the Court was careful to point out that: "The mere admission by an administrative tribunal of matter which under the rules of evidence applicable to judicial proceedings would be deemed incompetent . . . or mere error in reasoning upon evidence introduced, does not invalidate an order." And in [another case cited by the majority], where this Court set aside the rate fixed by a state commission as confiscatory, the method of valuation pursued by the commission was characterized as erroneous and open to review by this Court, as of course it is when the validity of the result is the subject of inquiry. But in no case hitherto has this Court assumed to set aside a rate fixed by a state commission, not found to be confiscatory, merely for what it conceived to be an erroneous method of valuation. If such an error in the deliberations of a state tribunal is a violation of the

Constitution, I should think that every error of a state court would present a federal question reviewable here.

It would seem that doubts, if any, as to the scope of our review of the action of a state commission in a case like the present, had been put at rest by our decision, two terms ago, in *Los Angeles Gas Corp.* v. *Railroad Commission,* 289 U. S. 287. There the commission made its valuation on the basis of prudent investment, a method repeatedly repudiated by this Court. It was argued that the erroneous method pursued by the commission vitiated its order, whether confiscatory or not. The Court emphatically repudiated that argument, saying: "We do not sit as a board of revision, but to enforce constitutional rights. . . . The legislative discretion implied in the rate-making power necessarily extends to the entire legislative process, embracing the method used in reaching the legislative determination as well as that determination itself. We are not concerned with either, so long as constitutional limitations are not transgressed. When the legislative method is disclosed, it may have a definite bearing upon the validity of the result reached, but the judicial function does not go beyond the decision of the constitutional question. That question is whether the rates as fixed are confiscatory. And upon that question the complainant has the burden of proof, and the Court may not interfere with the exercise of the state's authority unless confiscation is clearly established". Such should be our decision now.

West v. *Chesapeake & Potomac Telephone Co. of Baltimore City, 295 U. S. 662, 680 Decided June, 3, 1935*

Taxing Government Instrumentalities

THE POSITION OF STATE CONTRACTORS

CONSULTING engineers paid under protest an income tax on fees they received in 1917 for services rendered to states and political subdivisions. They sought to recover on the ground that the War Revenue Act of 1917 expressly exempted them from the tax and that Congress could not in any event tax such income because of the doctrine of the immunity of government instrumentalities. Both questions were determined in the opinion (slightly abridged below) of Justice Stone for a unanimous Court.

ALL OF THE ITEMS of income were received by the taxpayers as compensation for their services as consulting engineers under contracts with states or municipalities, or water or sewage districts created by state statute. In each case the service was rendered in connection with a particular project of water supply or sewage disposal, and the compensation was paid in some instances on an annual basis, in others on a monthly or daily basis, and in still others on the basis of a gross sum for the whole service.

The War Revenue Act provided for the assessment of a tax on net income; but § 201(a) . . . contains a provision for exemption from the tax as follows:

> "This title shall apply to all trades or businesses of whatever description, whether continuously carried on or not, except—
>
> "(a) In the case of officers and employees under the United States,

or any state, territory, or the District of Columbia, or any local subdivision thereof, the compensation or fees received by them as such officers or employees." * * *

We think it clear that neither of the plaintiffs in error occupied any official position in any of the undertakings to which their writ of error . . . relates. They took no oath of office; they were free to accept any other concurrent employment; none of their engagements was for work of a permanent or continuous character; some were of brief duration, and some from year to year, others for the duration of the particular work undertaken. Their duties were prescribed by their contracts and it does not appear to what extent, if at all, they were defined or prescribed by statute. We therefore conclude that plaintiffs in error have failed to sustain the burden cast upon them of establishing that they were officers of a state or a subdivision of a state within the exception of § 201(a).

An office is a public station conferred by the appointment of government. The term embraces the idea of tenure, duration, emolument and duties fixed by law. Where an office is created, the law usually fixes its incidents, including its term, its duties and its compensation. . . . The term "officer" is one inseparably connected with an office; but there was no office of sewage or water supply expert or sanitary engineer, to which either of the plaintiffs was appointed. The contracts with them, although entered into by authority of law and prescribing their duties, could not operate to create an office or give to plaintiffs the status of officers. . . . There were lacking in each instance the essential elements of a public station, permanent in character, created by law, whose incidents and duties were prescribed by law. . . .

Nor do the facts stated in the bill of exceptions establish that the plaintiffs were "employees" within the meaning of the statute. So far as appears, they were in the position of independent contractors. The record does not reveal to what extent, if at all, their services were subject to the direction or control of the public boards or officers engaging them. In each instance the performance of their contract involved the use of judgment and discretion on their part and they were required to use their best professional skill to bring about the desired result. This permitted to them liberty of action which excludes the idea of control or right of control by the employer which characterizes the relation of employer and employee and differentiates the employee or servant from the independent contractor. . . .

We pass to the more difficult question whether Congress had the constitutional power to impose the tax in question, and this must be answered by ascertaining whether its effect is such as to bring it within the purview of those decisions holding that the very nature of our constitutional system of dual sovereign governments is such as impliedly to prohibit the federal government from taxing the instrumentalities of a state government, and in a similar manner to limit the power of the states to tax the instrumentalities of the federal government. See, as to federal taxation on state instrumentalities [cases cited]. See, cases holding that the Sixteenth Amendment did not extend the taxing power to any new class of subjects [cited]. And, as to state taxation on federal instrumentalities, see [cases cited].

Just what instrumentalities of either a state or the federal government are exempt from taxation by the other cannot be stated in terms of universal application. But this Court has repeatedly held that those agencies through which either government immediately and directly exercises its sovereign powers, are immune from the taxing power of the other. Thus the employment of officers who are agents to administer its laws . . . , its obligations sold to raise public funds . . . , its investments of public funds in the securities of private corporations, for public purposes . . . , surety bonds exacted by it in the exercise of its police power . . . , are all so intimately connected with the necessary functions of government, as to fall within the established exemption; and when the instrumentality is of that character, the immunity extends not only to the instrumentality itself but to income derived from it . . . , and forbids an occupation tax imposed on its use. . . .

When, however, the question is approached from the other end of the scale, it is apparent that not every person who uses his property or derives a profit, in his dealing with the government, may clothe himself with immunity from taxation on the theory that either he or his property is an instrumentality of government within the meaning of the rule. . . .

As cases arise, lying between the two extremes, it becomes necessary to draw the line which separates those activities having some relation to government, which are nevertheless subject to taxation, from those which are immune. Experience has shown that there is no formula by which that line may be plotted with precision in advance. But recourse may be had to the reason upon which the rule rests, and which must be the guiding principle to control its operation. Its origin was due to the essential requirement of our constitutional system that the federal government must exercise its authority within the territorial limits of the states; and it rests on the conviction that each government in order that it may administer its affairs within its own sphere, must be left free from undue interference by the other. *McCulloch* v. *Maryland,* 4 Wheat. 316. . . .

In a broad sense, the taxing power of either government, even when exercised in a manner admittedly necessary and proper, unavoidably has some effect upon the other. The burden of federal taxation necessarily sets an economic limit to the practical operation of the taxing power of the states, and vice versa. Taxation by either the state or the federal government affects in some measure the cost of operation of the other.

But neither government may destroy the other nor curtail in any substantial manner the exercise of its powers. Hence the limitation upon the taxing power of each, so far as it affects the other, must receive a practical construction which permits both to function with the minimum of interference each with the other; and that limitation cannot be so varied or extended as seriously to impair either the taxing power of the government imposing the tax . . . or the appropriate exercise of the functions of the government affected by it. . . .

While it is evident that in one aspect the extent of the exemption must finally depend upon the effect of the tax upon the functions of the government alleged to be affected by it, still the nature of the governmental agencies or the mode of their constitution may not be disregarded in passing on the question of tax exemption; for it is obvious that an agency may be of such a character or so intimately connected with the exercise of a power or the performance of a duty by the one government, that any taxation of it by the other would be such a direct interference with the functions of government itself as to be plainly beyond the taxing power.

It is on this principle that, as we have seen, any taxation by one government of the salary of an officer of the other, or the public securities of the other, or an agency created and controlled by the other, exclusively to enable it to perform a governmental function . . . , is prohibited. But here the tax is imposed on the income of one who is neither an officer nor an employee of government and whose only relation to it is that of contract, under which there is an obligation to furnish service, for practical purposes not unlike a contract to sell and deliver a commodity. The tax is imposed without discrimination upon income whether derived from services rendered to the state or services rendered to private individuals. In such a situation it cannot be said that the tax is imposed upon an agency of government in any technical sense, and the tax itself cannot be deemed to be an interference with government, or an impairment of the efficiency of its agencies in any substantial way. . . .

As was said by this Court in *Baltimore Shipbuilding Co.* v. *Baltimore,* 195 U. S. 375 (in holding that a state might tax the interest of a corporation in a dry dock which the United States had the right to use under a contract entered into with the corporation):

"It seems to us extravagant to say that an independent private corporation for gain, created by a state, is exempt from state taxation, either in its corporate person, or its property, because it is employed by the United States, even if the work for which it is employed is important and takes much of its time."

And as was said in *Fidelity & Deposit Co.* v. *Pennsylvania,* 240 U. S. 319, in holding valid a state tax on premiums collected by bonding insurance companies on surety bonds required of United States officials:

"But mere contracts between private corporations and the United States do not necessarily render the former essential government agencies and confer freedom from state control."

These statements we deem to be equally applicable to private citizens engaged in the general practice of a profession or the conduct of a business in the course of which they enter into contracts with government from which they derive a profit. We do not suggest that there may not be interferences with such a contract relationship by means other than taxation which are prohibited. *Railroad Co.* v. *Peniston,* 18 Wall. 5, at page 36, recognizes that there may. Nor are we to be understood as laying down any rule that taxation might not affect agencies of this character in such a manner as directly to interfere with the functions of government and thus be held to be void. . . .

But we do decide that one who is not an officer or employee of a state, does not establish exemption from federal income tax merely by showing that his income was received as compensation for service rendered under a contract with the state; and when we take the next step necessary to a complete disposition of the question, and inquire into the effect of the particular tax, on the functioning of the state government, we do not find that it impairs in any substantial manner the ability of plaintiffs in error to discharge their obligations to the state or the ability of a state or its subdivisions to procure the services of private individuals to aid them in their undertakings. . . . We therefore conclude that the tax . . . was properly assessed.

Metcalf & Eddy v. *Mitchell*

269 U. S. 514 Decided January 11, 1926

INCOME FROM GOVERNMENT SECURITIES

MASSACHUSETTS amended its corporation excise tax law by including, in the measurement of net income for the preceding year, income derived from federal and state tax-exempt securities. The Supreme Court decided that this was a subterfuge to reach a non-taxable subject. Under the state constitution the tax could be upheld only if an excise. According to Justice Sutherland this levy on the privilege of doing business in corporate form was in reality a prohibited tax—a delusive name whereby to evade limitations on the state's taxing power—with the result that the immunity of national bonds was narrowed and the federal government was burdened.

Justice Stone felt that the inference of the majority was unwarranted: the Court had long upheld the principle of excises measured in part by tax-exempt securities. Justices Holmes and Brandeis agreed with this opinion:

THERE IS NO constitutional principle and no decision of this Court, of which I am aware, which would deny to the state the power so to tax the privileges which it has conferred upon petitioner [the Macallen Co., a Massachusetts corporation], even though all its property were tax-exempt securities of the United States and income derived from them. For seventy years this Court has consistently adhered to the principle that either the federal or state governments may constitutionally impose an excise tax on corporations for the privilege of doing business in corporate form, and measure the tax by the property or net income of the corporation, including the tax-exempt securities of the other or income derived from them. . . . In *Flint* v. *Stone Tracy Co.*, 220 U. S. 107, a federal tax on corporations "with respect to carrying on or doing business" measured by net income, was held to be an excise, not a direct tax on property or income, and so was valid, although not apportioned under Article I, § 2, cl. 3, § 9, cl. 4 of the Constitution and notwithstanding the fact that net income from tax-exempt municipal bonds was included in the measure of the tax. In no technical sense does this tax seem open to objection. Being an excise the tax is not one on property or income and may include either in its measurement although not directly taxable.

Upon like principle a state inheritance tax may be measured by including the value of United States bonds of the decedent. . . . Similarly an excise on a corporation may be measured by its outstanding capital stock . . . , or by its net income . . . , even though a part of its capital is used in or some of its income is derived from interstate commerce.

It would seem that only considerations of public policy of weight, which appear to be here wholly wanting, would justify overturning a principle so long established. It has survived a great war, financed by the sale of government obligations; and it has never even been suggested that in any practical way it has impaired either the dignity or credit of the national government.

I suppose a certain advantage would be enjoyed by a corporation if the exercise of its corporate franchise in the purchase and use of securities of one government could not be taxed by the other. Theoretically the advantage would inure to each government in the marketing of its securities, just as would be the case if such securities of the taxpayer could not be seized and sold for the payment of any taxes lawfully levied by the state or national government. But the advantage of the one would be gained only at the expense of the other, and it would seem that neither immunity could be claimed under any reasonably practical application of the rule that government instrumentalities may not be taxed.

In a broad sense, the taxing power of neither state nor national government can be exercised without having some effect on the other and there are many points at which the exercise of the undoubted power of one affects the other, but "the limitation upon the taxing power of each, so far as it affects the other, must receive a practical construction which permits both to function with the minimum of interference each with the other; and that limitation cannot be so varied or extended as seriously to impair either the taxing power of the government imposing the tax . . . or the appropriate exercise of the functions of the government affected by it". [Quoted from the *Metcalf & Eddy* case, *ante.*]

Granted that a statute otherwise valid may be deemed improper when intended as a covert means of directly burdening ownership of securities of the other sovereignty . . . , I can discern no such sinister purpose in the present legislation. It was, of course, the intention of the Massachusetts legislature in the amendment . . . to deal specifically not alone with federal bonds but with the tax-exempt securities of the Commonwealth and its municipalities by including them in the measure of the excise tax. The amendment did not aim at securities of the national government or discriminate against them. It was obviously designed to impose on corporations generally, a tax similar to the excise on national banks, measured by net income, recommended by the legislative committee as a means of avoiding a then existing discrimination. The inclusion in the measure of the tax of income from all tax-exempt securities tended only to effect this purpose, a similar computation of net income being contemplated for national banks.

But in neither case is there anything to suggest that the legislature intended to impose a direct tax on income or do more than to impose an excise tax, measured by income, including that upon federal bonds, which this Court has declared it may do. Its purpose was to prevent the evasion by corporations of payment of the tax which the Commonwealth had fixed as the price of the privilege of doing business within it in corporate form, by any course of investment of their funds in tax-exempt securities, state or national. As this seems to me to be a permissible purpose both on principle and by authority, I think the judgment below should be affirmed.

Macallen Co. v. *Massachusetts*
279 U. S. 620, 634 Decided May 27, 1929

The progress of Justice Stone's view may be noted. In 1931 he wrote the majority opinion in *Educational Films Corp. of*

America v. *Ward,* 282 U. S. 379, which ruled that a New York corporation was subject to an annual state franchise tax computed on the "entire net income" of a preceding year. The corporation had challenged the tax as inapplicable to royalties received from copyrights, instrumentalities of the federal government. The Justice said in part:

THIS COURT, in drawing the line which defines the limits of the powers and immunities of state and national governments, is not intent upon a mechanical application of the rule that government instrumentalities are immune from taxation, regardless of the consequences to the operations of government. The necessity for marking those boundaries grows out of our constitutional system, under which both the federal and the state governments exercise their authority over one people within the territorial limits of the same state. The purpose is the preservation to each government, within its own sphere, of the freedom to carry on those affairs committed to it by the Constitution, without undue interference by the other. . . .

Having in mind the end sought, we cannot say that the rule applied by this Court for some seventy years, that a nondiscriminatory tax upon corporate franchises is valid, notwithstanding the inclusion of tax-exempt property or income in the measure of it, has failed of its purpose, or has worked so badly as to require a departure from it now, or that the present tax, viewed in the light of actualities, imposes any such real or direct burden on the federal government as to call for the application of a different rule.

The inclusion of interest on government securities in the measure of a state franchise tax was fully sustained in 1932, when Justice Stone wrote the unanimous opinion in *Pacific Co.* v. *Johnson,* 285 U. S. 480. There a California corporation had acquired tax-exempt bonds before the state constitution was changed to authorize the tax. The Court held that the immunity was not broad enough to secure freedom from the tax, and therefore the obligation of the bond contracts was not impaired by it. "Grants of immunity from taxation, in derogation of a sovereign power of the state, are strictly construed," said Justice Stone.

THE AREA EXPANDED

A MANUFACTURER who sold a motorcycle to a Massachusetts city for the use of its police service paid a federal excise tax as required by the Revenue Act of 1924 and sued for recovery of the tax. From the Court of Claims came the question to the Supreme Court whether the transaction could be taxed consistently with the constitutional immunity of the state and its agencies. The United States argued that the tax was not on the city but on the manufacturer, who was not an agent of the state under the *Metcalf & Eddy* decision, *ante*.

Justice Van Devanter said for the Court that the immunity principle was applicable to all that lay in the field of governmental functions. He relied on the *Panhandle Oil* case, cited below, which ruled that a state could not apply an excise on the sale of oil to a federal instrumentality. He said the motorcycle tax was likewise on the sale, and not on the manufacture or on manufacture-and-sale.

Justice Holmes felt bound by the *Panhandle* case as controlling in principle. Justices Stone and Brandeis dissented:

I THINK the question should be answered in the affirmative. The implied immunity of one government, either national or state, from taxation by the other should not be enlarged. Immunity of the one necessarily involves curtailment of the other's sovereign power to tax. The practical effect of enlargement is commonly to relieve individuals from a tax, at the expense of the government imposing it, without substantial benefit to the government for whose theoretical advantage the immunity is invoked. . . .

This is especially the case where, as here, the sole ground of the immunity is that, although the tax is an excise collected by one government from an individual normally subject to it, the incidence of the tax may conceivably be shifted to the other government. In such a case it is not clear how a recovery by the taxpayer would benefit directly the government supposed to be burdened; and the assumption of indirect benefit in the case of a tax of this type necessarily rests upon speculation rather than reality. . . . It is significant that neither the federal nor any state government has appeared by intervention or otherwise to support this claim of immunity in cases in which the taxpayer has urged it upon us.

The Court has many times held, as recently as in *Educational Films Corp.* v. *Ward,* 282 U. S. 379, that an excise tax, imposed directly on the individual, is not invalid because indirectly it may burden either the state or the national government. . . . A bequest to the United States or a state may be subjected to an inheritance tax by the other . . . , although the consequent indirect burden is apparent. Even if it could be said that there is some reason, which the Court has never attempted to state, for the distinction which was made by the decision in *Panhandle Oil Co.* v. *Knox,* 277 U. S. 218, between an excise on sales to a government and one on legacies, the fact of the shifting of the burden would seem to be at least less apparent in the cases of a sale.

In the *Panhandle Oil* case, it was held that this shifting of the burden of a state tax from the seller to the buyer was sufficient to render the tax invalid where the buyer was an agency of the United States, and it was assumed that the burden of the sales tax involved was so inevitably passed on to the buyer as to require this result. With this assumption economists would not, I believe, generally agree. Many hold that whether the burden of any tax paid by the seller is actually passed on to the buyer depends upon considerations so various and complex as to preclude the assumption *a priori* that any particular tax at any particular time is passed on. In some conditions of the market, the burden remains with the seller, or even may be shifted back from the seller to the producer by the reduction of the producer's price, rather than forward to the consumer by an increase of the seller's price.

Whatever factors determine whether the burden does in fact shift, I do not think it can be said that a tax paid by the seller in any given case necessarily burdens the purchaser either more or less, because in form laid on the sale, as in the *Panhandle Oil* case, or upon transportation of goods sold f.o.b. destination . . . , or on manufacture alone of articles intended for sale . . . , or on both manufacture and sale.

These considerations are, to me, persuasive that the broad rule announced in the *Panhandle Oil* case ought not to be extended, even if we were not required by our own decisions to limit it; and that we ought not to strain the words of the statute to bring this case within the authority of that one. It seems to be conceded that if the tax in the present case were levied on manufacture alone, we would be bound to hold it valid . . .

The rule of the *Panhandle Oil* case has been limited in *Wheeler Lumber Co.* v. *United States,* 281 U. S. 572, holding that a tax on transportation, which in that case was necessary to effect delivery by the seller, was valid because not in terms a tax on the sale, as it was in the former. Even if verbal distinction, unfounded in economic realities, must be made between the two cases so that both may stand as authoritative expositions of the Constitution, considerations of substance rather than of form should lead us to choose that one which would restrict the doctrine of the *Panhandle Oil* case to the tax imposed in unqualified terms on sales to which it was applied in that case. The present tax is not levied in such terms, exclusively on sales, but is effective only when the seller both manufactures (or imports) and sells. With respect to the incidence of its burden on the buyer, so far as we can know, it does not differ from a tax on the manufacture of goods, payable when sold. . . . I think that the *Wheeler Lumber* case, rather than the *Panhandle Oil* case, should control in determining its validity.

Indian Motorcycle Co. v. *United States*
283 U. S. 570, 580   Decided May 25, 1931

Justice Stone registered a protest in *Missouri* v. *Gehner,* 281 U. S. 313, 322, to the theory of the majority that the Constitution required, when a state ascertained the taxable net worth of property, that tax-exempt bonds must be excluded from the computation as though they were not liable for the debts of the taxpayer. In a dissent joined by Justices Holmes and Brandeis he wrote:

THAT CONCLUSION appears to me to open a new and hitherto unsuspected field of operation for the immunity from taxation enjoyed by national and state securities as instruments of government, and to accord to their owners a privilege which is not justified by anything that has been decided or said by this Court. * * *

The immunity of government bonds from taxation does not carry with it immunity from liability for debts. * * * I suppose that the sale and market value of government bonds would be materially increased if we were to say that the Constitution *sub silentio* had forbidden their seizure for debts, or rendered their possessor immune from the various forms of state taxation to which this Court has said he is subject. But however desirable such a consequence may be thought to be, that could hardly be taken as a sufficient ground for saying it.

AN IRRECONCILABLE CONFLICT

INCOME of a private company from a lease of Oklahoma state-owned oil lands was not subject to tax where the state devoted its proceeds to the support of schools, the Court decided. The lease was an instrumentality of the state, and to tax the fruits of the lease would burden the state, said Justice McReynolds for the majority. He said the issue was controlled by *Gillespie* v. *Oklahoma,* 257 U. S. 501, (an opinion by Justice Holmes) invalidating a state tax on a lease of Indian oil lands. More recently, however, the Court had sustained a federal tax on income from leased Texas lands in *Group No. 1 Oil Corp.* v. *Bass,* 283 U. S. 279 (opinion by Justice Stone). While Justice McReynolds emphasized there was a distinction here, Stone declared there obviously was none, and in his dissent he decried "blind adherence" to precedent. "*Gillespie* v. *Oklahoma* should be overruled" as inconsistent with the principles affirmed in the later case. He said:

The State of Texas, like the State of Oklahoma, has set apart a portion of its public domain for educational purposes. It has granted oil and gas leases of these lands, not differing in any material respect from the Oklahoma lease involved in this case. The royalties received by the state from the leases are devoted to the University of Texas, as Oklahoma devotes the income derived from its leases to its public schools. In *Group No. 1 Oil Corp.* v. *Bass,* decided less than a year ago, this Court, notwithstanding its decision in the *Gillespie* case that the income of the lessees of Indian oil lands could not be taxed by Oklahoma, upheld the right of the national government to assess and collect a tax upon the income received by the lessee of one of the Texas leases, from the sale of oil produced from the leased land. It was pointed out that under Texas law the lessee, by virtue of his lease, became the owner of the oil underground and that the taxed income was derived from the sale of oil which was his own property. In upholding the tax the Court said [through Justice Stone]:

"Property sold or otherwise disposed of by the government, either state or national, in order to raise revenue for government purposes, is in a broad sense a government instrumentality, with respect to which neither the property itself before sale, nor its sale by one government, may be taxed by the other. But it does not follow that the same property in the hands of the buyer, or his use or enjoyment of it, or the income he derives from it, is also tax immune. . . . Theoretically, any tax imposed on the buyer with respect to the purchased property may have some effect on the price, and thus remotely and indirectly affect the selling government. We may assume that if the property is subject to tax after sale, the governmental seller will generally receive a less favorable price than if it were known in advance that the property in the hands of later owners, or even of the buyer alone, could not be taxed.

"But the remote and indirect effects upon the one government of such a non-discriminatory tax by the other have never been considered adequate grounds for thus aiding the one at the expense of the taxing power of the other. . . . This Court has consistently held that where property or any interest in it has completely passed from the government to the purchaser, he can claim no immunity from taxation with respect to it, merely because it was once government owned, or because the sale of it effect some government purpose. . . .

"Property which has thus passed from either the national or a state government to private ownership becomes a part of the common mass of property and subject to its common burdens. Denial to either government of the power to tax it, or income derived from it, in order to insure some remote and indirect antecedent benefit to the other, would be an encroachment on the sovereign power to tax, not justified by the implied constitutional restriction. . . ."

The doctrine thus announced was not a new one. More than fifty years before, and long before the decision in the *Gillespie* case, it had been definitely decided . . . that private mining claims granted by the government in the public lands of the United States, and the ores and minerals derived from them, are subject to state taxation.

In deciding the *Group No. 1 Oil Corp.* case, it was not necessary to determine whether the result in that case would have been different if the oil, from the sale of which the taxpayer derived his income, had become his only when severed from the soil, or whether there were other distinguishing features between that case and the *Gillespie* case. It was enough there, that, as the taxed income was derived from the lessee's sale of the oil, title to which was, by the lease, vested in him before severance, the case was definitely controlled by precedents whose avowed principles the Court approved. Now, we are concerned with a lease identical with that involved in the *Gillespie* case, and comparison of it with the Texas lease is unavoidable. If we can find no distinction of substance between the operation and effect of the Texas leases and the Oklahoma leases, the *Gillespie* case should no longer be followed. That no such distinction can be drawn is obvious.

The leasing by the national government of Indian oil lands in Oklahoma to private lessees, for the benefit of the Indians, and the leasing by Oklahoma of its school lands in like fashion, for the benefit of the schools of the state, are no more and no less governmental enterprises than the leasing by Texas of its oil lands for the benefit of the state university. Whatever the genesis of the particular public duty which each sovereignty has undertaken to perform, the method chosen and the instruments selected for its performance are the same. In each case there was the exercise of a function concededly governmental, but in each the only result, so far as the lessee was concerned, was the acquisition by him of certain property rights exclusively for his own benefit. In each the lessee was taxed on his profits, derived from his private business in the production and sale of oil and gas, which were his property.

It cannot be said that the identical tax, thus levied, has any effect on Oklahoma differing from that on Texas. The fact, if it is a fact, that under the Oklahoma leases the lessees do not acquire ownership of the oil or gas until they have severed it from the soil, but before its sale, while the lessees under the Texas leases acquire it immediately on receipt of their leases, presents no distinguishing feature. All acquire private rights by governmental grant, from the exploitation of which they have derived income which, upon principles consistently applied by this Court, except in the Indian oil lease cases, and reiterated in the *Group No. 1 Oil Corp.* case, may be taxed as other income is taxed.

Since comparison of the two methods of disposing of state assets reveals only formal differences, this Court must now deal with an irreconcilable conflict in the theories upon which two of its decisions rest. One, the *Gillespie* case, extends the doctrine of tax immunity, beyond any other case, to income from private business enterprises, merely because the property used in the business was acquired from a sovereign government which applies the proceeds of it to a governmental purpose. The other, and more recent, case, decided by the Court after full consideration of all the arguments now advanced as supporting the *Gillespie* case, restricted the immunity to the property of the sovereign government itself and to the income which the government derives from it.

It is plain that if we place emphasis on the orderly administration of justice, rather than on a blind adherence to conflicting precedents, the *Gillespie* case must be overruled. It is true that for ten years the State of Oklahoma has been deprived, by the decision in that case, of taxes upon the income derived from private business of lessees of Indian lands in that state, but that is no reason why it should continue to be so deprived or why the national government should now be denied the right to like taxes and at the same time be permitted to tax the income of the lessees under the Texas leases. No interest which could be subserved by so rigid an application of *stare decisis*, is superior to that of a system of justice based on a considered and consistent application of the Constitution of the United States.

[Justices Brandeis, Roberts and Cardozo joined in this opinion. Separately, Brandeis cited many instances where the Court had overruled its own decisions: "The Court bows to the lessons of experience and the force of better reasoning * * * . Moreover, the judgment of the Court in the earlier decision may have been influenced by prevailing views as to economic or social policy which have since been abandoned."]

Burnet v. *Coronado Oil & Gas Co.*
285 U. S. 393, 401 Decided April 11, 1932

[Six years later the Court expressly overruled *Gillespie* v. *Oklahoma* and *Burnet* v. *Coronado Oil & Gas Co.* as "out of harmony with correct principle", Chief Justice Hughes writing the opinion in *Helvering* v. *Mountain Producers Corp.*, 303 U. S. 376. He was supported by Justices Brandeis, Stone, Roberts and

Black. Justices Cardozo and Reed did not participate. Justices Butler and McReynolds were now the dissenters.]

THE DOCTRINE REPUDIATED

THE field of governmental immunity was narrowed further when the Court held that employees of the Port of New York Authority, a corporation created by New York and New Jersey, were subject to federal income tax. (*Helvering* v. *Gerhardt,* 304 U. S. 405.) State immunity was intended for the protection of state sovereignty and not to relieve such employees of the duty of financial support to the national government, said Justice Stone in the majority opinion. In a period of constant expansion of state activity into new enterprises, the federal taxing power might ultimately break down if the doctrine of immunity were pressed too far; and here the state obtained only a conjectural advantage.

Justices Butler and McReynolds protested that the decision "overrules a century of precedents" and insisted that the salaries of Port Authority employees were not distinguishable from salaries paid by states. Justice Black, on the other hand, acclaimed the recent overruling of the *Gillespie* and *Burnet* cases and asked for an examination of "the entire subject" in the light of the Sixteenth Amendment.

Finally, the Court rejected state taxation immunity claimed for the salary of an employee of a federal instrumentality, the Home Owners' Loan Corporation. Justice Stone said for the Court that Congress had intimated no purpose in this respect and that the tax laid no unconstitutional burden on the instrumentality, for the reasons stated in the *Gerhardt* decision. Such immunity, if allowed, would excessively restrict the states' taxing power. Cases relied upon by the claimant were overruled. Justice Frankfurter's concurring opinion called attention to this "important shift in constitutional doctrine * * * after a reconstruction in the membership of the Court". Justices Butler and McReynolds hewed to their line: the H. O. L. C. being an instrumentality hitherto deemed immune from state taxation, salaries paid to its employees were likewise immune. Stone's prevailing opinion follows:

WE ARE ASKED to decide whether the imposition by the State of New York of an income tax on the salary of an employee of the Home Owners' Loan Corporation places an unconstitutional burden upon the federal government.

Respondent, a resident of New York, was employed during 1934 as an examining attorney for the Home Owners' Loan Corporation at an annual salary of $2,400. In his income tax return for that year he included his salary as subject to the New York state income tax imposed by Art. 16 of the Tax Law of New York. . . . Subdivision 2f of § 359, since repealed, exempted from the tax "Salaries, wages and other compensation received from the United States of officials or employees thereof, including persons in the military or naval forces of the United States. * * * " Petitioners, New York State Tax Commissioners, rejected respondent's claim for a refund of the tax based on the ground that his salary was constitutionally exempt from state taxation because the Home Owners' Loan Corporation is an instrumentality of the United States Government and that he, during the taxable year, was an employee of the federal government engaged in the performance of a federal function.

On review by *certiorari* the Board's action was set aside by the Appellate Division of the Supreme Court of New York . . . , whose order was affirmed by the Court of Appeals. . . . Both courts held respondent's salary was free from tax on the authority of *New York ex rel. Rogers* v. *Graves,* 299 U. S. 401, which sustained the claim that New York could not constitutionally tax the salary of an employee of the Panama Rail Road Company, a wholly-owned corporate instrumentality of the United States. We granted *certiorari* . . . , the constitutional question presented by the record being of public importance.

The Home Owners' Loan Corporation was created pursuant to § 4(a) of the Home Owners' Loan Act of 1933 . . . , which was enacted to provide emergency relief to home owners, particularly to assist them with respect to home mortgage indebtedness. The corporation, which is authorized to lend money to home owners on mortgages and to refinance home mortgage loans within the purview of the Act, is declared by § 4(a) to be an instrumentality of the United States. Its shares of stock are wholly government-owned. . . . Its funds are deposited in the Treasury of the United States, and the compensation of its employees is paid by drafts upon the Treasury.

For the purposes of this case we may assume that the creation of the Home Owners' Loan Corporation was a constitutional exercise of the powers of the federal government. . . . As that government derives its authority wholly from powers delegated to it by the Constitution, its every action within its constitutional power is governmental action, and since Congress is made the sole judge of what powers within the constitutional grant are to be exercised, all activities of government constitutionally authorized by Congress must stand on a parity with respect to their constitutional immunity from taxation. . . . And when the national government lawfully acts through a corporation which it owns and controls, those activities are governmental functions entitled to whatever tax immunity attaches to those functions when carried on by the government itself through its departments. . . .

The single question with which we are now concerned is whether the tax laid by the state upon the salary of respondent, employed by a corporate instrumentality of the federal government, imposes an unconstitutional burden upon that government. The theory of the tax immunity of either government, state or national, and its instrumentalities, from taxation by the other, has been rested upon an implied limitation on the taxing power of each, such as to forestall undue interference, through the exercise of that power, with the governmental activities of the other. That the two types of immunity may not, in all respects, stand on a parity has been recognized from the beginning;

see *McCulloch* v. *Maryland,* 4 Wheat. 316, 435-36; and possibl differences in application, deriving from differences in the source nature and extent of the immunity of the governments and thei agencies were pointed out and discussed by this Court in detai during the last term. (*Helvering* v. *Gerhardt.*)

So far as now relevant, those differences have been thought t be traceable to the fact that the federal government is one o delegated powers in the exercise of which Congress is supreme so that every agency which Congress can constitutionally creat is a governmental agency. And since the power to create th agency includes the implied power to do whatever is needful o appropriate, if not expressly prohibited, to protect the agency there has been attributed to Congress some scope, the limits o which it is not now necessary to define, for granting or withhold ing immunity of federal agencies from state taxation. . . Whether its power to grant exemptions as an incident to th exercise of powers specifically granted by the Constitution ca ever, in any circumstances, extend beyond the constitutiona immunity of federal agencies which courts have implied, is a question which need not now be determined.

Congress has declared in § 4 of the Act that the Home Owners Loan Corporation is an instrumentality of the United States an that its bonds are exempt, as to principal and interest, from fed eral and state taxation, except surtaxes, estate, inheritance an gift taxes. The corporation itself, "including its franchise, it capital, reserves and surplus, and its loans and income," is like wise exempt from taxation; its real property is subject to tax to the same extent as other real property. But Congress has given no intimation of any purpose either to grant or withhold im munity from state taxation of the salary of the corporation's employees, and the congressional intention is not to be gathered from the statute by implication. . . .

It is true that the silence of Congress, when it has authority to speak, may sometimes give rise to an implication as to the congressional purpose. The nature and extent of that implication depend upon the nature of the congressional power and the effect of its exercise. But there is little scope for the application of that doctrine to the tax immunity of governmental instrumentalities. The constitutional immunity of either government from taxation by the other, where Congress is silent, has its source in an implied restriction upon the powers of the taxing government. So far as the implication rests upon the purpose to avoid interference with the functions of the taxed government or the imposition upon it of the economic burden of the tax, it is plain that there is no basis for implying a purpose of Congress to exempt the federal government or its agencies from tax burdens which are unsubstantial or which courts are unable to discern. Silence of Congress implies immunity no more than does the silence of the Constitution. It follows that when exemption from state taxation is claimed on the ground that the federal government is burdened by the tax, and Congress has disclosed no intention with respect to the claimed immunity, it is in order to consider the nature and effect of the alleged burden, and if it appears that there is no ground for implying a constitutional immunity, there is equally a want of any ground for assuming any purpose on the part of Congress to create an immunity.

The present tax is a non-discriminatory tax on income applied to salaries at a specified rate. It is not in form or substance a tax upon the Home Owners' Loan Corporation or its property or income, nor is it paid by the corporation or the government from their funds. It is measured upon income which becomes the property of the taxpayer when received as compensation for his services; and the tax laid upon the privilege of receiving it is paid from his private funds and not from the funds of the government, either directly or indirectly. The theory, which once won a qualified approval, that a tax on income is legally or economically a tax on its source, is no longer tenable. *New York ex rel. Cohn* v. *Graves* [page 253, this volume], *Helvering* v. *Gerhardt* [and other cases cited], and the only possible basis for implying a constitutional immunity from state income tax of the salary of an employee of the national government or of a governmental agency is that the economic burden of the tax is in some way passed on so as to impose a burden on the national government tantamount to an interference by one government with the other in the performance of its functions.

In the four cases in which this Court has held that the salary of an officer or employee of one government or its instrumentality was immune from taxation by the other, it was assumed, without discussion, that the immunity of a government or its instrumentality extends to the salaries of its officers and employees. This assumption, made with respect to the salary of a governmental officer in [cases cited] was later extended to confer immunity on income derived by a lessee from lands leased to him by a government in the performance of a governmental function, *Gillespie* v. *Oklahoma,* 257 U. S. 501; *Burnet* v. *Coronado* [page 176, this volume]; although the claim of a like exemption from tax on the income of a contractor engaged in carrying out a government project was rejected both in the case of a contractor with a state [*Metcalf & Eddy* v. *Mitchell,* page 163], and of a contractor with the national government. . . .

The ultimate repudiation in *Helvering* v. *Mountain Producers Corp.,* 303 U. S. 376, of the doctrine that a tax on the income of a lessee derived from a lease of government owned or controlled lands is a forbidden interference with the activities of the government concerned led to the reëxamination by this Court, in the *Gerhardt* case, of the theory underlying the asserted immunity from taxation by one government of salaries of employees of the other.

It was there pointed out that the implied immunity of one government and its agencies from taxation by the other should, as a principle of constitutional construction, be narrowly restricted. For the expansion of the immunity of the one government correspondingly curtails the sovereign power of the other to tax, and where that immunity is invoked by the private citizen it tends to operate for his benefit at the expense of the taxing government and without corresponding benefit to the government in whose name the immunity is claimed. . . .

It was further pointed out that, as applied to the taxation of salaries of the employees of one government, the purpose of the immunity was not to confer benefits on the employees by relieving them from contributing their share of the financial support of the other government, whose benefits they enjoy, or to give an advantage to that government by enabling it to engage employees at salaries lower than those paid for like services by other employers, public or private, but to prevent undue interference with the one government by imposing on it the tax burdens of the other.

In applying these controlling principles in the *Gerhardt* case the Court held that the salaries of employees of the New York Port Authority, a state instrumentality created by New York and New Jersey, were not immune from federal income tax, even though the Authority be regarded as not subject to federal taxation. It was said that the taxpayers enjoyed the benefit and protection of the laws of the United States and were under a duty, common to all citizens, to contribute financial support to the government; that the tax laid on their salaries and paid by them could be said to affect or burden their employer, the Port Authority, or the states creating it, only so far as the burden of the tax was economically passed on to the employer; that a non-discriminatory tax laid on the income of all members of the community could not be assumed to obstruct the function which New York and New Jersey had undertaken to perform, or to cast an economic burden upon them, more than does the general taxation of property and income which, to some extent, incapable of measurement by economists, may tend to raise the price level of labor and materials. The Court concluded that the claimed immunity would do no more than relieve the taxpayers from the duty of financial support to the national government in order to secure to the state a theoretical advantage, speculative in character and measurement and too unsubstantial to form the basis of an implied constitutional immunity from taxation.

The conclusion reached in the *Gerhardt* case that in terms of constitutional tax immunity a federal income tax on the salary of an employee is not a prohibited burden on the employer makes it imperative that we should consider anew the immunity here claimed for the salary of an employee of a federal instrumentality. As already indicated, such differences as there may be between the implied tax immunity of a state and the corresponding immunity of the national government and its instrumentalities may be traced to the fact that the national government is one of delegated powers, in the exercise of which it is supreme. Whatever scope this may give to the national government to claim immunity from state taxation of all instrumentalities which it may constitutionally create, and whatever authority Congress may possess as incidental to the exercise of its delegated powers to grant or withhold immunity from state taxation, Congress has not sought in this case to exercise such power. Hence these distinctions between the two types of immunity cannot affect the question with which we are now concerned.

The burden on government of a non-discriminatory income tax applied to the salary of the employee of a government or its instrumentality is the same, whether a state or national government is concerned. The determination in the *Gerhardt* case that the federal income tax imposed on the employees of the Port Authority was not a burden on the Port Authority made it unnecessary to consider whether the Authority itself was immune from federal taxation; the claimed immunity failed because even if the Port Authority were itself immune from federal income tax, the tax upon the income of its employees cast upon it no unconstitutional burden.

Assuming, as we do, that the Home Owners' Loan Corporation is clothed with the same immunity from state taxation as the government itself, we cannot say that the present tax on the income of its employees lays any unconstitutional burden upon it. All the reasons for refusing to imply a constitutional prohibition of federal income taxation of salaries of state employees, stated at length in the *Gerhardt* case, are of equal force when immunity is claimed from state income tax on salaries paid by the national government or its agencies. In this respect we perceive no basis for a difference in result whether the taxed income be salary or some other form of compensation, or whether the taxpayer be an employee or an officer of either a state or the national government, or of its instrumentalities.

In no case is there basis for the assumption that any such tangible or certain economic burden is imposed on the government concerned as would justify a court's declaring that the taxpayer is clothed with the implied constitutional tax immunity of the government by which he is employed. That assumption . . . is contrary to the reasoning and to the conclusions reached in the *Gerhardt* case and in *Metcalf & Eddy* v. *Mitchell*. . . . In their light the assumption can no longer be made. *Collector* v. *Day,* 11 Wall. 113, and *New York ex rel. Rogers* v. *Graves,* 299 U. S. 401 are overruled so far as they recognize an implied constitutional immunity from income taxation of the salaries of officers or employees of the national or a state government or their instrumentalities.

So much of the burden of a non-discriminatory general tax upon the incomes of employees of a government, state or national, as may be passed on economically to that government, through the effect of the tax on the price level of labor or materials, is but the normal incident of the organization within the same territory of two governments, each possessing the taxing power. The burden, so far as it can be said to exist or to affect the government in any indirect or incidental way, is one which the Constitution presupposes, and hence it cannot rightly be deemed to be within an implied restriction upon the taxing power of the national and state governments which the Constitution has expressly granted to one and has confirmed to the other. The immunity is not one to be implied from the Constitution, because if allowed it would impose to an inadmissible extent a restriction on the taxing power which the Constitution has reserved to the state governments.

Graves v. *New York ex rel. O'Keefe,*
306 U. S. 466 Decided March 27, 1939

[The Public Salary Act of 1939 provided that the federal income tax applied to state and local governmental employees.]

Regulation by the States

DESTRUCTION OF PROPERTY

VIRGINIA, faced with a choice of preserving one class of property or another which was of greater value to the public, enacted legislation permitting destruction of the former class. The Court decided that the law was not a violation of the due process clause of the Fourteenth Amendment. Voicing a unanimous opinion Justice Stone carefully rehearsed the conditions necessitating the statute and the fairness of its administrative procedure. In sum, the law was a reasonable safeguard of the public interest.

Under the Cedar Rust Act, the state entomologist ordered property owners to cut down a large number of ornamental red cedar trees growing on their property, to prevent the communication of a rust or plant disease, with which they were infected, to neighboring apple orchards. No compensation was afforded for the value of the standing cedars or for any decrease in the market value of the realty caused by their destruction, but a sum was allowed, after a court hearing, to cover the expense of removing the felled trees. The opinion continues:

THE VIRGINIA STATUTE presents a comprehensive scheme for the condemnation and destruction of red cedar trees infected by cedar rust. By § 1 it is declared to be unlawful for any person to "own, plant or keep alive and standing" on his premises any red cedar tree which is or may be the source or "host plant" of the communicable plant disease known as cedar rust, and any such tree growing within a certain radius of any apple orchard is declared to be a public nuisance, subject to destruction. Section 2 makes it the duty of the state entomologist, "upon the request in writing of ten or more reputable freeholders of any county or magisterial district, to make a preliminary investigation of the locality * * * to ascertain if any cedar tree or trees * * * are the source of, harbor or constitute the host plant for the said disease * * * and constitute a menace to the health of any apple orchard in said locality, and that said cedar tree or trees exist within a radius of two miles of any apple orchard in said locality". If affirmative findings are so made, he is required to direct the owner in writing to destroy the trees and, in his notice, to furnish a statement of the "fact found to exist whereby it is deemed necessary or proper to destroy" the trees and to call attention to the law under which it is proposed to destroy them. Section 5 authorizes the state entomologist to destroy the trees if the owner, after being notified, fails to do so. Section 7 furnishes a mode of appealing from the order of the entomologist to the circuit court of the county, which is authorized to "hear the objections" and "pass upon all questions involved", the procedure followed in the present case.

As shown by the evidence and as recognized in other cases involving the validity of this statute . . . cedar rust is an infectious plant disease in the form of a fungoid organism which is destructive of the fruit and foliage of the apple, but without effect on the value of the cedar. Its life cycle has two phases which are passed alternately as a growth on red cedar and on apple trees. It is communicated by spores from one to the other over a radius of at least two miles. It appears not to be communicable between trees of the same species, but only from one species to the other, and other plants seem not to be appreciably affected by it. The only practicable method of controlling the disease and protecting apple trees from its ravages is the destruction of all red cedars, subject to the infection, located within two miles of apple orchards.

The red cedar, aside from its ornamental use, has occasional use and value as lumber. It is indigenous to Virginia, is not cultivated or dealt in commercially on any substantial scale, and its value throughout the state is shown to be small as compared with that of the apple orchards of the state. Apple growing is one of the principal agricultural pursuits in Virginia. The apple is used there and exported in large quantities. Many millions of dollars are invested in the orchards, which furnish employment for a large portion of the population and have induced the development of attendant railroad and cold storage facilities.

On the evidence we may accept the conclusion of the [Virginia] Supreme Court of Appeals that the state was under the necessity of making a choice between the preservation of one class of property and that of the other wherever both existed in dangerous proximity. It would have been none the less a choice if, instead of enacting the present statute, the state, by doing nothing, had permitted serious injury to the apple orchards within its borders to go on unchecked. When forced to such a choice the state does not exceed its constitutional powers by deciding upon the destruction of one class of property in order to save another which, in the judgment of the legislature, is of greater value to the public. It will not do to say that the case is merely one of a conflict of two private interests and that the misfortune of the apple growers may not be shifted to cedar growers by ordering the destruction of their property; for it is obvious that there may be, and that here there is, a preponderant public concern in the preservation of the one interest over the other. . . . And where the public interest is involved preferment of that interest over the property interest of the individual, to the extent even of its destruction, is one of the distinguishing characteristics of every exercise of the police power which affects property. . . .

We need not weigh with nicety the question whether the infected cedars constitute a nuisance according to the common law; or whether they may be so declared by statute. . . . For where, as here, the choice is unavoidable, we cannot say that its exercise, controlled by considerations of social policy which are not unreasonable, involves any denial of due process. The injury to property here is no more serious, nor the public interest less, than in [cases cited].

The statute is not, as plaintiffs in error argue, subject to the vice which invalidated the ordinance considered by this Court in [case cited]. That ordinance directed the committee on streets of the city of Richmond to establish a building line, not less than five nor more than thirty feet from the street line whenever requested to do so by the owners of two-thirds of the property abutting on the street in question. No property owner might build beyond the line so established. Of this the Court said:

"It [the ordinance] leaves no discretion in the committee on streets as to whether the street [building, semble] line shall or shall not be established in a given case. The action of the committee is determined by two-thirds of the property owners. In other words, part of the property owners fronting on the block determine the extent of use that other owners shall make of their lots, and against the restriction they are impotent."

The function of the property owners there is in no way comparable to that of the "ten or more reputable freeholders" in the Cedar Rust Act. They do not determine the action of the state entomologist. They merely request him to conduct an investigation. In him is vested the discretion to decide, after investigation, whether or not conditions are such that the other provisions of the statute shall be brought into action; and his determination is subject to judicial review. The property of plaintiffs in error is not subjected to the possibly arbitrary and irresponsible action of a group of private citizens.

The objection of plaintiffs in error to the vagueness of the statute is without weight. The state court has held it to be applicable and that is enough when, by the statute, no penalty can be incurred or disadvantage suffered in advance of the judicial ascertainment of its applicability. . . .

Miller v. *Schoene*,
276 U.S. 272 *Decided February 20, 1928*

LEGISLATING PRICE LIMITS

A New York statute declared that the price of theater tickets was "affected with a public interest" and it limited brokers' surcharges to fifty cents per ticket to prevent exploiting the public. The Court invalidated the law as an invasion of private property rights, violating the due process clause of the Fourteenth Amendment. This was price-fixing, said Justice Sutherland; a right which was an inherent attribute of the business and not in the power of the legislature, whose declaration of "public interest" was unacceptable.

Of the four dissenters Justice Holmes observed that a state did not need to use such apologetic phrases as "police power" and "public interest" to do whatever it saw fit if not restrained by some express constitutional prohibition; at any rate, theaters were "as much devoted to public use as anything well can be". Justice Brandeis agreed. Both concurred in Justice Stone's opinion that the question here was not of legislative power to fix admission charges but of a right to exact exorbitant profits. Reviewing decisions sustaining price control, he declared that the category of cases under the vague term "public interest" was not a fixed one; that the power could be exerted where free competition between buyers and sellers was restricted. Justice Sanford agreed in general with Stone, who wrote:

I can agree with the majority that "constitutional principles, applied as they are written, it must be assumed, operate justly and wisely as a general thing, and they may not be remolded by lawmakers or judges to save exceptional cases of inconvenience, hardship, or injustice". But I find nothing written in the Constitution, and nothing in the case or common law development of the Fourteenth Amendment, which would lead me to conclude that the type of regulation attempted by the State of New York is prohibited.

The scope of our inquiry has been repeatedly defined by the decisions of this Court. As was said . . . by Chief Justice Waite, "For us the question is one of power, not of expediency. If no state of circumstances could exist to justify such a statute, then we may declare this one void, because in excess of the legislative power of the state. But if it could, we must presume it did. Of the propriety of legislative interference within the scope of legislative power, the legislature is the exclusive judge."

The attitude in which we should approach new problems in the field of price regulation was indicated in [a case cited]: "Against that conservatism of the mind which puts to question every new act of regulating legislation and regards the legislation invalid or dangerous until it has become familiar, government—state and national—has pressed on in the general welfare; and our reports are full of cases where in instance after instance the exercise of the regulation was resisted and yet sustained against attacks asserted to be justified by the Constitution of the United States. The dread of the moment having passed, no one is now heard to say that rights were restrained or constitutional guaranties impaired."

Again, in sustaining the constitutionality of the zoning ordinance under the Fourteenth Amendment, this Court has recently said, "Regulations, the wisdom, necessity and validity of which, as applied to existing conditions, are so apparent that they are now uniformly sustained, a century ago, or even half a century ago, probably would have been rejected as arbitrary and oppressive." . . .

The question with which we are here concerned is much narrower than the one which has been principally discussed by the Court. It is not whether there is constitutional power to fix the price which theater owners and producers may charge for admission. Although the statute in question declares that the price of tickets of admission to places of amusement is affected with a public interest, it does not purport to fix prices of admission. The producer or theater proprietor is free to charge any price he chooses. The statute requires only that the sale price, whatever it is, be printed on the face of the ticket, and prohibits the licensed ticket broker, an intermediary in the marketing process, from reselling the ticket at an advance of more than fifty cents above the printed price. Nor is it contended that this limit on the profit is unreasonable. It appears affirmatively that the business is now being carried on profitably by ticket brokers under this very restriction. But if it were not, there could be judicial relief without affecting the constitutionality of the measure. In these respects, the case resembles [case cited], where the attempt was not to fix the price of grain but to fix the price of the service rendered by the proprietors of grain elevators in connection with the transportation and distribution of grain, the cost of which entered into the price ultimately paid by the consumer. The statute there, as the statute here, was designed in part to protect a large class of consumers from exorbitant prices made possible by the strategic position of a group of intermediaries in the distribution of a product from producer to consumer.

There are about sixty first-class theaters in the borough of Manhattan. Brokers annually sell about two million tickets, principally for admission to these theaters. Appellant sells three hundred thousand tickets annually. The practice of the brokers, as revealed by the record, is to subscribe, in advance of the production of the play and frequently before the cast is chosen, for tickets covering a period of eight weeks. The subscriptions must be paid two weeks in advance and about twenty-five percent of the tickets unsold may be returned. A virtual monopoly of the best seats, usually the first fifteen rows, is thus acquired and the brokers are enabled to demand extortionate prices of theatergoers. Producers and theater proprietors are eager to make these advance sales which are effective insurance against loss arising from unsuccessful productions. The brokers are in a position to prevent the direct purchase of tickets to the desirable seats and to exact from the patrons of the successful productions a price sufficient to pay the loss of those which are unsuccessful, plus an excessive profit to the broker.

It is undoubtedly true as a general proposition that one of the incidents of the ownership of property is the power to fix the price at which it may be disposed. It may be also assumed that as a general proposition, under the decisions of this Court, the power of state governments to regulate and control prices may be invoked only in special and not well defined circumstances. But when that power is invoked in the public interest and in consequence of the gross abuse of private right disclosed by this record, we should make searching and critical examination of those circumstances which in the past have been deemed sufficient to justify the exercise of the power, before concluding that it may not be exercised here.

The phrase "business affected with a public interest" seems to me to be too vague and illusory to carry us very far on the way to a solution. It tends in use to become only a convenient expression for describing those businesses, regulation of which has been permitted in the past. To say that only those businesses affected with a public interest may be regulated is but another way of stating that all those businesses which may be regulated are affected with a public interest. It is difficult to use the phrase free of its connotations of legal consequences, and hence when used as a basis of judicial decision, to avoid begging the question to be decided. The very fact that it has been applied to businesses unknown to Lord Hale, who gave sanction to its use, should caution us against the assumption that the category has now become complete or fixed and that there may not be brought into it new classes of business or transactions not hitherto included, in consequence of newly devised methods of extortionate price exaction.

The constitutional theory that prices normally may not be regulated rests upon the assumption that the public interest and private right are both adequately protected when there is "free" competition among buyers and sellers, and that in such a state of economic society, the interference with so important an incident of the ownership of private property as price fixing is not justified and hence is a taking of property without due process of law.

Statutory regulation of price is commonly directed toward the prevention of exorbitant demands of buyers or sellers. An examination of the decisions of this Court in which price regulation has been upheld will disclose that the element common to all is the existence of a situation or a combination of circumstances materially restricting the regulative force of competition, so that buyers and sellers are placed at such a disadvantage in the bargaining struggle that serious economic consequences result to a very large number of members of the community. Whether this situation arises from the monopoly conferred upon public service companies or from the circumstances that the strategical position of a group is such as to enable it to impose its will in matters of price upon those who sell, buy or consume . . . , or from the predetermination of prices in the councils of those who sell, promulgated in schedules of practically controlling constancy . . . , or from a housing shortage growing out of a public emergency . . . , the result is the same. Self-interest is not permitted to invoke constitutional protection at the expense of the public interest, and reasonable regulation of price is upheld.

That should be the result here. We need not attempt to lay down any universal rule to apply to new and unknown situations. It is enough for present purposes that this case falls within the scope of the earlier decisions and that the exercise of legislative power now considered was not arbitrary. The question as stated is not one of reasonable prices, but of the constitutional right in the circumstances of this case to exact exorbitant profits beyond reasonable prices. The economic consequence of this regulation upon individual ownership is no greater, nor is it essentially different from that inflicted by regulating rates to be charged by laundries . . . , by anti-monopoly laws, Sunday laws, usury statutes . . . , the zoning ordinance . . . , or state statutes restraining the owner of land from leasing it to Japanese or Chinese aliens . . . , or state prohibition laws . . . , or legislation prohibiting option contracts for future sale of grain . . . , or invalidating sales of stock on margin or for "futures" . . . , or statutes preventing the maintenance of pool parlors . . . , or in numerous other cases in which the exercise of private rights has been restrained in the public interest. . . . Nor is the exercise of power less reasonable because the interests protected are in some degree less essential to life than some others. Laws against monopoly which aim at the same evil and accomplish their end by interference with private rights quite as much as the present law are not regarded as arbitrary or unreasonable or unconstitutional because they are not limited in their application to dealings in the bare necessities of life.

The problem sought to be dealt with has been the subject of earlier legislation in New York and has engaged the attention of the legislators of other states. That it is one involving serious injustice to great numbers of individuals who are powerless to protect themselves cannot be questioned. Its solution turns upon considerations of economics about which there may be reasonable differences of opinion. Choice between these views takes us from the judicial to the legislative field. The judicial function ends when it is determined that there is basis for legislative action in a field not withheld from legislative power by the Constitution as interpreted by the decisions of this Court. Holding these views, I believe the judgment below should be affirmed.

Tyson v. *Banton*

273 U. S. 418, 447 Decided February 28, 1927

WHEN "PUBLIC INTEREST" EXISTS

THE question of a business being "affected with a public interest" arose again when a New Jersey statute regulating employment agency fees was challenged. The Court observed that the phrase was the standard by which to judge validity of legislative price-control; only exceptional circumstances could justify the abridgement of freedom of contract. The business of employment agencies, Justice Sutherland said, was akin to that of ticket brokers, and the Court could not uphold, without disregarding its decision in the *Tyson* case, *ante,* "price-fixing legislation in respect of other brokers of like character". Justice Stone dissented. As against a hazy judicial concept he pitted economic realities, and Justices Holmes and Brandeis joined with him in this opinion:

THE QUESTION is whether a state has constitutional power to require employment agencies to charge only reasonable fees for their services to those seeking employment. As the case is presented we must take it that the New Jersey commissioner of labor was right in holding that Ribnik's list of fees was unreasonably high.

Under the decisions of this Court not all price regulation, as distinguished from other forms of regulation, is forbidden. As those decisions have been explained, price regulation is within the constitutional power of a state legislature when the business concerned is "affected with a public interest." That phrase is not to be found in the Constitution. Concededly it is incapable of any precise definition. It has and can have only such meaning as may be given to it by the decisions of this Court. As I read those decisions, such regulation is within a state's power whenever any combination of circumstances seriously curtails the regulative force of competition, so that buyers or sellers are placed at such a disadvantage in the bargaining struggle that a legislature might reasonably anticipate serious consequences to the community as a whole. . . .

The price regulation may embrace businesses "which, though not public at their inception, may be fairly said to have risen to be such and have become subject in consequence to some government regulation". . . . The use by the public generally of the specific thing or business affected is not the test. The nature of the service rendered, the exorbitance of the charges and the arbitrary control to which the public may be subjected without regulation, are elements to be considered in determining whether the "public interest" exists. . . . The economic disadvantage of a class and the attempt to ameliorate its condition may alone be sufficient to give rise to the "public interest" and to justify the regulation of contracts with its members . . . and obviously circumstances may so change in point of time or so differ in space as to clothe a business with such an interest which at other times or in other places would be a matter of private concern . . .

I cannot say *a priori* that the business of employment agencies in New Jersey lacks the requisite "public interest". We are judicially aware that the problem of unemployment is of grave public concern; that the conduct of the employment agency business bears an important relationship to that larger problem and affects vitally the lives of great numbers of the population, not only in New Jersey, but throughout the United States; that employment agencies, admittedly subject to regulation in other respects . . . and in fact very generally regulated, deal with a necessitous class, the members of which are often dependent on them for opportunity to earn a livelihood, are not free to move from place to place, and are often under exceptional economic compulsion to accept such terms as the agencies offer. We are not judicially ignorant of what all human experience teaches, that those so situated are peculiarly the prey of the unscrupulous and designing.

In *Adams* v. *Tanner,* 244 U. S. 590, a statute of Washington which in effect attempted to abolish the business was held unconstitutional because employment agencies were deemed not "inherently immoral or dangerous to public welfare," but, as was there emphasized, capable, under regulation, of being conducted in a useful and honest manner. But it was not questioned that the business was subject to grave abuses, involving frauds and impositions upon a peculiarly helpless class, among which the exaction of exorbitant fees was perhaps the least offensive. The Supreme Court of New Jersey, in an opinion in the present case, which was adopted by the Court of Errors and Appeals, said:

"It is common knowledge that an employment agency is a business dealing with a great body of our population, native and foreign born, which is susceptible to imposition, deception, and immoral influences. * * *"

In dealing with the question of power to require reasonable prices in this particular business, we should remember what was specifically pointed out by the Court in *Tyson* v. *Banton,* that whether a business is affected with a "public interest" turns "upon the existence of conditions, peculiar to the business under consideration". In the respects mentioned, or most of them, and in others to be pointed out, it seems to me that there is a marked difference between the character of this business and that of real estate brokers, ship brokers, merchandise brokers, and, more than all, of ticket brokers, who were involved in *Tyson* v. *Banton.* There the attempt was made to limit the advance which brokers might charge over box office prices for theater tickets, an expedient adopted to break up their monopolistic control of a luxury, not a necessity. Those affected by the practices of the ticket brokers constituted a relatively small part of the population within a comparatively small area of the state of New York. They were not necessitous. The consequences of the fraud and extortion practiced upon them were not visited upon the community as a whole in any such manner as are fraud and imposition practiced upon workers seeking employment. Here the effort is made, as in [other cases cited], first, to protect from abuses a class unable to protect itself, for whose welfare the police power has often been allowed broad play, and, second, to mitigate the evils which unemployment brings upon the community as a whole.

Some presumption should be indulged that the New Jersey legislature had an adequate knowledge of such local conditions as the circumstances of those seeking employment, the number and distribution of employment agencies, the local efficacy of competition, the prevalent practices with respect to fees. On this deserved respect for the judgment of the local lawmaker depends, of course, the presumption in favor of constitutionality, for the validity of a regulation turns "upon the existence of conditions, peculiar to the business under consideration". (*Tyson* v. *Banton.*) Moreover, we should not, when the matter is not clear, oppose our notion of the seriousness of the problem or the necessity of the legislation to that of local tribunals. "This Court, by an unbroken line of decisions from Chief Justice Marshall to the present day, has steadily adhered to the rule that every possible presumption is in favor of the validity of an act of Congress until overcome beyond rational doubt." (*Adkins* v. *Children's Hospital,* 261 U. S. 525, 544.) And the enactments of state legislatures are entitled to no less respect.

If, therefore, our consideration of the general conditions surrounding employment agencies, which it was thought in *Brazee* v. *Michigan,* 241 U. S. 340, made them subject to regulation, was to go no further than that of the Court, I should still have supposed that plaintiff in error had not sustained the burden which rests upon him to show that this law is unconstitutional. . . . But even if the presumption is not to be indulged, and the burden no longer to be cast on him who attacks the constitutionality of a law, we need not close our eyes to available data throwing light on the problem with which the legislature had to deal. (See *Muller* v. *Oregon,* 208 U. S. 412, 420-421.)

For thirty years or more the evils found to be connected with the business of employment agencies in the United States have been the subject of repeated investigations, official and unofficial, and of extensive public comment. They have been the primary reason for the establishment of public employment offices in the various states.

Quite apart from the other evils laid at the door of the private agencies, the data supplied by these investigations and reports afford a substantial basis for the conclusion of the New Jersey legislature that the business is peculiarly subject to abuses relating to fee charging, and that for the correction of these the restriction to a reasonable maximum charge is the only effective remedy. These data, to be gathered from numerous independent and public investigations, may be briefly summarized as follows:

First. They show that the agencies, left to themselves, very generally charge extortionate fees. * * * Exorbitant fees are taken for merely registering the applicants, no effort whatever being made to find them work. To stimulate the payment of such fees the agencies advertise for classes of laborers for whom no jobs are available. According to the Massachusetts Commission to Investigate Employment Offices, the ordinary forces of competition seem powerless to prevent or remedy this situation, because little capital is required to open an office, and because the clients of the agencies are constantly new.

Second. These data show that the fees charged are often discriminatory. It is made known in slack season that but few jobs are available, and that to these will be referred the applicants who tender the larger "extra fees" or "presents". There is ground for the belief that this is a particular danger in New Jersey, for a large proportion of its agencies specialize in employees for hotels and resorts, where the positions are seasonal and temporary. The whole supply of labor must, at the beginning and again at the end of the season, search for new positions at the same time.

Third. Fee-splitting has been a recurrent subject of complaint. It "is frequently practiced, part of the fee charged to the worker being paid over by the private employment agent to the employer or his foreman. This practice is closely akin to job selling by foremen and superintendents. * * * Both 'fee splitting' and 'job selling' result in short time employment and frequent discharges, for each time a job is filled a new fee is 'split' or a fresh price exacted. The resultant wastage from accelerated labor turnover, from extortionate and multiplied fees, from demoralization of workers, from unemployment and irregularity of employment, is incalculably great." (*Public Employment Offices in the United States,* U. S. Bureau of Labor Statistics Bulletin No. 241, 1918, p. 6.) While their fees are unregulated, the private agencies are free to charge those seeking employment enough to cover both the charge for their service and the gratuity paid to the foreman or employer. A legislature would certainly not be unreasonable in concluding that the fixing of a reasonable maximum fee was the appropriate and only effective method of assuring private agencies fair compensation while preventing them from abuses of this character.

Fourth. It is reported that at times of widespread unemployment the private agencies are known to raise their fees out of all proportion to the reasonable value of their services. There is a public interest at such times in bringing about a prompt readjustment of the labor supply to industry's need for labor. The additional barrier to a quick readjustment created by the agencies' raising of their rates affects that interest adversely. The establishment of a reasonable maximum rate is well calculated to obviate the abuse.

Fifth. Finally, it is pointed out that the private agencies charge the employee and do not charge the employer for a service that is rendered to both. The convenience of being furnished with employees is similar to that of being directed to a position; but less effort is required to collect compensation for the whole service from the employee alone. His necessities are normally greater. His bargaining power is normally weaker. The setting of a maximum fee need not mean—in New Jersey, does not mean—that an absolute limit is placed on the agency's return. The agency may still charge the employer in addition for such service as is rendered to him. The establishment of reasonable fees is thus, in one aspect, merely a method of providing that the patrons of the agency shall be required to pay only for the service rendered to them.

Legislation for the correction of these and other evils has been general throughout the United States. Among the earliest comprehensive schemes for that purpose was the Act of June 19, 1906 . . . adopted by Congress for the District of Columbia. For numerous classes of employees (including all domestic servants and farm help) it regulates not only the fee which may be charged to the applicant for work, but also the amount that the agency may receive from the employer. It requires a refund of half the fee if a fair opportunity for work is not secured in four days, and a refund of the whole fee and transportation expenses if no employment of the kind asked was vacant at the place to which the applicant was directed.

Among the states, twenty-one have limited the total fees that may be charged—ten by fixing a stated maximum, and eleven by restricting the charge to a named percentage of the salary earned during some period. In eight states the maximum registration fee is fixed by statute, and that fee is required to be returned if no work is found for the applicant. In seventeen states, if no work is furnished, the agency must return the entire fee collected.

It is of course true that the enactment of a particular type of legislation, even though general, and a widespread and competent opinion that it is wise and necessary, do not establish its constitutionality. But that such legislation has been enacted and continued in force over considerable periods of time and in widely separated areas, and is supported by a concurrence of informed public opinion, may not be disregarded in determining, first, whether the conditions peculiar to the business under consideration make it one in which, as in insurance companies, there is a paramount public concern; and, second, whether the regulation adopted is reasonably calculated to safeguard that interest. See *Muller* v. *Oregon*. . . .

Examination of the various reports of public bodies and the legislation referred to can, I think, leave no doubt that the practices of the private agencies with respect to their fees presented a problem for legislative consideration different from any other that this Court has passed on in ruling on the power to regulate prices, but certainly more akin to that in [cases previously cited] than to that in *Tyson* v. *Banton,* and, unless we are to establish once and for all the rule that only public utilities may be regulated as to price, the validity of the statute at hand would seem to me to be beyond doubt. Certainly it would be difficult to show a greater necessity for price regulation.

It is said that if there be abuses in this business, the business may be regulated but not by the fixing of reasonable prices, and that that was decided in *Tyson* v. *Banton*. So far as the significant facts in that case are concerned, it bears little resemblance to this one. Ticket brokers and employment brokers are similiar in name; in no other respect do they seem alike to me. To overcharge a man for the privilege of hearing the opera is one thing; to control the possibility of his earning a livelihood would appear to be quite another. And I shall not stop to argue that the state has a larger interest in seeing that its workers find employment without being imposed upon, than in seeing that its citizens are entertained. Here, too, if the business is subject to regulation, as seems to be admitted, the regulation which is appropriate and effective is some curtailment of the exorbitant fees charged and not some other form of control which would have no tendency to correct the evils aimed at.

I cannot accept as valid the distinction on which the opinion of the majority seems to me necessarily to depend, that granted constitutional power to regulate there is any controlling difference between reasonable regulation of price, if appropriate to the evil to be remedied, and other forms of appropriate regulation which curtail liberty of contract or the use and enjoyment of property. Obviously, even in the case of businesses affected with a public interest, other control than price regulation may be appropriate, and price regulation may be so inappropriate as to be arbitrary or unreasonable, and hence unconstitutional. To me it seems equally obvious that the Constitution does not require us to hold that a business, subject to every other form of reasonable regulation, is immune from the requirement of reasonable prices, where that requirement is the only remedy appropriate to the evils encountered. In this respect I can see no difference between a reasonable regulation of price and a reasonable regulation of the use of property, which affects its price or economic return. The privilege of contract and the free use of property are as seriously cut down in the one case as in the other.

To say that there is constitutional power to regulate a business or a particular use of property because of the public interest in the welfare of a class peculiarly affected, and to deny such power to regulate price for the accomplishment of the same end, when that alone appears to be an appropriate and effective remedy, is to make a distinction based on no real economic difference, and for which I can find no warrant in the Constitution itself nor any justification in the opinions of this Court.

The price paid for property or services is only one of the terms in a bargain; the effect on the parties is similar whether the restriction on the power to contract affects the price, or the goods or the services sold. Apart from the cases involving the historic public-callings, immemorially subject to the closest regulation, this Court has sustained regulations of the price in cases where the legislature fixed the charges which grain elevators . . . and insurance companies might make . . . , or required miners to be paid per ton of coal unscreened instead of screened . . . or required employers who paid their men in store orders to redeem them in cash . . . , or fixed the fees chargeable by attorneys appearing for injured employees before workmen's compensation commissions . . . , or fixed the rate of pay for overtime work . . . , or fixed the time within which the services of employees must be paid for . . . , or established maximum rents . . . , or fixed the maximum rate of interest chargeable on loans. . . . It sustained restrictions on the other element in the bargain where legislatures have established maximum hours of labor for men . . . or for women . . . , or prohibited the payment of wages in advance . . . , or required loaves of bread to be of a certain size . . . In each of these cases the police power of the state was held broad enough to warrant an interference with free bargaining in cases where, despite the competition that ordinarily attends that freedom, serious evils persisted.

Similar evils are now observed in the conduct of employment agencies. I see no reason why a state may not resort to the same remedy. There may be reasonable differences of opinion as to the wisdom of the solution here attempted. These I would be the first to admit. But a choice between them involves a step from the judicial to the legislative field. . . . That choice should be left where, it seems to me, it was left by the Constitution—to the states and to Congress.

Ribnik v. *McBride*
277 U. S. 350, 359. Decided May 28, 1928

[This view gained ascendancy in 1934 when Justice Roberts, speaking for a majority which sustained milk price-legislation in New York *(Nebbia* v. *New York,* 291 U. S. 502), said: the power of states to regulate business in the public interest extends to the control of price where price-regulation is a reasonable means of preventing public injury.]

COMPETITION FROM COÖPERATIVES

COTTON gins were public utilities, under Oklahoma law, and licenses were granted only on a showing of public necessity. After the statute was amended in 1925 to authorize the issuance of licenses to coöperatives without such a showing, a gin operator who already enjoyed a license contended that the grant of one to a coöperative invaded his property right. The Court majority agreed and said, through Justice Sutherland, that the private gin was also denied equal protection of the laws, for the coöperative was a stock company and the classification was arbitrary.

Justices Holmes, Brandeis and Stone dissented. One point made in a long opinion by Justice Brandeis was that the legislature had power at any time to abrogate the requirement of a certificate of necessity and open the business "to the competition of all comers" and that here the legislature had decided, in combating specific evils, to encourage farmers' coöperatives in their pursuit of economic democracy. Justice Stone reasoned that the complaint against the competition was without basis:

I AGREE with what Mr. Justice Brandeis has said. But there is one aspect of the decision now rendered to which I would especially direct attention. To me it would seem that there are such differences in organization, management, financial structure and practical operation between the business conducted by appellant, a single individual, and that conducted by a corporation organized as is appellee [Durant Coöperative Gin Company], as to justify the classification and discrimination made by the statute.

But, assuming there were no such differences, I fail to perceive any constitutional ground on which appellant can complain of a discrimination from which he has not suffered. His real and only complaint is not that he has been discriminated against either in the grant or enjoyment of his license, but that in the exercise of his non-exclusive privilege of carrying on the cotton ginning business he will suffer from competition by the corporate appellee, which, under local law, may secure a like privilege with possibly less difficulty than did appellant.

The proviso of the 1925 act [the amendment] is held unconstitutional solely on the ground that "an onerous restriction upon the right to engage in a public business" was "imposed by the statute upon appellant" and others similarly situated, which was not imposed on appellee. Appellant, if he had been denied a license, or if his exercise of the privilege, when granted, were more limited by the statute than that of appellee, might invoke the equal protection clause. But he now requires no such protection for he has received his license and is in full and unrestricted enjoyment of the same privilege as that which the appellee seeks. This is not less the case even if the statute be assumed to have made it more difficult for him than for appellee to secure a license.

Whether the grant appellant has received be called a franchise or a license would seem to be unimportant, for in any case it is not an exclusive privilege. Under the constitution and laws of Oklahoma the legislature has power to amend or repeal the franchise . . . , and injury suffered through an indefinite increase in the number of appellant's competitors by non-discriminatory legislation, would clearly be *damnum absque injuria* [loss without wrong]. A similar increase under the present alleged discriminatory statute would seem likewise to afford appellant no legal cause for complaint, for, a license not having been withheld from him, his position is precisely the same as though the statute authorized the grant of a license to him and to appellee on equal terms.

He is suffering, not from any application of the discriminatory feature of the statute, with which alone the Constitution is concerned . . . , but merely from the increase in the number of his competitors, an injury which would similarly have resulted from a non-discriminatory statute granting the privilege to all on terms more lenient than those formerly accorded appellant. Of such a statute, appellant could not complain and I can find no more basis for saying that constitutional rights are impaired where the discrimination which the statute authorizes has no effect, than where the statute itself does not discriminate.

Nor would appellant seem to be placed in any better position to challenge the constitutionality of the statute by recourse to the rule that the possessor of a non-exclusive franchise may enjoin competition unauthorized by the state. Appellee's business is not unauthorized. It is carried on under the sanction of a statute to which appellant himself can offer no constitutional objection, for even unconstitutional statutes may not be treated as though they had never been written. They are not void for all purposes and as to all persons. . . . For appellant to say that appellee's permit is void, and that its business may be enjoined, because conceivably someone else may challenge the constitutionality of the act, would seem to be a departure from the salutary rule consistently applied that only those who suffer from the unconstitutional application of a statute may challenge its validity. . . .

It seems to me that a fallacy, productive of unfortunate consequences, lurks in the suggestion that one may maintain a suit to enjoin competition of a business solely because hereafter someone else might suffer from an unconstitutional discrimination and enjoin it. But, more than that, even if the license had been withheld from appellant because he could not support the burden placed upon him by the statute, I should have thought it doubtful whether he would have been entitled to have had appellee's permit canceled—the relief now granted. He certainly could not have asked more than the very privilege which he now enjoys.

Frost v. *Corporation Commission of State of Oklahoma, et al.*
278 U. S. 515, 550 *Decided February 18, 1929*

WHEN A CITY COMPETES

JUSTICE STONE's views in the *Frost* case, *ante,* won acceptance five years later, when he wrote the prevailing opinion deciding that the City of Seattle, which operated an electric light and power service in competition with a private company, could impose a license tax on that company. The city ordinance imposed the same tax, three percent of the gross income from the business, on the city "so far as permitted by law". But the city had already issued bonds secured by the revenues of its electric business, and the company contended that this pledge being superior to all other charges, the city could not lawfully pay the tax; that even though the city paid the tax to itself, this would impose no actual burden; and therefore the burden placed on the company was a discrimination, a denial of equal protection, a deprivation of property without due process. Justice Stone observed that discrimination was permissible "with respect to things that are different" and that the Constitution gave no protection from the consequences of competition by a sovereign power. He wrote:

THERE IS NO contention that appellant's franchise or any contract relieves it generally from the duty of paying taxes. It is not contended that a state or municipality, merely because it fails or is unable to tax its own property or business, is prohibited from taxing like property or business. The contention here is that constitutional limitations are transgressed only because the tax affects a business with which the taxing sovereign is actively competing. For that reason it is argued that the taxation involves a forbidden discrimination and deprives appellant of its property without due process since the combined power of the city to tax and to compete may be used to destroy appellant's business. As appellant asserts that the tax can impose no effective burden on the city, its contention is, in effect, that the city, by virtue of the Fourteenth Amendment, upon entering the business forfeited its power to tax any competitor.

In conducting the business by state authority the city is exercising a part of the sovereign power of the state which the Constitution has not curtailed. The decisions of this Court leave no doubt that a state may, in the public interest, constitutionally engage in a business commonly carried on by private enterprise, levy a tax to support it . . . , and compete with private interests engaged in a like activity. . . .

We need not stop to inquire whether the equal protection clause was designed to protect the citizen from advantages retained by the sovereign, or to point out the extraordinary implications of appellant's argument when applied to expansions of government activities which have become commonplace. It is enough for present purposes that the equal protection clause does not forbid discrimination with respect to things that are different. The distinctions between the taxing sovereign and its taxpayers are many and obvious. The private corporation, whatever its public duties, carries on its business for private profit and is subject to the obligation, common to all, to contribute to the expense of government by paying taxes. The municipality, which is enabled to function only because it is a tax gatherer, may acquire property or conduct a business in the interest of the public welfare, and its gains if any must be used for public ends. Hence equal protection does not require a city to abstain from taxing the business of a corporation organized for profit merely because in the public interest the municipality has acquired like property or conducts a like business.

These differences are not lessened nor the constitutional exaction of uniformity increased because the city competes with a business which it taxes. . . . The state may tax different types of taxpayers differently even though they compete. . . . It could not plausibly be argued that a private nonprofit corporation distributing electric current to consumers at cost could not be exempted from taxes borne by others serving the same wants. . . . A business which in private hands might be exempted from taxation because not conducted for private profit is no less privileged because its capital is supplied by the government which controls it in the public interest. These considerations are in no way affected by calling the city's activity "proprietary" instead of governmental. . . .

The injury, which appellant fears may result, is the consequence of competition by the city, and not necessarily of the imposition of the tax. Even without the tax the possibility of injury would remain, for the city is not bound to conduct the business at a profit. The argument that some way must be found to interpret the due process clause so as to preclude the danger of such an injury fails to point the way. Legislation may protect from the consequences of competition, but the Constitution does not. . . . The Fourteenth Amendment does not purport to protect property from every injurious or oppressive action by a state . . . , nor can it relieve property of congenital defects. . . . It does not preclude competition, however drastic, between private enterprises or prevent unequal taxation of competitors who are different. Those were risks which appellant took when entering the field. No articulate principle is suggested calling for the conclusion that appellant is not subject to the same risks because the competing business is carried on by the state in the exercise of a power which has been constitutionally reserved to it from the beginning.

Such was the decision . . . where this Court pointed out that in the absence of any contract restriction the Fourteenth Amendment does not prevent a city from conducting a public water works in competition with private business or preclude taxation of the private business to help its rival to succeed. . . . Such must be our decision now.

The definition of gross income by § 2 of the ordinance, which is assailed as vague and indefinite, is that considered in [case cited]. By §§ 10 and 20 the comptroller of the city is required to make rules and regulations, having the force of law, for carrying the ordinance into effect, and to provide blank forms of return upon which the taxpayer is to enter such information as the comptroller may require to enable him to compute the tax. As appellant alleges that it has received its license and paid the first installment of the tax, it appears that a practical construction has been given to the ordinance by an administrative officer competent to give it, which the state court has upheld. It is thus apparent that the ordinance, as construed, is sufficiently definite to enable appellant to comply with it, and as appellant's return for taxation and the method of computing the tax are not disclosed by the record no constitutional infirmity in the ordinance is revealed. . . .

Appellant asserts a contract under its franchise to use the streets of the city for the purpose of carrying on its business for an unexpired term of years. It argues that the franchise is a contract license to carry on business, and that the exaction of a tax as a condition precedent to the enjoyment of the license will operate to destroy the privilege granted by the franchise.

This argument was made and answered in [cases cited]. Surrender of the state power to tax the privilege is not to be implied from the grant of it. Hence, appellant took its franchise subject to the power of the state to tax the granted privilege in common with all other privileges and property in the state. Without a clearly expressed obligation on the part of the city to surrender that power the contract clause does not limit it. . . .

Puget Sound Power & Light Co. v. *Seattle*
291 U. S. 618 Decided March 19, 1934

THE TEST OF INTERFERENCE

It was a direct interference with foreign commerce, a direct violation of the commerce clause, and not a proper exertion of police power, for Pennsylvania to require licenses to sell steamship tickets in foreign travel. This decision of the Court, delivered by Justice Butler, brought dissent from Justices Holmes, Brandeis and Stone. Brandeis said the statute did not affect the commerce except indirectly, and he cited various state regulations previously sustained although affecting it not less directly. Stone was not concerned with formal standards of direct and indirect interference; the method of deciding such cases was to search for "the actual effect" on the flow of commerce.

I AGREE with all that Mr. Justice Brandeis has said, but I would add a word with respect to one phase of the matter which seems to me of some importance. We are not here concerned with a question of taxation to which other considerations may apply, but with state regulation of what may be conceded to be an instrumentality of foreign commerce. As this Court has many times decided, the purpose of the commerce clause was not to preclude all state regulation of commerce crossing state lines, but to prevent discrimination and the erection of barriers or obstacles to the free flow of commerce, interstate or foreign.

The recognition of the power of the states to regulate commerce within certain limits is a recognition that these are matters of local concern which may properly be subject to state regulation and which, because of their local character, as well as their number and diversity, can never be adequately dealt with by Congress. Such regulation, so long as it does not impede the free flow of commerce, may properly be and for the most part has been left to the state by the decisions of this Court.

In this case the traditional test of the limit of state action by inquiring whether the interference with commerce is direct or indirect seems to me too mechanical, too uncertain in its application, and too remote from actualities, to be of value. In thus making use of the expressions, "direct" and "indirect interference" with commerce, we are doing little more than using labels to describe a result rather than any trustworthy formula by which it is reached.

It is difficult to say that such permitted interferences as those enumerated in Mr. Justice Brandeis' opinion are less direct than the interference prohibited here. But it seems clear that those interferences not deemed forbidden are to be sustained, not because the effect on commerce is nominally indirect, but because a consideration of all the facts and circumstances, such as the nature of the regulation, its function, the character of the business involved and the actual effect on the flow of commerce, lead to the conclusion that the regulation concerns interests peculiarly local and does not infringe the national interest in maintaining the freedom of commerce across state lines.

I am not persuaded that the regulation here is more than local in character or that it interposes any barrier to commerce. Until Congress undertakes the protection of local communities from the dishonesty of the sellers of steamship tickets, it would seem that there is no adequate ground for holding that the regulation here involved is a prohibited interference with commerce.

Di Santo v. *Pennsylvania*
273 U. S. 34, 43 *Decided January 3, 1927*

BARRIERS TO INTERSTATE COMMERCE

A South Carolina law limiting the width and weight of motor trucks on state highways was sustained by the Court as not an unlawful burden on interstate traffic passing through the state. Justice Stone pointed out that Congress had not undertaken such regulation of its own accord under the commerce clause but had left undisturbed the states' authority in this regard. The only question was whether, in the absence of congressional action, the legislature's choice was without rational basis.

Congress might determine whether burdens imposed by state regulation were excessive. "But that is a legislative, not a judicial, function," Justice Stone said in a unanimous opinion. Here use of the highways was prohibited to motor trucks and "semi-trailer motor trucks" exceeding 90 inches in width and 20,000 pounds in weight including load. Truckers and shippers argued that the statute not only imposed an unconstitutional burden on interstate commerce but also infringed the due process clause of the Fourteenth Amendment and was superseded by the Federal Motor Carrier Act of 1935.

The trial court enjoined enforcement of the weight provision against motor carriers passing over specified highways of the state, mostly concrete or asphalt-surfaced concrete; also the width provision, except in the case of vehicles exceeding 96 inches in width. This modified approval of the statute came before the Supreme Court, and Justice Stone analyzed it:

THE TRIAL COURT rested its decision that the statute unreasonably burdens interstate commerce, upon findings, not assailed here, that there is a large amount of motor truck traffic passing interstate in the southeastern part of the United States, which would normally pass over the highways of South Carolina, but which will be barred from the state by the challenged restrictions if enforced, and upon its conclusion that, when viewed in the light of their effect upon interstate commerce, these restrictions are unreasonable.

To reach this conclusion the court weighed conflicting evidence and made its own determinations as to the weight and width of motor trucks commonly used in interstate traffic and the capacity of the specified highways of the state to accommodate such traffic without injury to them or danger to their users. It found that interstate carriage by motor trucks has become a national industry; that from 85 to 90 percent of the motor trucks used in interstate transportation are 96 inches wide and of a gross weight, when loaded, of more than 10 tons; that only four other states prescribe a gross load weight as low as 20,000 pounds; and that the American Association of State Highway Officials and the National Conference on Street and Highway Safety in the Department of Commerce has recommended for adoption weight and width limitations in which weight is limited to axle loads of 16,000 to 18,000 pounds and width is limited to 96 inches.

It found in detail that compliance with the weight and width limitations demanded by the South Carolina act would seriously impede motor truck traffic passing to and through the state and increase its cost; that 2,417 miles of state highways, including most of those affected by the injunction, are of the standard construction of concrete or concrete base with asphalt surface, 7½ or 8 inches thick at the edges and 6 or 6½ inches thick at the center; that they are capable of sustaining without injury a wheel load of 8,000 to 9,000 pounds or an axle load of double those amounts, depending on whether the wheels are equipped with high-pressure or low-pressure pneumatic tires; that all but 100 miles of the specified highways are from 18 to 20 feet in width; that they constitute a connected system of highways which have been improved with the aid of federal money grants, as a part of a national system of highways; and that they constitute one of the best highway systems in the southeastern part of the United States.

It also found that the gross weight of vehicles is not a factor to be considered in the preservation of concrete highways, but that the appropriate factor to be considered is wheel or axle weight; that vehicles engaged in interstate commerce are so designed and the pressure of their weight is so distributed by their wheels and axles that gross loads of more than 20,000 pounds can be carried over concrete roads without damage to the surface; that a gross weight limitation of that amount, especially as applied to semi-trailer motor-trucks, is unreasonable as a means of preserving the highways; that it has no reasonable relation to safety of the public using the highways; and that the width limitation of 90 inches is unreasonable when applied to standard concrete highways of the state, in view of the fact that all other states permit a width of 96 inches, which is the standard width of trucks engaged in interstate commerce.

In reaching these conclusions, and at the same time holding that the weight and width limitations do not infringe the Fourteenth Amendment, the court proceeded upon the assumption that the commerce clause (Const. Art. I, § 8, cl. 3) imposes upon state regulations to secure the safe and economical use of highways a standard of reasonableness which is more exacting when applied to the interstate traffic than that required by the Fourteenth Amendment as to all traffic; that a standard of weight and width of motor vehicles which is an appropriate state regulation when applied to intrastate traffic may be prohibited because of its effect on interstate commerce, although the conditions attending the two classes of traffic with respect to safety and protection of the highways are the same.

South Carolina has built its highways and owns and maintains them. It has received from the federal government, in aid of its highway improvements, money grants which have been expended upon the highways to which the injunction applies. But as the District Court held, Congress has not undertaken to regulate the weight and size of motor vehicles in interstate motor traffic, and has left undisturbed whatever authority in that regard the states have retained under the Constitution.

While the constitutional grant to Congress of power to regulate interstate commerce has been held to operate of its own force to curtail state power in some measure, it did not forestall all state action affecting interstate commerce. Ever since [early cases cited] it has been recognized that there are matters of local concern, the regulation of which unavoidably involves some regulation of interstate commerce but which, because of their local character and their number and diversity, may never be fully dealt with by Congress. Notwithstanding the commerce clause, such regulation in the absence of congressional action has for the most part been left to the states by the decisions of this Court, subject to the other applicable constitutional restraints.

The commerce clause by its own force, prohibits discrimination against interstate commerce, whatever its form or method, and the decisions of this Court have recognized that there is scope for its like operation when state legislation nominally of local concern is in point of fact aimed at interstate commerce, or by its necessary operation is a means of gaining a local benefit by throwing the attendant burdens on those without the state. . . . It was to end these practices that the commerce clause was adopted. . . . The commerce clause has also been thought to set its own limitation upon state control of interstate rail carriers so as to preclude the subordination of the efficiency and convenience of interstate traffic to local service requirements.

But the present case affords no occasion for saying that the bare possession of power by Congress to regulate the interstate traffic forces the states to conform to standards which Congress might but has not adopted, or curtails their power to take measures to insure the safety and conservation of their highways which may be applied to like traffic moving intrastate. Few subjects of state regulation are so peculiarly of local concern as is the use of state highways. There are few, local regulation of which is so inseparable from a substantial effect on interstate commerce. Unlike the railroads, local highways are built, owned, and maintained by the state or its municipal subdivisions. The state has a primary and immediate concern in their safe and economical administration. The present regulations, or any others of like purpose, if they are to accomplish their end, must be applied alike to interstate and intrastate traffic both moving in large volume over the highways. The fact that they affect alike shippers in interstate and intrastate commerce in large number within as well as without the state is a safeguard against their abuse.

From the beginning it has been recognized that a state can, if it sees fit, build and maintain its own highways, canals, and railroads, and that in the absence of congressional action their regulation is peculiarly within its competence, even though interstate commerce is materially affected. . . . Congress not acting, state regulation of intrastate carriers has been upheld regardless of its effect upon interstate commerce. With respect to the extent and nature of the local interests to be protected and the unavoidable effect upon interstate and intrastate commerce alike, regulations of the use of the highways are akin to local regulation of rivers, harbors, piers, and docks, quarantine regulations, and game laws, which, Congress not acting, have been sustained even though they materially interfere with interstate commerce.

The nature of the authority of the state over its own highways has often been pointed out by this Court. It may not, under the guise of regulation, discriminate against interstate commerce. But, "In the absence of national legislation, especially covering the subject of interstate commerce, the state may rightly prescribe uniform regulations adapted to promote safety upon its highways and the conservation of their use, applicable alike to vehicles moving in interstate commerce and those of its own citizens". . . . This formulation has been repeatedly affirmed . . . and never disapproved. This Court has often sustained the exercise of that power, although it has burdened or impeded interstate commerce. It has upheld weight limitations lower than those presently imposed, applied alike to motor traffic moving interstate and intrastate. . . . Restrictions favoring passenger traffic over the carriage of interstate merchandise by truck have been similarly sustained . . . , as has the exaction of a reasonable fee for the use of the highways. . . .

In each of these cases regulation involves a burden on interstate commerce. But so long as the state action does not discriminate, the burden is one which the Constitution permits because it is an inseparable incident of the exercise of a legislative authority, which, under the Constitution, has been left to the states.

Congress, in the exercise of its plenary power to regulate interstate commerce, may determine whether the burdens imposed on it by state regulation, otherwise permissible, are too great, and may, by legislation designed to secure uniformity or in other respects to protect the national interest in the commerce, curtail to some extent the state's regulatory power. But that is a legislative, not a judicial, function, to be performed in the light of the congressional judgment of what is appropriate regulation of interstate commerce, and the extent to which, in that field, state power and local interests should be required to yield to the national authority and interest. In the absence of such legislation the judicial function, under the commerce clause as well as the Fourteenth Amendment, stops with the inquiry whether the state legislature in adopting regulations such as the present has acted within its province, and whether the means of regulation chosen are reasonably adapted to the end sought. . . .

Here the first inquiry has already been resolved by our decisions that a state may impose non-discriminatory restrictions with respect to the character of motor vehicles moving in interstate commerce as a safety measure and as a means of securing the economical use of its highways. In resolving the second, courts do not sit as legislatures, either state or national. They cannot act as Congress does when, after weighing all the conflicting interests, state and national, it determines when and how much the state regulatory power shall yield to the larger interests of a national commerce. And in reviewing a state highway regulation where Congress has not acted, a court is not called upon, as our state legislatures, to determine what, in its judgment, is the most suitable restriction to be applied of those that are possible, or to choose that one which in its opinion is best adapted to all the diverse interests affected. . . . When the action of a legislature is within the scope of its power, fairly debatable questions as to its reasonableness, wisdom, and propriety, are not for the determination of courts, but for the legislative body, on which rests the duty and responsibility of decision. . . . This is equally the case when the legislative power is one which may legitimately place an incidental burden on interstate commerce. It is not any the less a legislative power committed to the states because it affects interstate commerce, and courts are not any the more entitled, because interstate commerce is affected, to substitute their own for the legislative judgment. . . .

Since the adoption of one weight or width regulation, rather than another, is a legislative, not a judicial, choice, its constitutionality is not to be determined by weighing in the judicial scales the merits of the legislative choice and rejecting it if the weight of evidence presented in court appears to favor a different standard. . . . Being a legislative judgment it is presumed to be supported by facts known to the legislature unless facts judicially known or proved preclude that possibility. Hence, in reviewing the present determination, we examine the record, not to see whether the findings of the court below are supported by evidence, but to ascertain upon the whole record whether it is possible to say that the legislative choice is without rational basis. *Standard Oil Co.* v. *Marysville* [page 316, this volume]. Not only does the record fail to exclude that possibility but it shows affirmatively that there is adequate support for the legislative judgment.

At the outset it should be noted that underlying much of the controversy is the relative merit of a gross weight limitation as against an axle or wheel weight limitation. While there is evidence that weight stresses on concrete roads are determined by wheel rather than gross load weights, other elements enter into choice of the type of weight limitation. There is testimony to show that the axle or wheel weight limitation is the more easily enforced through resort to weighing devices adapted to ascertaining readily the axle or wheel weight. But it appears that in practice the weight of truck loads is not evenly distributed over axles and wheels; that commonly the larger part of the load—sometimes as much as 70 to 80 percent—rests on the rear axle, and that it is much easier for those who load trucks to make certain that they have complied with a gross load weight limitation than with an axle or wheel weight limitation. While the report of the National Conference on State and Highway Safety, on which the court below relied, suggested a wheel weight limitation of 8,000 or 9,000 pounds, it also suggested that a gross weight limitation might be adopted and should be subject to the recommended wheel weight limitation. But the Conference declined to fix the amount of gross weight limitation saying: "In view of the varying conditions of traffic, and lack of uniformity in highway construction in the several States, no uniform gross-weight limitations are here recommended for general adoption throughout the country".

The choice of a weight limitation based on convenience of application and consequent lack of need for rigid supervisory enforcement is for the legislature, and we cannot say that its preference for the one over the other is in any sense arbitrary or unreasonable. The choice is not to be condemned because the legislature prefers a workable standard, less likely to be violated than another under which the violations will probably be increased but more easily detected. It is for the legislature to say whether the one test or the other will in practical operation better protect the highways from the risk of excessive loads.

If gross load weight is adopted as the test, it is obvious that the permissible load must be somewhat lighter than if the axle or wheel test were applied. With the latter the gross weight of a loaded motor truck can never exceed twice the axle and four times the wheel limit. But the fact that the rear axle may and often does support as much as 70 or 80 percent of the gross load, with wheel weight in like proportion, requires that a gross load limit be fixed at considerably less than four times the permissible wheel limit.

There was testimony before the court to support its conclusion that the highways in question are capable of sustaining without inquiry a wheel load of 8,000 or 9,000 pounds, the difference depending upon the character of the tire in use, as against a wheel load of as much as 8,000 pounds, which would be possible under the statutory load limit of 20,000 as applied to motor trucks, and approximates the axle limit in addition to the gross load limit recommended by the National Conference on Street and Highway Safety.

Much of this testimony appears to have been based on theoretical strength of concrete highways laid under ideal conditions, and none of it was based on an actual study of the highways of South Carolina or of the sub-grade and other road building conditions which prevail there and which have a material bearing on the strength and durability of such highways. There is uncontradicted testimony that approximately 60 percent of the South Carolina standard paved highways in question were built without a longitudinal center joint which has since become standard practice, the portion of the concrete surface adjacent to the joint being strengthened by reinforcement or by increasing its thickness; and that owing to the distribution of the stresses on concrete roads when in use, those without a center joint have a tendency to develop irregular longitudinal cracks. As the concrete in the center of such roads is thinner than that at the edges, the result is that the highway is split into two irregular segments, each with a weak inner edge which, according to the expert testimony, is not capable of supporting indefinitely wheel loads in excess of 4,200 pounds.

There is little in the record to mark any controlling distinction between the application of the gross load weight limitation to the motor truck and to the semi-trailer motor truck. There is testimony which is applicable to both types of vehicle, that in case of accident the danger from the momentum of a colliding vehicle increases with gross load weight. The record is without convincing evidence of the actual distribution, in practice, of the gross load weight over the wheels and axles of the permissible types of semi-trailer motor trucks, but this does not enable us to say that the legislature was without substantial ground for concluding that the relative advantages of a gross load over a wheel weight limitation are substantially the same for the two types, or that it could not have concluded that they were so nearly alike for regulatory purposes as to justify the adoption of a single standard for both, as a matter of practical convenience. Even if the legislature were to accept appellees' assumption that net load weights are, in practice, evenly distributed over the wheels supporting the load of a permissible semi-trailer so that with the statutory gross limit the load on the rear axle would be about 8,000 pounds it might, as we have seen, also conclude that the danger point would then have been reached in the case of some 1,200 miles of concrete state roads constructed without a center joint.

These considerations, with the presumption of constitutionality, afford adequate support for the weight limitation without reference to other items of the testimony tending to support it. Furthermore, South Carolina's own experience is not to be ignored. Before adoption of the limitation South Carolina had had experience with higher weight limits. In 1924 it had adopted a combined gross weight limit of 20,000 pounds for vehicles of four wheels or less, and an axle weight limit of 15,000 pounds. In 1930 it had adopted a combined gross weight limit of 12½ tons with a five-ton axle weight limit for vehicles having more than two axles. . . . In 1931 it appointed a commission to investigate motor transportation in the state, to recommend legislation, and to report in 1932. The present weight limitation was recommended by the commission after a full consideration of relevant data, including a report by the state engineer who had constructed the concrete highways of the state and who advised a somewhat lower limitation as necessary for their preservation.

The fact that many states have adopted a different standard is not persuasive. The conditions under which highways must be built in the several states, their construction, and the demands made upon them, are not uniform. The road building art, as the record shows, is far from having attained a scientific certainty and precision, and scientific precision is not the criterion for the exercise of the constitutional regulatory power of the states. . . . The legislature, being free to exercise its own judgment, is not bound by that of other legislatures. It would hardly be contended that if all the states had adopted a single standard none, in the light of its own experience and in the exercise of its judgment upon all the complex elements which enter into the problem, could change it.

Only a word need be said as to the width limitation. While a large part of the highways in question are from 18 to 20 feet in width, approximately 100 miles are only 16 feet wide. On all the use of a 96-inch truck leaves but a narrow margin for passing. On the road 16 feet wide it leaves none. The 90-inch limitation has been in force in South Carolina since 1920, and the concrete highways which it has built appear to be adapted to vehicles of that width. The record shows without contradiction that the use of heavy loaded trucks on the highways tends to force other traffic off the concrete surface onto the shoulders of the road adjoining its edges, and to increase repair costs materially. It appears also that as the width of trucks is increased it obstructs the view of the highway, causing much inconvenience and increased hazard in its use. It plainly cannot be said that the width of trucks used on the highways in South Carolina is unrelated to their safety and cost of maintenance, or that a 90-inch width limitation, adopted to safeguard the highways of the state, is not within the range of the permissible legislative choice.

The regulatory measures taken by South Carolina are within its legislative power. They do not infringe the Fourteenth Amendment, and the resulting burden on interstate commerce is not forbidden.

South Carolina State Highway Dep't v. *Barnwell Bros.*
303 U. S. 177 *Decided February 14, 1938*

[Justice Stone concurred when the Court struck down an Arkansas law prohibiting entry into the state of any motor carrier having more than twenty gallons of gasoline in its tank without paying a tax on each gallon in excess. The facts disclosed that this was not a reasonable charge for the use of Arkansas roads but payment on gasoline to be transported beyond the state. "There are ways enough," Justice Stone observed, "in which the state can take its lawful toll without any suppression of the commerce which it taxes." (*McCarroll* v. *Dixie Greyhound Lines,* decided Feb. 12, 1940.)]

RECEIPTS FROM INTERSTATE SERVICE

JUSTICE Stone had written: "It was not the purpose of the commerce clause to relieve those engaged in interstate commerce from their just share of state tax burdens even though it increases the cost of doing the business * * * and the bare fact that one is carrying on interstate commerce does not relieve him from many forms of state taxation which add to the cost of his business." (*Western Live Stock* v. *Bureau of Revenue,* 303 U. S. 250 at 254, decided Jan. 2, 1938.)

However, he delivered a majority opinion holding a state "business activities" tax, measured by gross receipts, inapplicable to commissions earned by a marketing agent engaged in the business of shipping goods out of the state and selling them in other states. Close examination of the business facts showed that the tax was measured by the entire service in interstate commerce, which is protected by the commerce clause. But for this protection other states could exact similar taxes measured by the entire commerce, which would thus be subjected to burdens not borne by local commerce.

Justice Black in dissent regarded the taxing statute as nondiscriminatory, applying alike to all businesses in the state. He viewed the Court's judgment as operating to make the statute an instrument of discrimination against intrastate business. If valid state laws combined to hamper the free flow of commerce, the judiciary should not intervene but "Congress alone should adopt a broad national policy of regulation". Justice Stone repeated that other forms of taxation were still open to the state.

Here the State of Washington applied on a duly licensed corporation a tax for the "privilege of engaging in business activities", at the rate of one-half of one percent of gross income. The appellant corporation's business was that of marketing agent for fruit growers and growers' coöperatives in Washington—making sales and deliveries in other states and foreign countries, collecting the sales prices, and remitting the proceeds to its principals after proper deductions. Sometimes the fruit was shipped directly to purchasers, but more often was consigned to the company at extra-state points where it was stored pending sale or diverted to purchasers who bought the fruit while in transit. To representatives negotiating sales, shipments and collections at these points the company sent daily bulletins, and it spent large amounts for communications by telephone, telegraph and cable between itself in Washington and its representatives outside the state, Justice Stone pointed out.

Under contract with a federation of twelve Washington cooperative growers' organizations, the appellant marketing company was given exclusive authority to sell all apples and pears coming into the federation's control and to collect prices fixed by the federation, at a stipulated rate of commission. The Supreme Court of Washington, while conceding that the business involved interstate commerce, held that the company's activities in the state in promoting the commerce were a local business, subject to state taxation as was other business carried on in the state. Justice Stone's opinion continued:

WE NEED NOT STOP to consider which, if any, of appellant's activities in carrying on its business are in themselves transportation of the fruit in interstate or foreign commerce. For the entire service for which the compensation is paid is in aid of the shipment and sale of merchandise in that commerce. Such services are within the protection of the commerce clause . . . , and the only question is whether the taxation of appellant's gross receipts derived from them is such an interference with interstate commerce as to bring the tax within the constitutional prohibition.

While appellant is engaged in business within the state, and the state courts have sustained the tax as laid on its activities there, the interstate commerce service which it renders and for which the taxed compensation is paid is not wholly performed within the state. A substantial part of it is outside the state, where sales are negotiated and written contracts of sale are executed, and where deliveries and collections are made. Both the compensation and the tax laid upon it are measured by the amount of the commerce—the number of boxes of fruit transported from Washington to purchasers elsewhere; so that the tax, though nominally imposed upon appellant's activities in

Washington, by the very method of its measurement reaches the entire interstate commerce service rendered both within and without the state and burdens the commerce in direct proportion to its volume.

The constitutional effect of a tax upon gross receipts derived from participation in interstate commerce and measured by the amount or extent of the commerce itself has been so recently and fully considered by this Court that it is unnecessary now to elaborate the applicable principles. . . .

It has often been recognized that "even interstate business must pay its way" by bearing its share of local tax burdens . . . , and that in consequence not every local tax laid upon gross receipts derived from participation in interstate commerce is forbidden. . . . But it is enough for present purposes that under the commerce clause, in the absence of congressional action, state taxation, whatever its form, is precluded if it discriminates against interstate commerce or undertakes to lay a privilege tax measured by gross receipts derived from activities in such commerce which extend beyond the territorial limits of the taxing state. Such a tax, at least when not apportioned to the activities carried on within the state . . . , burdens the commerce in the same manner and to the same extent as if the exaction were for the privilege of engaging in interstate commerce and would, if sustained, expose it to multiple tax burdens, each measured by the entire amount of the commerce, to which local commerce is not subject.

Here the tax, measured by the entire volume of the interstate commerce in which appellant participates, is not apportioned to its activities within the state. If Washington is free to exact such a tax, other states to which the commerce extends may, with equal right, lay a tax similarly measured for the privilege of conducting within their respective territorial limits the activities there which contribute to the service. The present tax, though nominally local, thus in its practical operation discriminates against interstate commerce, since it imposes upon it, merely because interstate commerce is being done, the risk of a multiple burden to which local commerce is not exposed. . . . Such a multiplication of state taxes, each measured by the volume of the commerce, would reëstablish the barriers to interstate trade which it was the object of the commerce clause to remove. Unlawfulness of the burden depends upon its nature measured in terms of its capacity to obstruct interstate commerce, and not on the contingency that some other state may first have subjected the commerce to a like burden. * * *

For more than a century . . . it has been recognized that under the commerce clause, Congress not acting, some protection is afforded to interstate commerce against state taxation of the privilege of engaging in it. . . . For half a century . . . it has not been doubted that state taxation of local participation in interstate commerce, measured by the entire volume of the commerce, is likewise foreclosed. During that period Congress has not seen fit to exercise its constitutional power to alter or abolish the rules thus judicially established. Instead, it has left them undisturbed, doubtless because it has appreciated the destructive consequences to the commerce of the nation if their protection were withdrawn. Meanwhile Congress has accommodated its legislation, as have the states, to these rules as an established feature of our constitutional system. There has been left to the states wide scope for taxation of those engaged in interstate commerce, extending to the instruments of that commerce, to net income derived from it, and to other forms of taxation not destructive of it. . . .

Gwin, White & Prince v. *Henneford*
305 U. S. 434 Decided January 3, 1939

SALES TAXES IN INTERSTATE COMMERCE

FOR unemployment relief the New York state legislature authorized the City of New York to levy sales taxes upon all sales of goods for consumption within the state, to be paid by the purchaser and collected by the seller. The question for decision was whether the tax, as applied to a Pennsylvania corporation which sold and delivered to firms in New York coal mined in

Pennsylvania, infringed the commerce clause of the federal Constitution. The majority of the Supreme Court, speaking through Justice Stone, demonstrated that the tax was not a forbidden burden on interstate commerce.

On the other hand, Chief Justice Hughes and Justices McReynolds and Roberts considered it was a tax on interstate sales, "a direct burden" equivalent to a tariff, a state barrier to a free national market. Justice Stone again observed that the commerce clause was not intended to relieve those engaged in interstate commerce of "their just share of state tax burdens".

The city's authority did not extend to transactions originating or consummated outside its territorial limits. The municipal assembly fixed the tax as two percent of the receipts "from every sale in the City of New York" and commanded that the vendor charge the tax to the customer, collect it, and file returns. The vendor was made liable, as an insurer, for its payment to the city.

After setting forth the provisions of the law Justice Stone related that the Pennsylvania coal company maintained a sales office in the city, entered into contracts there, moved its product by rail from mine to Jersey City dock, thence in most cases by barge alongside the customers' public utility plants and steamships. He wrote:

SECTION 8 of the Constitution declares that "Congress shall have power * * * to regulate commerce with foreign Nations, and among the several States. * * *" In imposing taxes for state purposes a state is not exercising any power which the Constitution has conferred upon Congress. It is only when the tax operates to regulate commerce between the states or with foreign nations to an extent which impairs the authority conferred upon Congress, that the tax can be said to exceed constitutional limitations. See . . . *South Carolina Highway Dept.* v. *Barnwell Bros.,* [p. 220, this volume]. Forms of state taxation whose tendency is to prohibit the commerce or place it at a disadvantage as compared or in competition with intrastate commerce and any state tax which discriminates against the commerce, are familiar examples of the exercise of state taxing power in an unconstitutional manner, because of its obvious regulatory effect upon commerce between the states.

[Citing numerous cases in a footnote, the opinion points out: "Despite mechanical or artificial distinctions sometimes taken between the taxes deemed permissible and those condemned, the decisions appear to be predicated on a practical judgment as to the likelihood of the tax being used to place interstate commerce at a competitive disadvantage. * * * Lying back of these decisions is the recognized danger that, to the extent that the burden falls on economic interests without the state, it is not likely to be alleviated by those political restraints which are normally exerted on legislation where it affects adversely interests within the state."]

But it was not the purpose of the commerce clause to relieve those engaged in interstate commerce of their just share of state tax burdens, merely because an incidental or consequential effect of the tax is an increase in the cost of doing the business. . . . Not all state taxation is to be condemned because, in some manner, it has an effect upon commerce between the states, and there are many forms of tax whose burdens, when distributed through the play of economic forces, affect interstate commerce, which nevertheless fall short of the regulation of the commerce which the Constitution leaves to Congress. A tax may be levied on net income wholly derived from interstate commerce. Nondiscriminatory taxation of the instrumentalities of interstate commerce is not prohibited. The like taxation of property, shipped interstate, before its movement begins, or after it ends, is not a forbidden regulation. An excise for the warehousing of merchandise preparatory to its interstate shipment or upon its use, or withdrawal for use, by the consignee after the interstate journey has ended is not precluded. Nor is taxation of a local business or occupation which is separate and distinct from the transportation or intercourse which is interstate commerce, forbidden merely because in the ordinary course such transportation or intercourse is induced or occasioned by such business, or is prerequisite to it. . . .

In few of these cases could it be said with assurance that the local tax does not in some measure affect the commerce or increase the cost of doing it. But in them as in other instances of constitutional interpretation so as to insure the harmonious operation of powers reserved to the states with those conferred upon the national government, courts are called upon to reconcile competing constitutional demands, that commerce between the states shall not be unduly impeded by state action, and that the power to lay taxes for the support of state government shall not be unduly curtailed. . . .

Certain types of taxes may, if permitted at all, so readily be made the instrument of impeding or destroying interstate commerce as plainly as to call for their condemnation as forbidden regulations. Such are the taxes already noted which are aimed at or discriminate against the commerce or impose a levy for the privilege of doing it, or tax interstate transportation or communication or their gross earnings, or levy an exaction on merchandise in the course of its interstate journey. Each imposes a burden which intrastate commerce does not bear, and merely because interstate commerce is being done places it at a disadvantage in comparison with intrastate business or property in circumstances such that if the asserted power to tax were sustained, the states would be left free to exert it to the detriment of national commerce.

The present tax as applied to respondent is without the possibility of such consequences. Equality is its theme. . . . It does not aim at or discriminate against interstate commerce. It is laid upon every purchaser, within the state, of goods for consumption, regardless of whether they have been transported in interstate commerce. Its only relation to the commerce arises from the fact that immediately preceding transfer of possession to the purchaser within the state, which is the taxable event regardless of the time and place of passing title, the merchandise has been transported in interstate commerce and brought to its journey's end. Such a tax has no different effect upon interstate commerce than a tax on the "use" of property which has just been moved in interstate commerce, sustained in [cases cited], or the tax on storage or withdrawal for use by the consignee of gasoline, similarly sustained in [cases cited], or the familiar property tax on goods by the state of destination at the conclusion of their interstate journey. . . .

If, as guides to decision we look to the purpose of the commerce clause to protect interstate commerce from discriminatory or destructive state action, and at the same time to the purpose of the state taxing power under which interstate commerce admittedly must bear its fair share of state tax burdens, and to the necessity of judicial reconciliation of these competing demands, we can find no adequate ground for saying that the present tax is a regulation which, in the absence of congressional action, the commerce clause forbids. This Court has uniformly sustained a tax imposed by the state of the buyer upon a sale of goods, in several instances in the "original package", effected by delivery to the purchaser upon arrival at destination after an interstate journey, both when the local seller has purchased the goods extra-state for the purpose of resale . . . and when the extra-state seller has shipped them into the taxing state for sale there. . . . It has likewise sustained a fixed-sum license tax imposed on the agent of the interstate seller for the privilege of selling merchandise brought into the taxing state for the purpose of sale. . . .

The only challenge made to these controlling authorities is by reference to unconstitutional "burdens" on interstate commerce made in general statements which are inapplicable here because they are torn from their setting in judicial opinions and speak of state regulations or taxes of a different kind laid in different circumstances from those with which we are now concerned. . . . Others will presently be discussed. But unless we are now to reject the plain teaching of this line of sales tax decisions, extending back for more than seventy years . . . , the present tax must be upheld. As we have seen, the ruling of these decisions does not rest on precedent alone. It has the support of reason and of a due regard for the just balance between national and state power. In sustaining these taxes on sales, emphasis was placed on the circumstances that they were not so laid, measured, or conditioned as to afford a means of obstruction to the commerce or of discrimination against it, and that the extension of the immunity of the commerce clause contended for would be at the expense of state taxing power by withholding from taxation property and transactions within the state without the gain of any needed protection to interstate commerce. . . .

Apart from these more fundamental considerations which we think are of controlling force in the application of the commerce clause, we can find no adequate basis for distinguishing the present tax laid on the sale or purchase of goods upon their arrival at destination at the end of an interstate journey from the tax which may be laid in like fashion on the property itself. That the latter is a permissible tax has long been established by an unwavering line of authority. . . . As we have often pointed out, there is no distinction in this relationship between a tax on property, the sum of all the rights and powers incident to ownership, and the taxation of the exercise of some of its constituent elements. . . . If coal situated as that in the present case, was, before its delivery, subject to a state property tax . . . , transfer of possession of the coal upon a sale is equally taxable . . . , just as was the storage or use of the property in similar circumstances held taxable in [cases cited].

Respondent, pointing to the course of its business and to its contracts which contemplate the shipment of the coal interstate upon orders of the New York customers, insists that a distinction is to be taken between a tax laid on sales made, without previous contract, after the merchandise has crossed the state boundary, and sales, the contracts for which when made contemplate or require the transportation of merchandise interstate to the taxing state. Only the sales in the state of destination in the latter class of cases, it is said, are protected from taxation by the commerce clause, a qualification which respondent concedes is a salutary limitation upon the reach of the clause since its use is thus precluded as a means of avoiding state taxation of merchandise transported to the state in advance of the purchase order or contract of sale.

But we think this distinction is without the support of reason or authority. A very large part, if not most of the merchandise sold in New York City, is shipped interstate to that market. In the case of products like cotton, citrus fruits and coal, not to mention many others which are consumed there in vast quantities, all have crossed the state line to seek a market, whether in fulfillment of a contract or not. That is equally the case with other goods sent from without the state to the New York market, whether they are brought into competition with like goods produced within the state or not. We are unable to say that the present tax, laid generally upon all sales to consumers within the state, subjects the commerce involved where the goods sold are brought from other states, to any greater burden or affects it more, in any economic or practical way, whether the purchase order or contract precedes or follows the interstate shipment. Since the tax applies only if a sale is made, and in either case the object of interstate shipment is a sale at destination, the deterrent effect of the tax would seem to be the same on both. Restriction of the scope of the commerce clause so as to prevent recourse to it as a means of curtailing state taxing power seems as salutary in the one case as in the other.

True, the distinction has the support of a statement *obiter* in [case cited] and seems to have been tacitly recognized in [two other cases cited], although in each case a tax on the sale of goods brought into the state for sale was upheld. But we have sustained the tax where the course of business and the agreement for sale plainly contemplated the shipment interstate in fulfillment of the contract. . . . In the same circumstances the Court has upheld a property tax on the merchandise transported . . . , upon its use . . . , and upon its storage. . . . Taxation of property or the exercise of a power over it immediately preceding its previously contemplated shipment interstate has been similarly sustained. . . . For reasons already indicated all such taxes upon property or the exercise of the powers of ownership stand in no different relation to interstate commerce and have no different effect upon it than has the present sales tax upon goods whose shipment interstate into the taxing state was contemplated when the contract was entered into.

It is also urged that the conclusion which we reach is inconsistent with the long line of decisions of this Court . . . , which have held invalid license taxes to the extent that they have sought to tax the occupation of soliciting orders for the purchase of goods to be shipped into the taxing state. In some instances the tax appeared to be aimed at suppression or placing at a disadvantage this type of business when brought into competition with competing intrastate sales. . . . In all, the statute, in its practical operation, was capable of use, through increase in the tax, and in fact operated to some extent to place the merchant thus doing business interstate at a disadvantage in competition with untaxed sales at retail stores within the state. While a state, in some circumstances may by taxation suppress or curtail one type of intrastate business to the advantage of another type of competing business which is left untaxed . . . , it does not follow that interstate commerce may be similarly affected by the practical operation of a state taxing statute. . . . It is enough for present purposes that the rule of *Robbins* v. *Shelby County Taxing District,* 120 U. S. 489 [the earliest decision cited], has been narrowly limited to fixed-sum license taxes imposed on the business of soliciting orders for the purchase of goods to be shipped interstate . . . and that the actual and potential effect on the commerce of such a tax is wholly wanting in the present case.

Finally it is said that the vice of the present tax is that it is measured by the gross receipts from interstate commerce and thus in effect reaches for taxation the commerce carried on both within and without the taxing state. . . . It is true that a state tax upon the operations of interstate commerce measured either by its volume or the gross receipts derived from it has been held to infringe the commerce clause, because the tax if sustained would exact tribute for commerce carried on beyond the boundaries of the taxing state, and would leave each state through which the commerce passes free to subject it to a like burden not borne by intrastate commerce. . . .

In [case cited], a tax on gross receipts, so far as laid by the state of the seller upon the receipts from sales of goods manufactured in the taxing state and sold in other states, was held invalid because there the court found the receipts derived from activities in interstate commerce, as distinguished from the receipts from activities wholly intrastate, were included in the measure of the tax, the sales price, without segregation or apportionment. It was pointed out . . . that had the tax been conditioned upon the exercise of the taxpayer's franchise or its privilege of manufacturing in the taxing state, it would have been sustained, despite its incidental effect on interstate commerce since the taxpayer's local activities or privileges were sufficient to support such a tax, and that it could fairly be measured by the sales price of the goods.

The rationale of the [cited] case does not call for condemnation of the present tax. Here the tax is conditioned upon a local activity, delivery of goods within the state upon their purchase for consumption. It is an activity which apart from its effect on the commerce, is subject to the state taxing power. The effect of the tax, even though measured by the sales price, as has been shown, neither discriminates against nor obstructs interstate commerce more than numerous other state taxes which have repeatedly been sustained as involving no prohibited regulation of interstate commerce.

In two instances * * * respondent's contracts with Austin, Nichols & Co. and with the New England Steamship Co. call for delivery of the coal at points outside of New York, in the one case f.o.b. at the mines in Pennsylvania, and in the other at the pier in Jersey City, New Jersey, and deliveries were made accordingly.

Respondent asked the state courts to rule that the taxing act did not apply to these transactions, particularly because the enabling statute expressly prohibits the city from imposing a tax upon "any transaction originating and/or consummated outside the territorial limits of the City". . . . This question the state courts left unanswered, the Court of Appeals resting its decision wholly on the constitutional ground.

Upon the remand of this clause for further proceedings not inconsistent with this decision, the state court will be free to decide the state question, and the remand will be without prejudice to the further presentation to this Court of any federal question remaining undecided here, if the state courts shall determine that the taxing statute is applicable.

McGoldrick v. *Berwind-White Coal Mining Co.*
Decided January 29, 1940

State Taxing Powers

FIRST PRINCIPLES OF TAXATION

An Ohio tax on income from intangible property, as applied to trust certificates issued under deeds on land within and without the state, was invalidated by the Supreme Court. Justice McReynolds held that the tax on interests represented by the certificates was an unconstitutional levy on land situate beyond the state, not on a species of intangible personal property. Referring to legal writings on the conflicting theories, he cited an article written by Justice Stone when dean of the Columbia School of Law.

Justice Stone, joined in dissent by Justices Holmes and Brandeis, gave a complete description of the certificates to show that they were within the control and protection of the taxing state and subject to its taxing power. Validity did not depend on the label which had been used to describe a nontaxable interest; and this included labels used by writers on legal theory. He wrote:

Tax laws are neither contracts nor penal laws. The obligation to pay taxes arises from the unilateral action of government in the exercise of the most plenary of sovereign powers, that to raise revenues to defray the expenses of government and to distribute the burden among those who must bear it. . . . To that obligation are subject all rights of persons and property which enjoy the protection of the sovereign and are within the reach of its power.

For centuries no principle of law has won more ready or universal acceptance. Even now that it is doubted, the doubt is rested on no more substantial foundation than the want of "jurisdiction" to tax, and the assertion that the Fourteenth Amendment is endowed with a newly discovered efficacy to forbid "double taxation" when the sovereignty imposing the tax is that of two or more states. . . . But as no opinion of this Court has undertaken to define the taxation which is thus forbidden because it is double, or to declare that different legal rights founded upon the same economic interest may never, under any circumstances, be compelled to contribute to the cost of government of two states whose protection they respectively enjoy, it would still seem to be open to inquiry whether the particular tax now imposed infringes any constitutional principle capable of statement and definition.

When we speak of the jurisdiction to tax land or a chattel, as being exclusively in the state where it is located, we mean no more than that, in the ordinary sense of ownership of tangible property, the legal interests of ownership enjoy the benefit and protection of the laws of that state alone, and that it alone can effectively reach the interests protected for the purpose of subjecting them to the payment of the tax. Other states are said to be without jurisdiction, and so without constitutional power to tax, if they afford no protection to the ownership of the property and cannot lay hold of any interest in the property in order to compel payment of the tax. . . .

But when new and different legal interests, however named, are created with respect to land or a chattel, of such a character that they do enjoy the benefits of the laws of another state and are brought within the reach of its taxing power, I know of no articulate principle of law or of the Fourteenth Amendment which would deny to the state the right to tax them. No one would doubt the constitutional power of a state to tax its residents on their shares of stock in a foreign corporation whose only property is real estate or chattels located elsewhere . . . , or to tax a valuable contract for the purchase of land or chattels located in another state . . . , or to tax a mortgage of real estate located without the state even though the land affords the only source of payment. . . . Each of these legal interests, it is true, finds its only economic source in the value of the land, and the rights which are elsewhere subjected to the tax can be brought to their ultimate economic fruition only through some means of control of the land itself. But the means of control may be subjected to taxation in the state of its owner, whether it be a share of stock or a contract or a mortgage. There is no want of jurisdiction to tax these interests where they are owned, in the sense that the state lacks power to appropriate them to the payment of the tax. No court has condemned such action as capricious, arbitrary or oppressive. The Fourteenth Amendment does not forbid it, for it is universally recognized that these interests of themselves are in some measure clothed with the legal incidents of property in the taxing state and enjoy there the benefit and protection of its laws.

Similarly, I do not doubt that the state may tax the income of its citizen derived from land in another state. The right to impose the tax is founded upon the power to exact it, coupled with the protection which the state affords to the taxpayer in the receipt and enjoyment of his income. . . . I can perceive no more constitutional objection to imposing such a tax than to the taxation of a citizen on income derived from a business carried on by the taxpayer in another state, and subject to taxation there, which we upheld in [case cited], or to the tax on income derived from securities having a tax *situs* in another state, upheld in [case cited]. The fact that it is now thought to be necessary to discredit or overrule [case cited] in order to overturn the tax imposed here, should lead us to doubt the result, rather than the authority which plainly challenges it, and should give us pause before reading into the Fourteenth Amendment so serious and novel a restriction on the vital elements of the taxing power.

The present tax, measured by income, is upon intangible property interests owned by a citizen of Ohio. They are represented by the transferable certificates, issued, by trustees of land, under contracts by which each trustee undertakes to hold the title of specified lands in trust for the benefit of the certificate holders; to receive the income and to pay it over to them ratably, after meeting expenses and depreciation; and to receive and distribute ratably the proceeds of sale of the land if sold under existing options. In the event of default by the lessee, the trustee is given plenary authority to terminate the lease, take possession of the land and sell it, as fully as though it were the sole legal and equitable owner. The trustee is authorized to settle claims upon contract and tort made against the trustee or the trust estate, and is entitled to indemnity from the estate for all personal liability and expenses. It is authorized to borrow money and to give the trust estate as security.

The beneficiaries have no right to possession or to partition of the property, and can maintain no action at law with respect to it. They cannot be assessed, and incur no liability by virtue of the administration of the trust estate. The trust certificates are freely transferable, as are shares of stock in a corporation. The rights of the beneficiaries are so identified with the certificates that they may be transferred only on surrender of the certificate to the trustee. Certificates lost, stolen, or destroyed may be replaced by the trustee at its option and in its discretion. . . .

There is thus created an active trust of land, under which the trustee is clothed with all the incidents of legal ownership, and which is given the status of a business entity separate and distinct, for all practical purposes, from the interests of the certificate holders. . . . The beneficiaries have none of the incidents of legal ownership. They can neither take nor defend possession of the land. But they are clothed with rights *in personam,* in form both contractual and equitable, enforcible against the trustee by suit in equity for an accounting, to compel performance of the trust or to restrain breaches of it. Such actions are transitory and maintainable wherever the trustee may be found. . . .

The ownership of the certificates in Ohio is thus vested with valuable rights, differing from those of ordinary ownership, including those enforcible rights against the trustee within as well as without the state. They are brought within the control of the state. These rights, the physical certificates with which they are identified, and the receipt and enjoyment of their income by the owner, are each protected by Ohio laws. If we look to substance rather than form, to the principles which underlie and justify the taxing power, rather than to descriptive terminology which, merely as a matter of convenience, we may apply to the interest taxed, it would seem to be as much subject to the taxing power as any other tangible interest brought within the control and protection of the state, even though its ultimate economic enjoyment may be dependent wholly on property located and taxed elsewhere. . . .

It is unimportant what labels writers on legal theory, the courts of Ohio, or this Court may place upon this interest. The Fourteenth Amendment did not adopt as ultimate verities the quaint distinctions taken three centuries ago by Sir Edward Coke between things that savour of the realty and other forms of right, and between corporeal and incorporeal rights. In applying the Fourteenth Amendment we may recognize, what he failed to realize, that all rights are incorporeal and that whether they are rightly subjected to state taxing power must be determined by recourse to the principles upon which taxes have universally been laid and collected, rather than by the choice of a label which, by definition previously agreed upon, will infallibly mark the interest as nontaxable.

In every practical aspect—and taxation is a practical matter—the trust certificate holder stands in the same relationship to the land as the stockholder of a land-owning corporation. It is not denied that the petitioner receives as much benefit and protection from the State of Ohio with respect to his certificates as does the owner of corporate stock, or that his interest is as much within the reach of the state power. Only by resort to subtle refinements of legal doctrine, devised without reference to the problems of taxation and irrelevant to them, or by treating the Fourteenth Amendment as an instrument for giving effect to our own peculiar convictions of what is morally or economically desirable, is it possible to sustain the taxation of the one and not the other.

Even though the tax be destroyed so far as it is imposed on petitioner's interest in the trusts of lands outside of Ohio, it cannot, for any reason advanced to support that conclusion, be deemed invalid as applied to appellant's interest in the Ohio trusts. The opinion of the Court suggests no other reason.

Whatever name we may give to the interest taxed, Ohio is not without jurisdiction of the land, the trustee, the certificates, or the owners of them. All are within the state. The objection to double taxation by a single sovereign is no more potent under the Fourteenth Amendment than the objection that a tax otherwise valid has been doubled. . . . The imposition of a tax on a particular interest in land already taxed *ad valorem* does not infringe any constitutional immunity. . . .

The fact that the certificates are taxed, and the owners of interests in trusts of land not represented by certificates are untaxed, plainly involves no forbidden discrimination. The owners of transferable certificates, representing an equitable interest in a trust of land divided into shares, enjoy privileges and advantages not attaching to other forms of ownership, which are an adequate basis for a difference in taxation. . . .

The judgment now given cannot rest on the Delphic concession of counsel, that the state has "no power to tax land or interests in land situate beyond its borders", and that if situate within the state, there is no power to tax them "in any other manner than by uniform rule according to value". The concession, so far as it relates to the Ohio trusts, plainly has reference to requirements of the state and not the federal Constitution. For the Fourteenth Amendment does not restrict a state to the taxation of all interests in land uniformly according to value.

We are not concerned with the validity of the tax under the state constitution. The state court has plenary power to settle that question for the litigants and for us . . . , as it has done by sustaining the tax. No concession of counsel about his theory of law requires us to adopt his theory, however mistaken or irrelevant, for decision of the federal question which alone is before us. None can confer on us jurisdiction to review on appeal the decision of a state question by the highest court of the state, or excuse the abuse of power involved in our reversing its judgment on state grounds.

The objections to the tax affecting the Ohio trusts present no substantial federal question or any which the Court has deemed it necessary to consider. The tax affecting the extra-state trusts should be sustained as not infringing any constitutional guarantee.

Senior v. *Braden*
295 U. S. 422, 433 Decided May 20, 1935

INCOME FROM LAND IN ANOTHER STATE

A RESIDENT of New York sought a refund of state taxes paid on income from land in New Jersey. The Supreme Court, through Justice Stone, held that her rents and interest were properly included in her taxable income; by reason of domicil in New York she enjoyed the state's protection and was responsible for a share of the costs of government; these benefits and responsibilities were not affected by the character of the source of the income. Justice Butler (with Justice McReynolds) dissented: previous decisions of the Court had established that a tax on income from the use of land was in effect a tax on the land itself. Justice Stone made the distinction clear.

The New York law, imposing a tax upon the "entire net income" of residents of the state, defined gross income as including interest and rent; amended in 1935, it enumerated among the items of taxable income, rent from real property outside the state and expressed the intention "to include all the foregoing items without regard to the source thereof, location of the property thereof, or any other factor except only a rare case where the inclusion thereof would be violative of constitutional restrictions". The ground on which recovery was sought was that the tax was actually on real estate and tangible property located outside New York and thus violated the Fourteenth Amendment. Was there anything in the Amendment which precluded the state from taxing the income?

Justice Stone's analysis follows:

INCOME FROM RENTS. That the receipt of income by a resident of the territory of a taxing sovereignty is a taxable event is universally recognized. Domicil itself affords a basis for such taxation. Enjoyment of the privileges of residence in the state and the attendant right to invoke the protection of its laws are inseparable from responsibility for sharing the costs of government. "Taxes are what we pay for civilized society . . ." [Justice Holmes]. A tax measured by the net income of residents is an equitable method of distributing the burdens of government among those who are privileged to enjoy its benefits. The tax, which is apportioned to the ability of the taxpayer to pay it, is founded upon the protection afforded by the state to the recipient of the income in his person, in his right to receive the income and in his enjoyment of it when received. These are rights and privileges which attach to domicil within the state. To them and to the equitable distribution of the tax burden, the economic advantage realized by the receipt of the income and represented by the power to control it, bears a direct relationship. . . .

Neither the privilege nor the burden is affected by the character of the source from which the income is derived. For that reason income is not necessarily clothed with the tax immunity enjoyed by its source. A state may tax its residents upon net income from a business whose physical assets, located wholly without the state, are beyond its taxing power. . . . It may tax net income from bonds held in trust and administered in another state . . . , although the taxpayer's equitable interest may not be subjected to the tax. . . . It may tax net income from operations in interstate commerce, although a tax on the commerce is forbidden. . . . Congress may lay a tax on net income derived from the business of exporting merchandise in foreign commerce, although a tax upon articles exported is prohibited by constitutional provision. . . .

Neither analysis of the two types of taxes, nor consideration of the basis upon which the power to impose them rests, supports the contention that a tax on income is a tax on the land which produces it. The incidence of a tax on income differs from that of a tax on property. Neither tax is dependent upon the possession by the taxpayer of the subject of the other. His income may be taxed, although he owns no property, and his property may be taxed, although it produces no income. The two taxes are measured by different standards, the one by the amount of income received over a period of time, the other by the value of the property at a particular date. Income is taxed but once; the same property may be taxed recurrently. The tax on each is predicated upon different governmental benefits; the protection offered to the property in one state does not extend to the receipt and enjoyment of income from it in another.

It would be pressing the protection which the due process clause throws around the taxpayer too far to say that because a state is prohibited from taxing land which it neither protects nor controls, it is likewise prohibited from taxing the receipt and command of income from the land by its resident, who is subject to its control and enjoys the benefits of its laws. The imposition of these different taxes, by the same or different states, upon these distinct and separable taxable interests, is not subject to the objection of double taxation, which has been successfully urged in those cases where two or more states have laid the same tax upon the same property interest in intangibles or upon its transfer at death. . . . These considerations lead to the conclusion that income derived from real estate may be taxed to the recipient at the place of his domicil, irrespective of the location of the land, and that the state court rightly upheld the tax.

Nothing which was said or decided in *Pollock* v. *Farmers Loan & Trust Co.,* 157 U. S. 429, calls for a different conclusion. There the question for decision was whether a federal tax on income derived from rents of land is a direct tax requiring apportionment under Article I, § 2, Cl. 3 of the Constitution. In holding that the tax was "direct" the Court did not rest its decision upon the ground that the tax was a tax on the land, or that it was subject to every limitation which the Constitution imposes on property taxes. It determined only that for purposes of apportionment there were similarities in the operation of the two kinds of tax which made it appropriate to classify both as direct, and within the constitutional command. And in [case cited], decided ten years after the *Pollock* case, the present question was thought not to be foreclosed.

It is by a parity of reasoning that the immunity of income-producing instrumentalities of one government, state or national, from taxation by the other, has been extended to the income. It was thought that the tax, whether on the instrumentality or on the income produced by it, would equally burden the operations of government. . . . But as we have seen, it does not follow that a tax on land and a tax on income derived from it are identical in their incidence or rest upon the same basis of taxing power, which are controlling factors in determining whether either tax infringes due process.

In *Senior* v. *Braden, ante,* on which appellant relies, no question of taxation of income was involved. By concession of counsel, on which the Court rested its opinion, if the interest taxed was "land or an interest in land situate within or without the state", the tax was invalid, and the Court held that the interest represented by the certificates subjected to the tax was an equitable interest in the land. Here the subject of the tax is the receipt of income by a resident of the taxing state, and is within its taxing power, even though derived from property beyond its reach.

Income from bonds secured by New Jersey mortgages. What has been said of the power to tax income from land without the state is decisive of the objection to the taxation of the income from interest on bonds because they are secured by mortgages on land without the state. . . . Appellant also argues that the interest from the bonds is immune from taxation by New York because they have acquired a business situs in New Jersey within the doctrine of [cases cited]. This contention, if pertinent to the present case, is not supported by the record. The stipulation of facts discloses only that the bonds and mortgages were located in New Jersey. . . . The burden rested on the taxpayer to present further facts which would establish a "business situs". . . .

Retroactive application of the tax. Appellant insists that in upholding the tax upon her income for 1931 and 1932 the state court infringed due process by giving retroactive effect to the 1935 amendment of § 359 of the New York Tax Law, which specifically declared that rents, embraced in taxable income by the section before amendment, should include rent from real property without the state. In support of this contention appellant points to the decision . . . that rents from land outside the state were not taxed by that section before its amendment, and to the dismissal by this Court of the writ of *certiorari* to review the judgment for want of a properly presented federal question. . . .

It is unnecessary for us to determine whether, or to what extent, the state court, in sustaining the tax in this case, rested its decision on the amendment of 1935, or whether it regarded it as anything more than a clarifying act pointing out the meaning properly attributable to the section before amendment. The record does not disclose that appellant raised in the state court the objection, which she presses here, to the retroactive application of the statute. In reviewing the judgment of a state court, this Court will not pass upon any federal question not shown by the record to have been raised in the state court or considered there, whether it be one arising under a different or the same clause in the Constitution with respect to which other questions are properly presented. . . .

New York ex rel. Cohn v. *Graves*
300 U. S. 308 Decided March 1, 1937

JURISDICTION OF INTANGIBLES

We find it impossible to say that taxation of intangibles can be reduced in every case to the mere mechanical operation of locating at a single place, and there taxing, every legal interest growing out of all the complex legal relationships which may be entered into between persons. This is the case because in point of actuality those interests may be too diverse in their relationships to various taxing jurisdictions to admit of unitary treatment without discarding modes of taxation long accepted and applied before the Fourteenth Amendment was adopted, and still recognized by this Court as valid. . . . The Fourteenth Amendment cannot be carried out with such mechanical nicety without infringing powers which we think have not yet been withdrawn from the states. We have recently declined to press to a logical extreme the doctrine that the Fourteenth Amendment may be invoked to compel the taxation of intangibles by only a single state by attributing to them a situs within that state. We think it cannot be pressed so far here.

If we enjoyed the freedom of the framers it is possible that we might, in the light of experience, devise a more equitable system of taxation than that which they gave us. But we are convinced that that end cannot be attained by the device of ascribing to intangibles in every case a locus for taxation in a single state despite the multiple legal interests to which they may give rise and despite the control over them or their transmission by any other state and its legitimate interest in taxing the one or the other. While fictions are sometimes invented in order to realize the judicial conception of justice, we cannot define the constitutional guaranty in terms of a fiction so unrelated to reality without creating as many tax injustices as we would avoid and without exercising a power to remake constitutional provisions which the Constitution has not given to the courts. . . .

Excerpted from majority opinion: Curry v. *McCanless*
307 U. S. 357 Decided May 29, 1939

CLASSIFICATIONS: PERMISSIBLE AND DISCRIMINATORY

In passing upon a Vermont income tax law the Supreme Court validated two exemptions—dividends derived from corporate business carried on within the state and income from investments in property within the state—but held that the exemption of income from money loaned within the state at not more than 5 percent interest was an arbitrary discrimination against loans made outside the state. This was as capricious, Justice Sutherland said, as if the tax were "upon all income from loans except those made on Mondays". The provision violated the equal protection and the privileges and immunities clauses of the Fourteenth Amendment; the tax abridged the privilege of a citizen of the United States "to loan money * * * in any part of the United States".

Justice Stone justified the exemption, which the Court said was forbidden, as a permissible classification. In addition, he argued against expansion of the privileges and immunities clause to cover interstate transactions:

I think that the exemption, from the tax, of net income from money loaned within the state at not more than 5 percent, like the exemption of income from dividends of corporations earned within the state, does not deny equal protection or infringe any privilege or immunity of citizens of the United States, and that the judgment should be affirmed in its entirety. Unless the constitutional validity of the exemptions is to turn upon the ground that we approve laws enacted to avoid taxing the same economic interest twice, but disapprove those to encourage residents to invest their funds at home, it would seem that the considerations which have led to upholding the one exemption would not admit of condemning the other. . . .

1. It is not denied that the effect of both exemptions is to place a burden on income derived from sources or investments made without the state which they do not place on income derived from like sources or investments made within it. But that affords no ground for saying that either is invalid. The equal protection clause does not forbid inequalities in state taxation. A state may select the objects to be taxed, and selection, which is but the converse of exemption, involves the imposition of a tax burden on some which is not placed on others. As this Court has repeatedly held, inequalities resulting from the singling out of one particular class for taxation or exemption, regardless of the reason for the choice, or even if there is no discernible reason, are not to be pronounced invalid where there is no clear indication that the purpose or effect is a hostile or oppressive discrimination against particular persons or classes. . . .

The end sought by the classification is of significance in passing upon the constitutionality of the tax only in so far as it serves to show that the discrimination is not invidious. If it appears or may fairly be assumed that it is for the purpose of promoting a permissible public aim, it cannot be condemned because one class must pay a tax which another does not. Where the public interest is served, one business may be left untaxed and another taxed, in order to promote the one . . . , or to restrict or suppress the other. . . . But it is not necessary to go so far to support the present exemption. There is no serious contention that its purpose or effect is to suppress the lending of money without the state or to injure appellant or his fellow residents of Vermont who may prefer to invest their funds elsewhere. Nor can it be said that the exemption was not granted in furtherance of a permissible state policy, which was the legislative objective rather than an invidious discrimination against appellant and others similarly situated.

It seems to be conceded that if the statute had placed upon the tax gatherers the burden of ascertaining whether money loaned within the state is invested in property there, and had limited the exemption to money so loaned and invested, the tax would be sustained because of the benefit which would result from the increase of wealth in the state and the enlarged opportunity to obtain additional revenue. The attack is thus narrowed to the single objection that there are exempted loans, some of which, although made within the state, are or may be withdrawn and used elsewhere. It is assumed that money thus loaned and withdrawn can be of no possible benefit to the state, and it is declared that since such transactions may occur the Court cannot determine whether the exemption will have any beneficent effect and that it is therefore invalid.

But there are benefits other than the increase of its taxable wealth which a state is at liberty to stimulate by its taxing policy, and exemptions have been sustained on the broader ground that they foster some form of domestic industry. . . . If Vermont chooses to encourage, by tax exemption, loans at favorable rates of interest within the state, because it believes that local interests will be benefited, it can hardly be said for that reason to be contravening a Constitution that has known a protective tariff for more than a hundred years. . . . It is true that a state may not lay taxes on imports or burden interstate commerce . . . , but it is too late for this Court to declare that a state may not favor domestic interests by granting exemptions in the exercise of its taxing power.

It is not for us to say that the Vermont legislature was unmindful of these broader advantages, or to declare that the presence within the state of investment funds offered at 5 percent or less to borrowers there, including those who are carrying on the business and industry of the state, is not beneficial; or that if any loans made within the state are used elsewhere they are or ever would be more than negligible in amount; or if they were that they could not have a favorable effect on interest rates within the state, which is a matter of state concern. When the Vermont legislature adopted the present exemption, it had before it the reports of two committees specially appointed to investigate the tax system of the state, which clearly indicate their judgment, based on a study of conditions in the state, that the existing system was driving investment capital from the state or into secured and noncommercial loans, and that a tax exemption embracing both secured and commercial loans would tend to increase the supply of investment capital for both and to reduce interest rates in the state. This Court has no basis for saying that those committees were wrong and no authority to say it. The state Supreme Court has stated in the present case that the legislature did have in mind these broader advantages, for it rested its decision on the ground that the exemption was made "in the interests of thrift and state development" and "for the assistance of the agricultural and industrial interests of the state".

If, in the face of so much which is persuasive of the legitimate purpose and effect of this legislation, we are to declare that we cannot say whether the benefits intended either will or will not result, it does not follow that the Vermont legislature is similarly uninformed. We must assume that it is not, unless we are to discard the salutary principle of decision, that, out of a decent respect to an independent branch of the government, legislative acts must be taken to be based on facts which support their constitutional validity unless the contrary reasonably appears. This Court, it is true, has held discriminations invalid where, upon the facts disclosed by the record or within the range of judicial notice, it has felt able to say that there could be no state of facts which could rationally support them. . . . But in no case has it rendered such a judgment where it has declared that it is unable to say that consequences which would justify the discriminations will not result. . . . Unless, as we profess not to do, . . . we are to sit as a superlegislature, or as triers of the facts on which a legislature is to say what shall and what shall not be taxed, we are not free to say that the exemption will not induce residents to offer to lend their funds within the state and at lower interest rates than they otherwise would, or that opportunities thus afforded will not be availed of by borrowers requiring funds for carrying on the commerce and industry of the state.

Even if we are to assume, in the absence of any actual knowledge, that money loaned in the state at favorable rates would not benefit it if used elsewhere, and, further, that in fact some money is so loaned and used, there is no discernible reason why those circumstances should be deemed to invalidate the tax, and none is stated by the Court. It is irrelevant that the state, which has selected domestic loans for exemption in furtherance of a state policy, has not excluded from the exemption every transaction which conceivably might not advance its purpose. Whether the legislative object is completely achieved is of no concern to this Court, once it appears that the exemption is made for a permissible end and bears some reasonable relation to that end. Purpose or motive of the selection of the objects of taxation and exemption is material only so far as it is needful to ascertain whether the discrimination is invidious. If the choice is not condemned for that reason, it has never been held that an exemption must fail because it may benefit some who do not advance the legislative purpose. A classification for a permissible end is not to be condemned because it operates to prohibit transactions in themselves harmless, or fails to reach others which are harmful. . . .

All taxes must of necessity be levied by general rules capable of practical administration. In drawing the line between the taxed and the untaxed, the equal protection clause does not command the impossible or the impractical. Unless the line which the state draws is so wide of the mark as palpably to have no reasonable relation to the legitimate end, it is not for the judicial power to reject it and say that another must be substituted. . . .

As the purpose of the exemption appears to be to encourage the lending of money within Vermont by its residents, at low rates of interest, and as it appears reasonably calculated to have that effect, and as we cannot say that such loans will not be of benefit to the state by tending to establish the interest rate of 5 percent or less, and by stimulating loans to borrowers for the purpose of carrying on business and industry within the state, the conclusion seems inescapable that the equal protection clause does not forbid it.

2. Feeble indeed is an attack on a statute as denying equal protection which can gain any support from the almost forgotten privileges and immunities clause of the Fourteenth Amendment. The notion that that clause could have application to any but the privileges and immunities peculiar to citizenship of the United States, as distinguished from those of citizens of states, has long since been rejected. . . . It created no new privileges and immunities of United States citizenship . . . and, as they are derived exclusively from the Constitution and laws enacted under it, the states were powerless to abridge them before the adoption of the Fourteenth Amendment as well as after. . . .

Before the Amendment the privilege of passing from state to state for the purpose of approaching the seat of the national government, of transacting business with it, and of gaining access to its courts, its public officers, and its ports, was declared in *Crandall* v. *Nevada,* 6 Wall. 35, to be a right of national citizenship which could be exercised independently of the will of the state. Upon this ground was placed the decision in that case that a state capitation tax on passengers transported out of the state by railroad or stagecoach infringed the Constitution. No one could doubt that if the decision had been made at any time after [an 1874 case] and until the present moment, it would have been rested on the commerce clause. This Court has many times pointed out that movements of persons across state boundaries are a part of interstate commerce, subject to the regulation and entitled to the protection of the national government under the commerce clause. . . . And it has specifically pointed out that *Crandall* v. *Nevada* is overruled so far as it referred the protection of such commerce to the privileges and immunities clause rather than to the commerce clause. . . .

The privileges and immunities clause has consistently been construed as protecting only interests growing out of the relationship between the citizen and the national government, created by the Constitution and federal laws. . . . Appeals to this Court to extend the clause beyond these limitations have uniformly been rejected and even those basic privileges and immunities secured against federal infringement by the first eight Amendments have been held not to be protected from state action by the privileges and immunities clause. . . . The protection and control of intercourse between the states, not carried on in pursuance of the relationship between the citizen and the national government, has been left to the interstate commerce clause, to the due process and equal protection clauses of the Fourteenth Amendment, and to Article IV, § 2, guaranteeing to the citizens of each state the privileges and immunities of citizens in the several states. . . . In no case since the adoption of the Fourteenth Amendment has the privileges and immunities clause been held to afford any protection to movements of persons across state lines or other form of interstate transaction.

The reason for this reluctance to enlarge the scope of the clause has been well understood since the decision of the *Slaughter House Cases,* 16 Wall. 36. If its restraint upon state action were extended more than is needful to protect relationships between the citizen and the national government, and it did more than duplicate the protection of liberty and property secured to persons and citizens by the other provisions of the Constitution, it would enlarge judicial control of state action and multiply restrictions upon it to an extent difficult to define, but sufficient to cause serious apprehension for the rightful independence of local government. That was the issue fought out in the *Slaughter House Cases,* with the decision against the enlargement. Since the adoption of the Fourteenth Amendment, at least 44 cases have been brought to this Court in which state statutes have been assailed as infringements of the privileges and immunities clause. Until today, none has held that state legislation infringed that clause.

If its sweep were now to be broadened to include protection of every transaction across state lines, regardless of its connection with any relationship between the citizen and the national government, a step would be taken, the gravity of which might well give us concern. But it is necessary to go much further before the present tax can be condemned. If protection of the freedom of the citizen to pass from state to state were the object of our solicitude, that privilege is adequately protected by the commerce clause, even though the purpose of his going be to effect insurance or transact any other kind of business which is in itself not commerce. But protection of the citizen's freedom of movement, whether by the privileges and immunities clause or by the commerce clause, will afford appellant no relief from the present tax. The record does not show that he was ever outside the State of Vermont, and for aught that appears he acquired his extra-state investments, which are in the form of negotiable corporate securities, by gift or purchase in Vermont. Nor does it appear that the physical securities or payments of income of which appellant has had the benefit have crossed state lines. He can be saved from the tax only by the extension of the immunity to his income merely because the property from which it has been derived, or the corporation paying it, is located in another state.

Such is the contention now made: that the privilege of acquiring, owning, and receiving income from investments without the state is a privilege of federal citizenship. And the suggestion is that the privilege is infringed by taxing this income just as the commerce clause is infringed by state taxation burdening the privilege of carrying on commerce across state lines. In any case the privileges and immunities clause is said to be infringed by taxing this income at a different rate than income from investments made within the state.

The novel application thus given to the clause, and the arguments used to support it, leave one in doubt whether it is thought to preclude all differences of taxation of the two classes of income, or only to forbid such inequality as is in some sense arbitrary and unreasonable. If the former, the clause becomes an inexhaustible source of immunities, incalculable in their benefit to taxpayers and in their harm to local government, by imposing on the states the heavy burden of an exact equality of taxation wherever transactions across state lines may be involved. If the latter, it would seem to add nothing to the guarantee of the equal protection clause, which extends to all "persons", including citizens of the United States. In that case, discourse upon the privileges and immunities clause would appear to be a gratuitous labor of supererogation.

If the privilege of making investments without the state is one protected by the privileges and immunities clause and a tax upon the income derived from them is analogous to a tax upon the privilege of carrying on interstate commerce, we must not only accept the view that the privilege is infringed by the present tax, but it would follow that any taxation of the income is forbidden. The answer is, of course, that a state tax on net income derived from interstate commerce has never been regarded as a burden on commerce or as an infringement of the commerce clause. . . . Far less could it be thought that a tax on property, or income from it, is an interference with commerce because the property had at some time been, or might sometime become, the subject of such commerce. . . . In applying the privileges and immunities clause, as now interpreted, no ground is suggested, or well could be, for regarding a tax on income from investments without the state as infringing the privilege of carrying on interstate transactions, any more than a tax on net income derived from interstate commerce or from property which had at some time moved in interstate commerce infringes the commerce clause.

The contention that a state tax indirectly affecting transactions carried on across state lines, not forbidden by the commerce clause (Art. I, § 8, cl. 3) or by Article IV, § 2, can be condemned under the privileges and immunities clause, was definitely rejected by this Court in *Williams* v. *Fears,* 179 U. S. 270. There a state occupation tax upon those engaged in hiring laborers for employment outside the state was held not to infringe the privileges and immunities clause or the equal protection clause.

So far as the objection is addressed to bare inequality of taxation affecting interstate transactions, if valid, it must be accepted as compelling equality of taxation by the state of the citizen's residence and as well by the state into which the transaction extends. More than this, since the exercise of the privilege involves both states, it would seem to be infringed not only by an unequal tax imposed by either, but by any tax imposed at the normal rate by both.

Starting with the dubious assumption that the protection of every movement of the citizen interstate, an acknowledged subject of the commerce clause, is independently a subject of the privileges and immunities clause, the protection afforded by the latter is expanded until it affords a refuge to the citizen from taxation which has no necessary relation to his movements interstate, and is in fact not shown to impose any restraint upon them. A tax immunity created avowedly for the protection of the citizen's privilege of movement from state to state is thus pressed far beyond the requirements of the interest put forward to justify it, and to a point which has never been thought needful or even desirable for the protection of the commerce of the nation. It is a transition effected only by ignoring the decision of this Court in *Williams* v. *Fears.*

If mere difference in taxation is made the test of infringement, the iron rule of equality of taxation which the equal protection and due process clauses have failed to impose . . . is the first fruit of this expansion of the protection of the privileges and immunities clause. To gain the benefits of its shelter the citizen has only to acquire, by a transaction wholly intrastate, an investment outside his state. I can find in the language and history of the privileges and immunities clause no warrant for such a restriction upon local government and policy. Citizens of the United States are given no privilege not to pay taxes. It would seem that a subordination of state taxing power to the interests of the individual, of such debatable wisdom, could be justified only by a pointed command of the Constitution of plain import.

If we turn from the reasoning by which this application of the privileges and immunities clause to state taxation is supported to the decision now actually made, it seems that the clause is thought to prohibit only these inequalities in taxation which are considered to be arbitrary and unreasonable. The exemption of dividends derived from corporate business carried on within the state, and the taxation of similar dividends from without the state, are held not to be an infringement of the clause. Exemption of income from investments in property within the state and taxation of like income from without the state are thought to be valid. But the privileges and immunities clause, it is declared, forbids any difference in the taxation of income from investment made within the state and income from investment made without, a conclusion which can only be attributed to the belief that this discrimination, as distinguished from the others, is arbitrary and unreasonable.

We are thus returned to the point of beginning, to a discussion of the question whether the exemption in the present tax is so unreasonable, so without support of a permissible state policy, as to infringe constitutional limitations. If the exemption does not merit condemnation as a denial of the equal protection which the Fourteenth Amendment extends to every person, nothing can be added to the vehemence or effectiveness of the denunciation by invoking the command of the privileges and immunities clause.

Colgate v. *Harvey*
296 U. S. 404, 436   Decided December 16, 1935

[Only Justices Brandeis and Cardozo joined in this dissenting opinion. Four years later the majority opinion was overturned.

A case involved a Kentucky statute which imposed a higher tax on deposits in banks outside the state than on those within the state. Appeal was made to *Colgate* v. *Harvey,* but the Court now said through Justice Reed that the decision there "must be and is overruled". *Madden* v. *Kentucky,* decided Jan. 29, 1940.]

A Range of Federal Powers

EVASIONS OF ESTATE TAXES

To prevent evasions of the estate tax and loss of revenue to the federal government the 1916 Revenue Act provided that gifts between living persons (*inter vivos*), if made "in contemplation of death", were to be taxed as a part of the decedents' estates. But motive was hard to prove, so a gift tax was enacted, levying on gifts at the same rates as legacies. This attempt to stop the leak was found ineffective, and Congress repealed it in 1926, providing instead that all gifts made within two years of death were to be deemed made in contemplation of death, regardless of the donor's motive.

This presumption, the Supreme Court said, was a taking of property without due process. It was arbitrary and unreasonable, Justice Sutherland stated, for it might apply to a "young man in abounding health, bereft of life by a stroke of lightning within two years after making a gift" and because the presumption excluded consideration of real motives.

Justice Stone dissented, joined by Justice Brandeis. The Court was concerned only with the power of Congress to tax this class of gifts, which it plainly had. Presumption was immaterial. Congress could "aim at the evil where it exists", as disclosed by ten years' experience with the estate tax. Countering the majority's hypothetical "young man," Justice Stone arrayed the elderly donors in 102 litigated cases, which he analyzed:

THE PRESENT federal estate tax, enacted in 1916 . . . has been continued in each successive Revenue Act. Although levied upon the privilege of transferring property passing at death and imposed on the estates of decedents, the prescribed tax was not limited to such transfers. By § 202(b) and (c) of the 1916 Act it was extended to gifts *inter vivos,* made in contemplation of death, and to gifts of property upon joint tenancy or tenancy by entirety, the benefit of which inured to the surviving tenant upon the death of the donor. Both classes of gifts were taxed as a part of the decedent's estate at the rates prescribed by the estate tax. The obvious purpose of these provisions was to prevent or compensate for the withdrawal of property by gifts *inter vivos* from the operation of the estate tax. The 1918 Revenue Act . . . included in the donor's estate, subject to the estate tax, all gifts effected by any trust taking effect in possession or enjoyment at the time of the donor's death, and the proceeds in excess of $40,000 of life insurance purchased by the decedent in his lifetime and payable to named beneficiaries at his death.

As a further measure for preventing avoidance of the tax by gifts *inter vivos,* Congress in 1924 adopted the gift tax . . . That it was adopted as a measure to prevent avoidance of the estate tax sufficiently appears from the fact that the graduated rates and exemptions of the tax were the same as in the case of testamentary transfers . . . and from the fact that in the Revenue Act of 1926 the retroactive reductions in rates of the estate tax were extended to the rates of the gift tax. . . . Provisions were also made for crediting the gift tax against the estate tax where the amount of the gift was later required to be included in the decedent's gross estate. . . .

Because of inequalities and inconvenience, expense and other difficulties in its operation and administration, the gift tax was repealed by § 1200 of the Revenue Act of 1926 . . . and as a result of ten years' experience in the administration of the estate tax and particularly of the provision taxing gifts in contemplation of death, the present provision of § 302 of the Revenue Act of 1926 . . . was added, which operates to impose the tax on all gifts made within two years of death, regardless of the purpose or motive of the donor. The Ways and Means Committee of the House of Representatives, in its report recommending this legislation . . . pointed out that the tax on gifts in contemplation of death had been ineffective in its practical administration, with a great loss of revenue to the government in consequence, and that "the difficulty of enforcement will be even more serious in view of the repeal of the gift tax". It stated, without qualification, that the amendment was one imposing the tax on all gifts made within two years of death, and said that "the inclusion of this provision will prevent most of the evasion and is the only way in which it can be prevented".

As we are concerned here only with the power of Congress to tax such gifts, I shall take no time in discussing the particular form of language by which Congress has sought to accomplish its purpose. In this statute taxing gifts *inter vivos,* as though they were legacies, it can be of no consequence whether the enactment says that all gifts within two years of death of the donor are irrebuttably presumed to be in contemplation of death or whether more directly it imposes the tax on all gifts made within two years of the donor's death. In either case, we are concerned only with the power which, here, the legislative body has indisputably sought to exert, and not with the particular choice of words by which it has expressed that purpose.

The question, reduced to its simplest terms, is whether Congress possesses the power to supplement an estate tax, and protect the revenue derived from it, as was its declared purpose, by a tax on all gifts *inter vivos,* made within two years of the death of the donor, at the same rate and in the same manner as though the gift were made at death. I think it has.

At the outset it is to be borne in mind that gifts *inter vivos* are not immune from federal taxation. Whatever doubts may formerly have been entertained, it is now settled that the national government may tax all gifts *inter vivos* and at rates comparable to those which may be imposed on gifts at death. . . . That the present gifts were *inter vivos,* made in the lifetime of the donors and effected as are any other dispositions of property passing from the donors independently of death, is not in dispute. The question then is, not whether they may be taxed, but, more narrowly, whether the congressional selection of some such gifts—those made within two years of death—and their taxation as though made at death, as an adjunct to the estate tax, is so arbitrary and unreasonable as to amount to a taking of property without due process of law, prohibited by the Fifth Amendment.

That question was not answered by *Schlesinger* v. *Wisconsin*, 270 U. S. 230 [cited by the majority]. If it had been, this case could and doubtless would be disposed of *per curiam* on the authority of that one. This case comes to us after ten years of experience in the administration of the estate tax, an experience which was not available, or at least not presented, in the *Schlesinger* case. There, all gifts made within six years of death were taxed. Here, only those within two years of death are within the statute. There, the tax was a succession tax and so was a burden on the right to receive . . . and necessarily payable by the donee, but at rates and valuations prevailing at the time of the donor's death. Here, the tax was upon the transfer effected by the donor's gift after the enactment of the statute, and is payable from the donor's estate at the same rates and values as though it had passed at his death. It burdens the estate of the donor before distribution, exactly as does the estate tax. . . .

In the *Schlesinger* case the Court declared (p. 240) that the gifts were "subjected to graduated taxes which could not properly be laid on all gifts or, indeed, upon any gifts without testamentary character". And in stating the argument presented and rejected there, the Court said (p. 240): "The presumption and consequent taxation are defended upon the theory that, exercising judgment and discretion, the legislature found them necessary in order to prevent evasion of inheritance taxes. That is to say 'A' may be required to submit to an exactment forbidden by the Constitution if this seems necessary in order to enable the State readily to collect lawful charges against 'B'."

Here, a graduated tax imposed by Congress on gifts *inter vivos* is not forbidden . . . and the case is not one where A's property is taxed to enable the government to collect lawful charges against B. Here A's gifts, which may be lawfully taxed, is in this instance, taxed because it removes property from the operation of another tax, which, but for the gift, would be applied to the property at A's death. Concededly, there is nothing in the federal Constitution which necessarily precludes taxation of gifts at the same rate and value as if they had passed at the donor's death, rather than at the rate and value prevailing at the time of the gift. The tax upheld in *Bromley* v. *McCaughn,* 280 U. S. 124, taxed all gifts *inter vivos* at the same rates and with the same exemptions as in the case of testamentary transfers. In [another case cited] a selected class of gifts *inter vivos,* which were not testamentary although made in contemplation of death, were so taxed as a part of the donor's estate. . . . In [another case] we upheld taxation, as a part of the donor's estate, of another selected class of gifts *inter vivos,* estates by the entirety donated by one spouse for the benefit of both, although the gift was not testamentary and neither title, possession, nor enjoyment passed at death. Similar taxation of gifts made *inter vivos,* but finally effective only at death, was sustained in [cases cited]. * * *

No tax has been held invalid under the Fifth Amendment because based on an improper classification, and it is significant that in the entire one hundred and forty years of its history, the only taxes held condemned by the Fifth Amendment were those deemed to be arbitrarily retroactive. . . .

It is, I think, plain, then, that this tax cannot rightly be held unconstitutional on its face. These gifts *inter vivos,* not being immune from taxation, and the obvious and permissible purpose of the present and related sections being to protect the revenue derived from the taxation of estates, want of due process in taxing them can arise only because the selection of this class of gifts within two years of death, for taxation at the prescribed rates, is so remote from the permissible policy of taxing transfers at death or so unrelated to it as to be palpably arbitrary and unreasonable.

It is evident that the practice of disposing of property by gift *inter vivos,* if generally adopted, would, regardless of the age or motive of the donor, defeat or seriously impair the operation of the estate tax, and that the practice would be encouraged if such gifts, made shortly before the death of the donor, were left free of any form of taxation. That in itself would be a legitimate ground for taxing all gifts at the same rates as legacies, as was done by the gift tax; but since the object is to protect the revenue to be derived from the estate tax, the government is not bound to tax every gift without regard to its relation to the end sought or the convenience and expense of the government in levying and collecting it. It may aim at the evil where it exists and select for taxation that class of gifts which experience has shown tends most to defeat the estate tax. This Court has held explicitly that the Fourteenth Amendment does not forbid the selection of subjects for one form of taxation for the very reason that they may not be readily or effectively reached by another tax which it is the legislative policy to maintain. . . . And since the imposition of the one tax is induced by the purpose to compensate for the loss of the other, the effect in accomplishing this result may itself be the basis of the selection of subjects of taxation. . . .

That being the object here, it is not imperative that the motive of the donor be made the exclusive basis of the selection of these gifts for taxation, as in the case of gifts made in contemplation of death. The fact that such gifts, made shortly before death, regardless of motive, chiefly contribute to the withdrawal of property from operation of the estate tax, is enough to support the selection, even though they are not conscious evasions of the estate tax, and opprobrious epithets can not certainly be applied to them.

The opinion of the Court does not deny that Congress has the power to select, on this basis, certain gifts to be taxed as estates are taxed. In fact, this Court has recently held that Congress does possess that power and has said so in language completely applicable to the present tax. In *Tyler* v. *United States,* 281 U. S. 497, 505, the tax on estates by the entirety, as a part of the decedent's estate passing to the surviving spouse, was upheld regardless of the motive which inspired it, and the decision was rested on the sole and only possible ground that "the evident and legitimate aim of Congress was to prevent an avoidance in whole or in part, of the estate tax by this method of disposition during the lifetime of the spouse who owned the property or whose separate funds had been used to procure it; and the provision under review is an adjunct of the general scheme of taxation of which it is a part entirely appropriate as a means to that end". . . .

The gifts taxed may, in some instances, as the present opinion states, bear no relation whatever to death, except that all are near death. But that all do have an intimate and vital relation to the policy of taxing the estates of decedents at death cannot be gainsaid, for what would otherwise be taxed is, by the gift, withdrawn from the operation of the taxing act, and the revenue derived from the taxation of estates necessarily impaired, unless the act which impairs it, the giving away of property *inter vivos,* is itself taxed. It cannot be said generally that gifts made near the time of death do not have a greater tendency to defeat the estate tax than gifts made at periods remote from it, both because of the greater number and amounts of the former and because such gifts more certainly withdraw the property from the operation of the estate tax than do the earlier and relatively infrequent gifts of property which may be lost or destroyed before the donor's death. Gifts in excess of $5,000 to one donee in any one year, which alone are taxed, are usually made from substantial fortunes which, in the generality of cases, are accumulated late in life, and the great bulk of which, if not given away in life, would pass at death. Nor can it be denied that the cost and inconvenience of collecting the tax on earlier, generally smaller, and less frequent gifts, which led to the repeal of the gift tax, may not themselves require or justify a distinction between them and gifts made nearer to the time of death.

Since Congress has power to make the selection if the facts warrant, we cannot say *a priori* that such facts do not exist or that in making the selection which it did, Congress acted arbitrarily or without the exercise of the judgment or discretion which rightfully belong to it. . . . As was said in *Ogden* v. *Saunders*, 12 Wheat. 213, 270, it is but a proper ". . . respect due to the wisdom, the integrity, and the patriotism of the legislative body by which any law is passed, to presume in favor of its validity, until its violation of the Constitution is proved beyond all reasonable doubt". The existence of facts underlying constitutionality is always to be presumed, and the burden is always on him who assails the selection of a class for taxation to establish that there could be no reasonable basis for the legislative judgment in making it.

But even if that presumption is not to be indulged, in passing on the power of Congress to impose this tax, we cannot rightly disregard the nature of the difficulties involved in the effective administration of a scheme for taxing transfers at death, and we cannot close our eyes to those perhaps less apparent, which have been disclosed by the experience with this form of taxation in the United States, which led to the enactment of the present statute.

It is evident that the estate tax, if not supplemented by an effective provision taxing gifts tending to defeat it, would, to a considerable extent, fail of its purpose. The tax on gifts made in contemplation of death, devised for this purpose, has been upheld by this Court . . . , but the difficulties of its successful administration have become apparent. The donor of property which would otherwise be subject to heavy taxes at his death does not usually disclose his purpose in making the gift, even if he does not conceal it. He may not, and often does not, analyze his motives or determine for himself whether his dominating purpose is to substitute the gift for a testamentary disposition which would subject it to the tax . . . , or whether it is so combined with other motives as to preclude its taxation, even though in making it the donor cannot be unaware that he, like others, must die and that his donation will, in the natural course of events, escape the tax which will be imposed on his other property passing at death. . . . The difficulty of searching the motives and purposes of one who is dead, the proofs of which, so far as they survive, are in the control of his personal representatives, need not be elaborated. As the event has proved, the difficulties of establishing the requisite mental state of the deceased donor has rendered the tax on gifts in contemplation of death a weak and ineffective means of compensating for the drain on the revenue by the withdrawal of vast amounts of property from the operation of the estate tax.

The government has been involved in 102 cases arising under § 202(b) of the 1916 Revenue Act and its successors. This number does not include any of the cases arising under § 302(c) of the Revenue Act of 1926, the statute under present consideration. And it includes only those cases, decision of which was determined by the answer made to the question of fact, whether a gift had been made in contemplation of death.

In twenty cases involving gifts of approximately $4,250,000, the government was successful. In three it was partially successful, and in 78 involving gifts largely in excess of $120,000,000 it was unsuccessful. In another the jury disagreed.

In 56 of the total of 78 cases decided against the government, the gifts were made within two years of death. In this group of 56 donors, two were more than ninety years of age at the time of death; ten were between eighty and ninety; twenty-seven were between seventy and eighty; six were between sixty and seventy; six were between fifty and sixty, and only one was younger than fifty. There was one gift of $46,000,000 made within two months of death by a donor seventy-one years of age at death; one of $36,790,000 made by a donor over eighty, who consulted a tax expert before making the gift; one of over $10,400,000 made by a donor aged seventy-six, six months before death; and one by a donor aged seventy-five at death, in which the tax assessed was over $1,000,000. There was one other in excess of $2,000,000; five others largely in excess of $1,000,000, four others in excess of $500,000; and thirteen in excess of $250,000, and fourteen in excess of $100,000. The value of the gifts was not shown definitely in three cases; twelve involved gifts totaling less than $100,000. In the remaining twenty-two cases the gifts were made more than two years before the death of the donor.

The judgment of the Ways and Means Committee that the provision of § 302(c) of the 1926 Act was required to stop the drain on the revenues from the estate tax, is strikingly confirmed by these 56 cases. The value of the gifts in those cases alone was $113,401,157, a total that does not include realty and personalty of undetermined value or the very large gifts on which the government, in the case already noted, sought to collect a tax of more than $1,000,000.

In many of the cases, notably those in which large amounts were involved, the gift was substantially all the donor's estate. In others the addition of the amount of the gifts to the estate of the donor would place the tax on the gifts in the higher brackets, so that the total amount of the tax that might have been collected is much larger than the tax that would have been payable on the gifts considered separately from the estates of which they had been part. It is also fairly inferable that the cases actually litigated constitute only a small portion of the instances in which large gifts were made within two years of the donor's death.

These are but a few of the many details of the administration of the Act, supporting the conclusion of congressional committees that large amounts of money and property were being withdrawn from the operation of the estate tax by gifts *inter vivos* under circumstances which clearly indicated that but for the gifts all would have been taxed as a part of the donors' estates, and that by far the greater number and amount of such gifts had been made within two years of death by persons of advanced age.

The present tax, if objectionable, is not so because motive or intention of the donor is not made the basis of the classification. It is not so because it does not tend to prevent or compensate for the evil aimed at. It is not so because the revenue leak will not be effectively stopped by including in the estate tax all gifts made within two years of death. Legislation to accomplish that end, and reasonably adapted to it, cannot be summarily dismissed as being arbitrary and capricious. Nor can it be deemed invalid on the assumption that Congress has acted arbitrarily in drawing the line between all gifts made within two years of death and those made before. Congress cannot be held rigidly to a choice between taxing all gifts or taxing none, regardless of the practical necessities of preventing tax avoidance, and regardless of experience and practical convenience and expense in administering the tax. Even the equal protection clause of the Fourteenth Amendment has not been deemed to impose any such inflexible rule of taxation.

The very power to classify involves the power to recognize and distinguish differences in degree between those things which are near and those which are remote from the object aimed at. . . . It has never occurred to anyone to suggest that a state could not, by statute, fix the age of consent, or the age of competence to make a will or conveyance, although some included within the class selected as competent might be less competent than some who are excluded. In the exercise of the police power, classification may be based on mere numbers or amounts where the distinction between the class appropriately subject to classification and that not chosen for regulation is one of degree.

As all taxes must be levied by general rules, there is a still larger scope for legislative action in framing revenue laws, even under the Fourteenth Amendment, with its guaranty of equal protection of the laws. The legislature may grant exemptions. . . . It may impose graduated taxes on gifts, inheritances, or on income. . . . It may impose a tax that falls more heavily on ownership of chain stores than on ownership of a smaller number. . . . And generally it may create classes for taxation wherever there is basis for the legislative judgment that differences in degree produce differences in kind.

The purpose here being admittedly to impose a tax on a privilege—that of making gifts *inter vivos*—to the extent that its exercise substantially impairs the operation of the tax on estates, it was for Congress to say how far that impairment extends and how far it is necessary to go in the taxation of gifts either to prevent or to compensate for it. Unless the line it draws is so wide of the mark as palpably to have no relation to the end sought, it is not for the judicial power to reject it and substitute another, or to say that no line may be drawn.

The objection that the gifts are taxed as a part of the donor's estate, and at the same rates and on values as of the donor's death, has no more force than that made to the selection for taxation of gifts made within two years of death. Since the basis of the tax is that it compensates for the drain on the estate tax, and since it is paid by the donor's estate which would otherwise be compelled to pay the estate tax on transmission at death, the whole object of the tax on the gifts would be defeated if levied on another basis.

In determining the reasonableness of a tax which, like this one, is levied in lieu of another, it is of course necessary to consider all the statutes affecting the subject matter. . . . Where the very purpose and justification of the one tax is that it is compensatory for the loss of the other, it is no objection that the one is made the exact equivalent of the other, thus avoiding inequality which, under some circumstances, might be objectionable. . . . No one has yet indicated precisely in what way this method of measuring the tax works any greater injustice or hardship than the tax on estates. It is certainly not greater where, as here, the tax is paid from the estate of the donor who, regardless of his age, in giving away his property after the statute was in force, took his chances that death within two years would bring it into his estate for taxation where it would have been if the gift had not been made. . . . A very different case would be presented if the taxed gift were made before the enactment of the taxing statute and many years before the death, as in [cases cited]. . . . The application of the estate tax to the other types of gift *inter vivos* mentioned in the Act has uniformly been upheld, even though the gift was made more than two years before death. . . .

I cannot say that the tax on all gifts made in contemplation of death, supplemented by that imposed on all others made within two years of death, is not adapted to a legitimate legislative object. The history of the litigation over gifts made in contemplation of death, to which reference has been made, and the reports of congressional committees prepared after extensive investigation and with expert aid, plainly indicate that it is. I can find no adequate reason for saying that the tax is invalid. The denial of its validity seems to me to rest on no substantial ground and to be itself an arbitrary and unreasonable restriction of the sovereign power of the federal government to tax, for which neither the words of the Fifth Amendment nor any judicial interpretation of it affords justification.

Heiner v. *Donnan*
285 U. S. 312, 332 Decided March 21, 1932

GOLD PAYMENTS: I

A $10,000 gold bond of the United States, issued in 1918, provided for payment in "United States gold coin of the present standard of value". A Joint Resolution of 1933 abrogated the gold clause in all obligations. The weight of the gold dollar was reduced by Presidential proclamation in 1934. Later that year the bondholder demanded redemption by the payment of $16,931.25 in legal tender currency. The Court of Claims certified two questions to the Supreme Court: (1) Was the claimant entitled to an amount in legal tender currency in excess of the face amount of the bond? (2) Was the United States liable in damages?

The Supreme Court held that the Joint Resolution was invalid so far as it overrode the government obligation created by the bond. "The contractual obligation still exists, and, despite infirmities of procedure, remains binding upon the conscience of the sovereign," said Chief Justice Hughes for the majority. But as the action was for breach of contract, and as plaintiff had not shown any loss in relation to buying power and was "not entitled to be enriched," the suit could not be entertained.

Four dissenters, Justices McReynolds, Van Devanter, Sutherland and Butler, not only insisted that the challenged enactments would result in confiscation of property rights; they declared the damage was demonstrable as the 69 cents difference between the old dollar and the new dollar. Justice Stone, in a separate opinion, concurred in part of the majority's conclusion but maintained that it was unnecessary to decide that the government was immune from liability by reason of its power to regulate the value of money. Should Congress decide to resume gold payments or adopt other stabilization measures, the Court's opinion might be an obstacle unless the government withdrew the privilege of suit.

I AGREE that the answer to the first question is "No", but I think our opinion should be confined to answering that question and that it should essay an answer to no other.

I do not doubt that the gold clause in the government bonds, like that in the private contracts just considered, calls for the payment of value in money, measured by a stated number of gold dollars in the standard defined in the clause. . . .

In the absence of any further exertion of governmental power that obligation plainly could not be satisfied by payment of the same number of dollars, either specie or paper, measured by a gold dollar of lesser weight, regardless of their purchasing power or the state of our internal economy at the due date.

I do not understand the government to contend that it is any the less bound by the obligation than a private individual would be, or that it is free to disregard it except in the exercise of the constitutional power "to coin money" and "regulate the value thereof". In any case, there is before us no question of default apart from the regulation by Congress of the use of gold as currency.

While the government's refusal to make the stipulated payment is a measure taken in the exercise of that power, this does not disguise the fact that its action is to that extent a repudiation of its undertaking.

As much as I deplore this refusal to fulfill the solemn promise of bonds of the United States, I cannot escape the conclusion, announced for the Court, that in the situation now presented the government, through the exercise of its sovereign power to regulate the value of money, has rendered itself immune from liability for its action. To that extent it has relieved itself of the obligation of its domestic bonds, precisely as it has relieved the obligors of private bonds in *Norman* v. *Baltimore & Ohio Railroad Company* [294 U. S. 240], decided this day.

In this posture of the case it is unnecessary, and I think undesirable, for the Court to undertake to say that the obligation of the gold clause in government bonds is greater than in the bonds of private individuals, or that in some situation not described, and in some manner and in some measure undefined, it has imposed restrictions upon the future exercise of the power to regulate the currency.

I am not persuaded that we should needlessly intimate any opinion which implies that the obligation may so operate, for example, as to interpose a serious obstacle to the adoption of measures for stabilization of the dollar, should Congress think it wise to accomplish that purpose by resumption of gold payments, in dollars of the present or any other gold content less than that specified in the gold clause, and by the reëstablishment of a free market for gold and its free exportation.

There is no occasion now to resolve doubts, which I entertain, with respect to these questions. At present they are academic. Concededly, they may be transferred wholly to the realm of speculation by the exercise of the undoubted power of the government to withdraw the privilege of suit upon its gold-clause obligations.

We have just held that the Court of Claims was without power to entertain the suit in *Nortz* v. *United States* [295 U. S. 317] because, regardless of the nature of the obligation of the gold certificates, there was no damage. Here it is declared that there is no damage because Congress, by the exercise of its power to regulate the currency, has made it impossible for the plaintiff to enjoy the benefits of gold payments promised by the government.

It would seem that this would suffice to dispose of the present case, without attempting to prejudge the rights of other bondholders, and of the government under other conditions which may never occur. It will not benefit this plaintiff, to whom we deny any remedy, to be assured that he has an inviolable right to performance of the gold clause.

Moreover, if the gold clause be viewed as a gold value contract, as it is in *Norman* v. *Baltimore & Ohio Railroad Company, supra,* it is to be noted that the government has not prohibited the free use by the bondholder of the paper money equivalent of the gold clause obligation; it is the prohibition, by the Joint Resolution of Congress, of payment of the increased number of depreciated dollars required to make up the full equivalent, which alone bars recovery.

In that case it would seem to be implicit in our decision that the prohibition, at least in the present situation, is itself a constitutional exercise of the power to regulate the value of money.

I, therefore, do not join in so much of the opinion as may be taken to suggest that the exercise of the sovereign power to borrow money on credit, which does not override the sovereign immunity from suit, may nevertheless preclude or impede the exercise of another sovereign power, to regulate the value of money; or to suggest that although there is and can be no present cause of action upon the repudiated gold clause, its obligation is nevertheless, in some manner and to some extent, not stated, superior to the power to regulate the currency which we now hold to be superior to the obligation of the bonds.

Perry v. *United States*
294 U. S. 330, 358 Decided February 18, 1935

[To offset new suits seeking to show damages Congress passed, at the President's request, a bill barring suits against the government for damages that might be charged to dollar revaluation and abrogation of the gold clause.]

GOLD PAYMENTS: II

After the *Perry* case decision, *ante,* the Treasury called for redemption of gold bonds in advance of their stated maturity date. When a bondholder was refused payment in gold dollars he contended that the Treasury notice of redemption was void and he presented an interest coupon for the next period following the accelerated date. The Supreme Court, by Justice Cardozo, held that the notice did not commit the government to a forbidden medium of payment; that it effectively terminated the running of interest. Disagreeing, Justices McReynolds, Sutherland and Butler insisted that as the bond's redemption clause promised payment in gold coin, a notice divorced from that purpose was "a dishonest effort to defeat the contract"; and the Court had acknowledged the obligation of the contract in the *Perry* case.

To Justice Stone, concurring in the result, it was apparent that the time had come to determine the power of Congress to suspend gold payments.

I THINK the court below . . . correctly interpreted the bonds involved in these cases as reserving to the government the privilege of accelerating their maturity by paying them or standing ready to pay them on any interest date according to their tenor, and upon giving the specified notice fixing the "date of redemption". The words "redeemed" and "redemption" as used in the bonds point the way in which the privilege was to be exercised as plainly as when they are written in the bonds of a private lender. . . . If payment, or readiness to pay the bonds in accordance with their terms was essential to "redemption", the one or the other, equally with the required notice, was a condition of acceleration.

The obligation of the bonds, read in the light of long established custom and of our own decision in *Holyoke Water Power Co.* v. *American Writing Paper Co.,* 300 U. S. 324, 336, decided since the *Perry* case [*ante*], must, I think, be taken to be a "gold value" undertaking to pay in gold dollars of the specified weight and fineness or their equivalent in lawful currency. . . . The suppression of the use of gold as money, and the restriction on its export and of its use in international exchange, by acts of Congress, . . . did not relieve the government of its obligation to pay the stipulated gold value of the bonds in lawful currency. Hence it has not complied, or ever stood ready to comply, with one of the two conditions upon performance of which the bonds "may be redeemed and paid" in advance of their due date—the payment to the bondholder of the currency equivalent of the stipulated gold value.

It will not do to say that performance of this condition can be avoided or dispensed with by the adoption of any form of words in the notice. Nor can it be said that a declaration, in the notice, of intention to pay whatever can be collected in court (see *Perry* case) is equivalent to a notice of readiness to pay the currency equivalent of the gold value stipulated to be paid, or that a statement of purpose to pay what will constitutionally satisfy the debt suffices to accelerate although no payment of the currency equivalent is made or contemplated or is permitted by the statutes. It follows that judgment must go for the bondholders unless the Joint Resolution of Congress of June 5, 1933, . . . requiring the discharge of all gold obligations "dollar for dollar" in lawful currency, and declaring void as against public policy all provisions of such obligations calling for gold payments, is to be pronounced constitutional.

Decision of the constitutional question being in my opinion now unavoidable, I am moved to state shortly my reasons for the view that government bonds do not stand on any different footing from those of private individuals and that the Joint Resolution in the one case, as in the other, was a constitutional exercise of the power to regulate the value of money. . . . Without elaborating the point, it is enough for present purposes to say that the undertaking of the United States to pay its obligations in gold, if binding, operates to thwart the exercise of the constitutional power in the same manner and to the same degree *pro tanto* as do bonds issued by private individuals . . . , except insofar as the government resorts to its sovereign immunity from suit. Had the undertaking been given any force in the *Gold Clause Cases,* or the meaning which we have since attributed to it when used in private contracts, it would, if valid and but for the immunity from suit, have defeated the government policy of suspension of gold payments and devaluation of the dollar. . . .

The very fact of the existence of such immunity, which admits of the creation of only such government obligations as are enforceable at the will of the sovereign, is persuasive that the power to borrow money "on the credit" of the United States cannot be taken to be a limitation of the power to regulate the value of money. Looking to the purposes for which that power is conferred upon the national government, its exercise, if justified at all, is as essential in the case of bonds of the national government as it is in the case of bonds of states, municipalities, and private individuals. . . . Its effect on the bondholders is the same in every case. . . . No reason of public policy or principle of construction of the instrument itself has ever been suggested, so far as I am aware, which would explain why the power to regulate the currency, which is not restricted by the Fifth Amendment in the case of any obligation, is controlled, in the case of government bonds, by the borrowing clause which imposes no obligation which the government is not free to discard at any time through its immunity from suit. I cannot say that the borrowing clause which is without force to compel the sovereign to pay nevertheless renders the government powerless to exercise the specifically granted authority to regulate the value of money with which payment is to be made.

Smyth v. *United States*
302 U. S. 329, 360 Decided December 13, 1937

THE OBLIGATION OF THE BOND

THE bonds of a railroad, issued and sold in 1912, provided for payment in gold dollars or the equivalent in foreign currencies. Congress having abrogated gold payments in 1933, the bondholders in bankruptcy reorganization proceedings three years later asserted their optional right in Dutch guilder value—which would have amounted to a greater number of dollars than promised, because of the currency devaluation. Through Justice Black the Supreme Court declared that the optional provision of the bonds was, by reason of the Joint Resolution of Congress, contrary to public policy and unenforceable. Taking a dig at this "major operation of statutory reconstruction", Justice Stone dissented, joined by Chief Justice Hughes and Justices McReynolds and Butler.

WITHOUT considering the question whether the bondholders in these cases have properly exercised their options, I cannot agree that the Joint Resolution of Congress of June 5, 1933, has set at naught the promise of the bonds to pay guilders to the holders at their election.

In each case the bonds contained alternative and mutually exclusive undertakings. The holder could if he wished demand payment in United States gold dollars of a fixed standard or their equivalent in United States currency. The alternative promise is for payment abroad of specified amounts of any one of several foreign currencies, without reference to their gold value at the time of payment. Its performance is as independent of gold or gold value as if it had called for the delivery of a specified amount of wheat, sugar or coffee, or the performance of specified services.

Any construction of the gold clause resolution which would in the circumstances of the present case preclude payment in foreign money would equally forbid performance of an alternative promise calling for the delivery of a commodity or the rendition of services. Hence the decisive question is whether the resolution admits of a construction which would compel one whose contract stipulates for delivery at his option of a cargo of sugar to accept instead payment of a specified amount in legal tender dollars, merely because by the terms of his contract he might have demanded, though he did not, an equal number of gold dollars.

When the Joint Resolution was adopted there were many obligations of American citizens payable abroad exclusively in foreign currency, and the attendant devaluation of the dollar greatly increased the burden of performance of such contracts through the necessity of purchasing with depreciated dollars the foreign exchange required for their fulfillment. But it must be conceded that Congress did not undertake to relieve any American citizen of that burden, and it is not contended that the Joint

Resolution provided for the discharge of any obligations payable in foreign currency, not measured in gold, except in the case where the promise to pay in foreign currency is an alternative for the promise to pay in dollars. After devaluation of the dollar the burden on American citizens of meeting obligations abroad by payment in foreign currencies may well have been as great whether the undertaking was unconditional or to pay upon a condition which had happened, or whether the obligation was to pay in a foreign currency or to supply goods which must be acquired by the expenditure of depreciated dollars.

We can find nothing in the legislative history of the Joint Resolution or its language to suggest any congressional policy to relieve from the one form of obligation more than another, or to indicate that the resolution was aimed at anything other than provisions calling for payment in gold value or gold dollars or their equivalent, which Congress explicitly named and described as the evil to be remedied, both in the Joint Resolution itself and in the committee reports attending its adoption. . . .

The Joint Resolution of Congress and the committee reports make no mention of obligations dischargeable in foreign currencies or by delivery of commodities or performance of services. If it was the purpose of Congress to control such obligations through the exercise of its power to regulate the value of money, that fact must be discoverable from the language of the resolution or from some underlying public policy, to which its words and the records of Congress give no clue. Shortly before the adoption of the resolution, Congress had authorized the President to devalue the dollar. By appropriate legislation and executive action, gold payments by the Treasury had been suspended, the hoarding of gold and its exportation had been prohibited, and all persons had been required to deliver gold owned by them to the Treasury. . . . It was obvious that these measures, aimed at the suppression of the use of gold as a standard of currency value, would fail of their purpose unless all payments in gold of the established standard or its equivalent were outlawed. The reports of the congressional committees recommending the adoption of the resolution indicate clearly enough that such was its purpose. They give no hint that more was intended. . . .

The recitals of the Joint Resolution declare that it is aimed at "the holding of or dealing in gold" and the "provisions of obligations which purport to give the obligee a right to require payment in gold or a particular kind of coin or currency of the United States, or in an amount in money of the United States measured thereby". No other purpose is suggested. The enacting part of the resolution proscribes "every provision * * * which purports to give the obligee a right to require payment in gold or a particular kind of coin or currency, or in an amount in money of the United States measured thereby", and declares "Every obligation, heretofore or hereafter incurred, whether or not any such provision is contained therein or made with respect thereto, shall be discharged upon payment, dollar for dollar, in any coin or currency which at the time of payment is legal tender * * *" "Obligation", it states, "means an obligation * * * payable in money of the United States." Thus the resolution proclaims that it is aimed at gold clauses and declares, if language is to be taken in its plain and most obvious sense, that provisions requiring payment in gold dollars or measured by gold are illegal and that every promise or obligation "payable in money of the United States" (not in guilders) shall be discharged "dollar for dollar" in legal tender currency.

To arrive at the conclusion that the resolution compels the present bondholders to accept dollars instead of the guilders for which they have contracted, it is necessary to say that "obligation", which the Joint Resolution defines as obligation "payable in money of the United States" and requires to be discharged "dollar for dollar" in legal tender, includes the obligation payable in guilders. This difficulty is bridged by recourse to a major operation of statutory reconstruction. It is said that "obligation" means, not the obligation or promise which is defined by the resolution as that "payable in money of the United States" and in which the gold clause provision is "contained" and "with respect" to which the provision is "made", but includes all obligations, although not dischargeable in money of the United States or in gold, which may be written into the instrument or document containing alternative promises, one of which is to pay in dollars. The "obligation" of the resolution "with respect" to which the gold clause is "made" is thus treated as synonymous with the instrument containing the multiple obligations, and all the provisions in it (not alone the promise to pay dollars) are now held to be dischargeable in dollars merely because one of the alternative promises "contained" a provision payable in "money of the United States", although the bondholder is entitled by his contract to demand performance of a promise to pay guilders not measured by gold. Thus, starting with a resolution avowedly directed at gold clauses, we are brought to the extraordinary conclusion that a promise to pay foreign currency is void if expressed in an instrument containing an alternative promise to pay in money of the United States whether of gold standard or not.

The argument is not persuasive, both because it rests upon a strained and unnatural construction of the resolution and upon an assumption that there was a congressional policy to strike down provisions for the alternative discharge of dollar obligations by payment in foreign currency not tied to gold, which finds no support in the language of the Joint Resolution or in its legislative history. It seems fair to suppose that if Congress proposed to end all possibility of creating an international market for bonds payable in dollars or alternatively abroad in foreign currencies, both without gold value, it would have given some more explicit indication of that purpose than is exhibited by the Joint Resolution. Even if we assume that Congress would have struck down such alternative currency clauses had it considered the matter, we are not free to do what Congress might have done but did not, or what we may think it ought to have done to lessen the rigors of our own currency devaluation for those who had made contracts for payment abroad in foreign currency without gold value.

In any case it seems plain that if Congress had made the attempt it would not have chosen to do so in terms which, if the

Court's construction of the Joint Resolution be accepted, are broad enough to strike down every conceivable provision for payment in foreign currency, delivery of commodities, or performance of services as an alternative for a promise to pay dollars, whether of gold standard or not.

Guaranty Trust Co. v. *Henwood*
307 U. S. 247, 260 Decided May 22, 1939

SPENDING TO REGULATE AGRICULTURE

To reëstablish farm prices at an economic level the Agricultural Adjustment Act of 1933 encouraged acreage reduction by benefit payments to farmers signing agreements. The funds were to be paid out of taxes on the processing of agricultural products. The Hoosac Mills failed to pay such processing taxes and won a reversal of a district court order in the Circuit Court of Appeals. The government contended that the tax was a proper excise, and once the money was in the federal treasury it could be expended for proper purposes without interference by the taxpayer.

In the opinion of the Supreme Court majority Justice Roberts said: The Act regulated agricultural production and thus exercised a power not granted to the federal government but reserved to the states. The end being unconstitutional, the tax, as an incident of this regulation, must be invalid. The general welfare clause of the Constitution, which permitted Congress to lay taxes and spend money, could not be used to coerce farmers and effectuate an illegitimate purpose.

The opinion set up hypothetical illustrations of the application of the doctrine embodied in the Act. A possible result of sustaining the claimed spending power "would be that every business group which thought itself underprivileged might demand that a tax be laid on its vendors or vendees, the proceeds to be appropriated to the redress of its efficiency of income. . . . The supposed cases are no more improbable than would the present Act have been deemed a few years ago."

To this Justice Stone retorted that the suggestion of curtailing the spending power "by judicial fiat because it may be abused by unwise use hardly rises to the dignity of argument". Justice Roberts envisioned obliteration of the independence of the states, but the minority (including Justices Brandeis and Cardozo) were not fearful. Justice Stone made an elaborate defense of the power of Congress to lay down conditions incident to spending:

THE PRESENT STRESS of widely held and strongly expressed differences of opinion of the wisdom of the Agricultural Adjustment Act makes it important, in the interest of clear thinking and sound result, to emphasize at the outset certain propositions which should have controlling influence in determining the validity of the Act. They are:

1. The power of courts to declare a statute unconstitutional is subject to two guiding principles of decision which ought never to be absent from judicial consciousness. One is that courts are concerned only with the power to enact statutes, not with their wisdom. The other is that, while unconstitutional exercise of power by the executive and legislative branches of the government is subject to judicial restraint, the only check upon our own exercise of power is our own sense of self-restraint. For the removal of unwise laws from the statute books appeal lies not to the courts but to the ballot and to the processes of democratic government.

2. The constitutional power of Congress to levy an excise tax upon the processing of agricultural products is not questioned. The present levy is held invalid, not for any want of power in Congress to lay such a tax to defray public expenditures, including those for the general welfare, but because the use to which its proceeds are put is disapproved.

3. As the present depressed state of agriculture is nation-wide in its extent and effects, there is no basis for saying that the expenditure of public money in aid of farmers is not within the specifically granted power of Congress to levy taxes to "pro-

vide for the general welfare". The opinion of the Court does not declare otherwise.

4. No question of a variable tax fixed from time to time by fiat of the Secretary of Agriculture, or of unauthorized delegation of legislative power, is now presented. The schedule of rates imposed by the Secretary in accordance with the original command of Congress has since been specifically adopted and confirmed by act of Congress, which has declared that it shall be the lawful tax. . . . That is the tax which the government now seeks to collect. Any defects there may have been in the manner of laying the tax by the Secretary have now been removed by the exercise of the power of Congress to pass a curative statute validating an intended, though defective tax. . . . The Agricultural Adjustment Act as thus amended declares that none of its provisions shall fail because others are pronounced invalid.

It is with these preliminary and hardly controverted matters in mind that we should direct our attention to the pivot on which the decision of the Court is made to turn. It is that a levy unquestionably within the taxing power of Congress may be treated as invalid because it is a step in a plan to regulate agricultural production and is thus a forbidden infringement of state power. The levy is not any the less an exercise of taxing power because it is intended to defray an expenditure for the general welfare rather than for some other support of government. Nor is the levy and collection of the tax pointed to as effecting the regula tion. While all federal taxes inevitably have some influence on the internal economy of the states, it is not contended that the levy of a processing tax upon manufacturers using agricultural products as raw material has any perceptible regulatory effect upon either their production or manufacture. The tax is unlike the penalties which were held invalid in the *Child Labor* tax case [and other cases cited], because they were themselves the instruments of regulation by virtue of their coercive effect on matters left to the control of the states. Here regulation, if any there be, is accomplished not by the tax but by the method by which its proceeds are expended, and would equally be accomplished by any like use of public funds, regardless of their source.

The method may be simply stated. Out of the available fund payments are made to such farmers as are willing to curtail their productive acreage, who, in fact, do so and who in advance have filed their written undertaking to do so with the Secretary of Agriculture. In saying that this method of spending public moneys is an invasion of the reserved powers of the states, the Court does not assert that the expenditure of public funds to promote the general welfare is not a substantive power specifically delegated to the national government, as Hamilton and Story pronounced it to be. It does not deny that the expenditure of funds for the benefit of farmers and in aid of a program of curtailment of production of agricultural products, and thus of a supposedly better ordered national economy, is within the specifically granted power. But it is declared that state power is nevertheless infringed by the expenditure of the proceeds of the tax to compensate farmers for the curtailment of their cotton acreage. Although the farmer is placed under no legal compulsion to reduce acreage, it is said that the mere offer of compensation for so doing is a species of economic coercion which operates with the same legal force and effect as though the curtailment were made mandatory by act of Congress. In any event it is insisted that even though not coercive the expenditure of public funds to induce the recipients to curtail production is itself an infringement of state power, since the federal government cannot invade the domain of the states by the "purchase" of performance of acts which it has no power to compel.

Of the assertion that the payments to farmers are coercive, it is enough to say that no such contention is expressed by the taxpayer, and no such consequences were to be anticipated or appear to have resulted from the administration of the Act. The suggestion of coercion finds no support in the record or in any data showing the actual operation of the Act. Threat of loss, not hope of gain, is the essence of economic coercion. Members of a long depressed industry have undoubtedly been tempted to curtail acreage by the hope of resulting better prices and by the proffered opportunity to obtain needed ready money. But there is nothing to indicate that those who accepted benefits were impelled by fear of lower prices if they did not accept, or that at any stage in the operation of the plan a farmer could say whether, apart from the certainty of cash payments at specified times, the advantage would lie with curtailment of production plus compensation, rather than with the same or increased acreage plus the expected rise in prices which actually occurred. Although the Agricultural Adjustment Act was put in operation in June, 1933, the official reports of the Department of Agriculture show that 6,343,000 acres of productive cotton land, fourteen percent of the total, did not participate in the plan in 1934, and 2,790,000 acres, six percent of the total, did not participate in 1935. Of the total number of farms growing cotton estimated at 1,500,000, thirty-three percent in 1934 and thirteen percent in 1935 did not participate.

It is significant that in the congressional hearings on the bill that became the Bankhead Act . . . , which imposes a tax of fifty percent on all cotton produced in excess of limits prescribed by the Secretary of Agriculture, there was abundant testimony that the restriction of cotton production attempted by the Agricultural Adjustment Act could not be secured without the coercive provisions of the Bankhead Act. . . . The Senate and House committees so reported. . . . The report of the Department of Agriculture on the administration of the Agricultural Adjustment Act (February 15, 1934, to December 31, 1934) page 50, points out that the Bankhead Act was passed in response to a strong sentiment in favor of mandatory production control "that would prevent non-coöperating farmers from increasing their own plantings in order to capitalize upon the price advances that had resulted from the reductions made by contract signers." The presumption of constitutionality of a statute is not to be overturned by an assertion of its coercive effect which rests on nothing more substantial than groundless speculation.

It is upon the contention that state power is infringed by purchased regulation of agricultural production that chief reliance is placed. It is insisted that, while the Constitution gives to Congress, in specific and unambiguous terms, the power to tax and spend, the power is subject to limitations which do not find their origin in any express provision of the Constitution and to which other expressly delegated powers are not subject.

The Constitution requires that public funds shall be spent for a defined purpose, the promotion of the general welfare. Their expenditure usually involves payment on terms which will insure use by the selected recipients within the limits of the constitutional purpose. Expenditures would fail of their purpose and thus lose their constitutional sanction if the terms of payment were not such that by their influence on the action of the recipients the permitted end would be attained. The power of Congress to spend is inseparable from persuasion to action over which Congress has no legislative control. Congress may not command that the science of agriculture be taught in state universities. But if it would aid the teaching of that science by grants to state institutions, it is appropriate, if not necessary, that the grant be on the condition, incorporated in the Morrill Act . . . that it be used for the intended purpose. Similarly it would seem to be compliance with the Constitution, not violation of it, for the government to take and the university to give a contract that the grant would be so used. It makes no difference that there is a promise to do an act which the condition is calculated to induce. Condition and promise are alike valid since both are in furtherance of the national purpose for which the money is appropriated.

These effects upon individual action, which are but incidents of the authorized expenditure of government money, are pronounced to be themselves a limitation upon the granted power, and so the time-honored principle of constitutional interpretation that the granted power includes all those which are incident to it is reversed. "Let the end be legitimate," said the great Chief Justice [Marshall]. "Let it be within the scope of the Constitution, and all means which are appropriate, which are plainly adapted to that end, which are not prohibited, but consist with the letter and spirit of the Constitution are constitutional." *McCullough* v. *Maryland,* 4 Wheat. 316, 421. This cardinal guide to constitutional exposition must now be rephrased so far as the spending power of the federal government is concerned. Let the expenditure be to promote the general welfare; still, if it is needful in order to insure its use for the intended purpose to influence any action which Congress cannot command because within the sphere of state government, the expenditure is unconstitutional. And taxes otherwise lawfully levied are likewise unconstitutional if they are appropriated to the expenditure whose incident is condemned.

Congress through the Interstate Commerce Commission has set aside intrastate railroad rates. It has made and destroyed intrastate industries by raising or lowering tariffs. These results are said to be permissible because they are incidents of the commerce power and the power to levy duties on imports. . . . The only conclusion to be drawn is that results become lawful when they are incidents of those powers but unlawful when incident to the similarly granted power to tax and spend.

Such a limitation is contradictory and destructive of the power to appropriate for the public welfare, and is incapable of practical application. The spending power of Congress is in addition to the legislative power and not subordinate to it. This independent grant of the power of the purse, and its very nature, involving in its exercise the duty to insure expenditure within the granted power, presuppose freedom of selection among divers ends and aims, and the capacity to impose such conditions as will render the choice effective. It is a contradiction in terms to say that there is power to spend for the national welfare, while rejecting any power to impose conditions reasonably adapted to the attainment of the end which alone would justify the expenditure.

The limitation now sanctioned must lead to absurd consequences. The government may give seeds to farmers, but may not condition the gift upon their being planted in places where they are most needed or even planted at all. The government may give money to the unemployed but may not ask that those who get it shall give labor in return, or even use it to support their families. It may give money to sufferers from earthquake, fire, tornado, pestilence or flood, but may not impose conditions —health precautions designed to prevent the spread of disease, or induce the movement of population to safer and more sanitary areas. All that, because it is purchased regulation infringing state powers, must be left for the states, who are unable or unwilling to supply the necessary relief.

The government may spend its money for vocational rehabilitation . . . , but it may not, with the consent of all concerned, supervise the process which it undertakes to aid. It may spend its money for the suppression of the boll weevil, but may not compensate the farmers for suspending the growth of cotton in the infected areas. It may aid state reforestation and forest-fire prevention agencies . . . , but may not be permitted to supervise their conduct. It may support rural schools . . . , but may not condition its grant by the requirement that certain standards be maintained. It may appropriate moneys to be expended by the Reconstruction Finance Corporation "to aid in financing agriculture, commerce and industry" and to facilitate "the exportation of agricultural and other products." Do all its activities collapse because, in order to effect the permissible purpose, in myriad ways, the money is paid out upon terms and conditions which influence action of the recipients within the states, which Congress cannot command? The answer would seem plain. If the expenditure is for a national public purpose, that purpose will not be thwarted because payment is on condition which will advance that purpose. The action which Congress induces by payments of money to promote the general welfare, but which it does not command or coerce, is but an incident to a specifically granted power, but a permissible means to a legitimate end. If appropriation in aid of a program of curtailment of agricultural production is constitutional, and it is not denied that it is, payment to farmers on condition that they reduce their crop acreage is constitutional. It is not any the less so because the farmer at his own option promises to fulfill the condition.

That the governmental power of the purse is a great one is not now for the first time announced. Every student of the history of government and economics is aware of its magnitude and of its existence in every civilized government. Both were well understood by the framers of the Constitution when they sanctioned the grant of the spending power to the federal government, and both were recognized by Hamilton and Story, whose views of the spending power as standing on a parity with the other powers specifically granted have hitherto been generally accepted.

The suggestion that it must now be curtailed by judicial fiat because it may be abused by unwise use hardly rises to the dignity of argument. So may judicial power be abused. "The power to tax is the power to destroy," but we do not, for that reason, doubt its existence or hold that its efficacy is to be restricted by its incidental or collateral effects upon the states. . . . The power to tax and spend is not without constitutional restraints. One restriction is that the purpose must be truly national. Another is that it may not be used to coerce action left to state control. Another is the conscience and patriotism of Congress and the Executive. "It must be remembered that legislators are the ultimate guardians of the people in quite as great a degree as the courts." Justice Holmes, in *Missouri, Kansas & Texas R. R. Co.* v. *May,* 194 U. S. 267, 270.

A tortured construction of the Constitution is not to be justified by recourse to extreme examples of reckless congressional spending which might occur if courts could not prevent—expenditures which, even if they could be thought to effect any national purpose, would be possible only by action of a legislature lost to all sense of public responsibility. Such suppositions are addressed to the mind accustomed to believe that it is the business of courts to sit in judgment on the wisdom of legislative action. Courts are not the only agency of govern ment that must be assumed to have capacity to govern. Congress and the courts both unhappily may falter or be mistaken in the performance of their constitutional duty. But interpretation of our great charter of government which proceeds on any assumption that the responsibility for the preservation of our institutions is the exclusive concern of any one of the three branches of government, or that it alone can save them from destruction is far more likely, in the long run, "to obliterate the constituent members" of "an indestructible union of indestructible states" than the frank recognition that language, even of a constitution, may mean what it says: That the power to tax and spend includes the power to relieve a nation-wide economic maladjustment by conditional gifts of money.

United States v. *Butler*
297 U. S. 1, 78 *Decided January 6, 1936*

[The principle of the A.A.A. decision was later abandoned by the Court. The Agricultural Adjustment Act of 1938, which exercised control of production by means of marketing quotas in interstate commerce, was sustained by a new majority, with Justice Roberts again as spokesman. *Mulford* v. *Smith,* decided April 17, 1939.]

SUBORDINATION OF THE STATES

THE State of California was subjected to a fine for violating a federal statute which required automatic couplers on cars of railroads in interstate transportation. The state, owning such a common carrier, argued that Congress had no power to impose a penalty upon a state engaged in the discharge of a sovereign function. The Supreme Court unanimously held the state-owned railroad within the scope of the federal law, in an opinion by Justice Stone excerpted below.

THE STATE urges that it is not subject to the Federal Safety Appliance Act. It is not denied that the omission charged would be a violation if by a privately-owned rail carrier in interstate commerce. But it is said that as the state is operating the railroad without profit, for the purpose of facilitating the commerce of the port, and is using the net proceeds of operation for harbor improvement . . . it is engaged in performing a public function in its sovereign capacity and for that reason cannot constitutionally be subjected to the provisions of the federal Act. In any case it is argued that the statute is not to be construed as applying to the state acting in that capacity.

Despite reliance upon the point both by the government and the state, we think it unimportant to say whether the state conducts its railroad in its "sovereign" or in its "private" capacity. That in operating its railroad it is acting within a power reserved to the states cannot be doubted. . . . The only question we need consider is whether the exercise of that power, in whatever capacity, must be in subordination to the power to regulate interstate commerce, which has been granted specifically to the national government. The sovereign power of the states is necessarily diminished to the extent of the grants of power to the federal government in the Constitution. The power of a state to fix intrastate railroad rates must yield to the power of the national government when their regulation is appropriate to the regulation of interstate commerce. . . . A contract between a state and a rail carrier fixing intrastate rates is subject to regulation and control by Congress, acting within the commerce clause . . . , as are state agencies created to effect a public purpose. . . . In each case the power of the state is subordinate to the constitutional exercise of the granted federal power.

The analogy of the constitutional immunity of state instrumentalities from federal taxation, on which respondent relies, is not illuminating. That immunity is implied from the nature of our federal system and the relationship within it of state and national governments, and is equally a restriction on taxation by either of the instrumentalities of the other. Its nature requires that it be so construed as to allow to each government reasonable scope for its taxing power, [*Metcalf & Eddy* v. *Mitchell,* page 163, this volume], which would be unduly curtailed if either by extending its activities could withdraw from the taxing power of the other subjects of taxation traditionally within it. . . . Hence we look to the activities in which the states have traditionally engaged as marking the boundary of the restriction upon the federal taxing power. But there is no such limitation upon the plenary power to regulate commerce. The state can no more deny the power if its exercise has been authorized by Congress than can an individual.

California, by engaging in interstate commerce by rail, has subjected itself to the commerce power, and is liable for a violation of the Safety Appliance Act as are other carriers, unless the statute is to be deemed inapplicable to state-owned railroads because it does not specifically mention them. The Federal Safety Appliance Act is remedial, to protect employees and the public from injury because of defective railway appliances . . . , and to safeguard interstate commerce itself from obstruction and injury due to defective appliances upon locomotives and cars used on the highways of interstate commerce, even though their individual use is wholly intrastate. . . . The danger to be apprehended is as great and commerce may be equally impeded whether the defective appliance is used on a railroad which is state-owned or privately-owned. No convincing reason is advanced why interstate commerce and persons and property concerned in it should not receive the protection of the Act whenever a state, as well as a privately-owned carrier, brings itself within the sweep of the statute, or why its all-embracing language should not be deemed to afford that protection.

In [case cited] it was held that a state, upon engaging in the business, became subject to a federal statute imposing a tax on those dealing in intoxicating liquors, although states were not specifically mentioned in the statute. The same conclusion was reached in [case cited]. Similarly the Interstate Commerce Commission has regarded this and other state-owned interstate rail carriers as subject to its jurisdiction, although the Interstate Commerce Act does not in terms apply to state-owned rail carriers.

Respondent invokes the canon of construction that a sovereign is presumptively not intended to be bound by its own statute unless named in it. . . . This rule has historical basis in the English doctrine that the Crown is unaffected by acts of Parliament not specifically directed against it. . . . The presumption is an aid to consistent construction of statutes of the enacting sovereign when their purpose is in doubt, but it does not require that the aim of a statute fairly to be inferred be disregarded because not explicitly stated. . . . We can perceive no reason for extending it so as to exempt a business carried on by a state from the otherwise applicable provisions of an act of Congress, all-embracing in scope and national in its purpose, which is as capable of being obstructed by state as well as by individual action. Language and objectives so plain are not to be thwarted by resort to a rule of construction whose purpose is but to resolve doubts, and whose application in the circumstances would be highly artificial.

United States v. *California*
297 U. S. 175 *Decided February 3, 1936*

PRESCRIBING A CONDITION

THE Interstate Commerce Commission did not exceed its authority in conditioning approval of a railroad consolidation by a requirement protecting the welfare of affected workers. The conditional order was warranted by the "public interest", the Supreme Court unanimously held, answering the contention that the public interest in an adequate transportation system did not extend, by law, to employees. On other occasions the Court had recognized the obligation of business "to carry the burden of employee wastage", Justice Stone reminded, although in the *Railroad Pension* case (*Railroad Retirement Board* v. *Alton R.R. Co.,* 295 U. S. 330), the Court invalidated pension regulation. He was one of the dissenters in that case, but now he wrote the decision which in effect cancelled the reasoning and conclusion there.

Here the trustees of two railroads, both in bankruptcy, applied to the I.C.C. for authority to lease one of the lines to the other; by combining the operations of the two lines they would effect savings in costs through elimination of the accounting offices of the leased road. Section 5 of the Interstate Commerce Act empowered the Commission to approve such a lease, "subject to such terms and conditions and such modification as it shall find to be just and reasonable", if the lease "will promote the public interest". The Commission found that the lease would not affect rates, routes, or service; that the elimination of the accounting offices would bring an annual saving of $100,000 by the dismissal of 49 employees and the transfer of 20 others from Texas to the Chicago offices of the lessee.

The Commission also found that the welfare of the employees affected by the change was one of the matters of public interest which it must consider in these proceedings. It accordingly authorized the lease on these conditions: that for a period not exceeding five years each retained employee should be compensated for any reduction in salary so long as he was unable, in the exercise of his seniority rights under existing rules and practices, to obtain a position with compensation equal to his pay at the date of the lease; that dismissed employees unable to obtain equivalent employment be paid partial compensation for the loss of their employment in specified amounts and for specified periods depending on the length of their service, and that the transferred employees be paid their traveling and moving expenses including losses incurred through being forced to sell their homes. The maximum cost of compliance with the conditions would be $290,000 spread over five years, during which the savings by the lease would be not less than $500,000.

Section 5 of the Interstate Commerce Act was a part of the Transportation Act of 1920, by which Congress gave the Commission new power to secure a more adequate and efficient transportation system. The Court recognized the term "public interest" as used in a restricted sense defined by reference to the purposes of the latter Act. According to the trustees, a carrier's employees were not part of the public whose interest was to be promoted by the lease.

Justice Stone said the issue was "narrowed to a single question whether we can say, as matter of law, that the granting or withholding of the protection afforded to the employees by the prescribed conditions can have no influence or effect upon the maintenance of an adequate and efficient transportation system which the statute recognizes as a matter of public concern". After a thorough preliminary statement he continued:

THE PROPOSED LEASE in its relation to the transfer or dismissal of employees and to an adequate and efficient transportation system, is not to be viewed as an isolated transaction or apart from the Commission's plan for consolidation of the railroads. As a result of the enactment of the Transportation Act in 1920, consolidation of the railroads of the country, in the interest of economy and efficiency, became an established national policy, and the effective consolidation of the railroads in conformity to the provisions of the Act and to the plan of consolidation which the Commission was directed to prepare became a matter of public interest. The policy of consolidation is so intimately related to the maintenance of an adequate and efficient rail transportation system that the "public interest" in the one cannot be dissociated from that in the other. Hence, in considering whether the public interest under § 5(4)(b) will be promoted by the conditions of an order authorizing a consolidation or lease, the Commission is free to consider their effect upon the national policy of consolidation as well as their more immediate effect on the adequacy and efficiency of the transportation system.

Obedient to the mandate of § 5(2) of the Act the Commission has prepared and published a plan under which it is proposed that the railroads of the country be consolidated into a limited number of large systems. . . . By § 5 of the Act the ban on consolidation of railway carriers was removed, and acting under it the Commission has granted authority for numerous consolidations and leases in furtherance of the plan. In the preparation and execution of the plan it speedily became apparent that the great savings which would result from consolidation could not be effected without profoundly affecting the private interests of those immediately concerned in the maintenance of the existing nationwide railway system, the railroad security holders and employees.

The security holders are usually, though not always, favorably affected by economies resulting from consolidation. But the Commission has estimated in its report on unification of the railroads that 75% of the savings will be at the expense of railroad labor. Not only must unification result in wholesale dismissals and extensive transfers, involving expense to transferred employees, but in the loss of seniority rights which, by common practice of the railroads, are restricted in their operation to those members of groups who are employed at specified points or divisions. It is thus apparent that the steps involved in carrying out the congressional policy of railroad consolidation in such manner as to secure the desired economy and efficiency will unavoidably subject railroad labor relations to serious stress and its harsh consequences may so seriously affect employee morale as to require their mitigation both in the interest of the successful prosecution of the congressional policy of consolidation and of the efficient operation of the industry itself, both of which are of public concern within the meaning of the statute.

One must disregard the entire history of railroad labor relations in the United States to be able to say that the just and reasonable treatment of railroad employees in the mitigation of the hardship imposed on them in carrying out the national policy of railway consolidation has no bearing on the successful prosecution of that policy and no relationship to the maintenance of an adequate and efficient transportation system. As was pointed out by Commissioner Eastman in his concurring opinion in this case the protection afforded to employees by the challenged conditions is substantially that provided in event of consolidation by an agreement entered into in May, 1936, between

219, the great majority, of the railroad lines of the country, and 21 labor organizations. He also directed attention to the fact that the Committee of Six, three of whom were railroad executives, in their report to the President of December 23, 1938, recommended that the federal agency passing upon railroad consolidation "require as a prerequisite to approval a fair and equitable arrangement to protect the interests of * * * employees", and that this report had been approved by the directors of the Association of American Railroads.

We can hardly suppose that the railroads, in entering into this agreement and endorsing this recommendation left out of account their own interest in the maintenance of transportation service or that their interest in this respect differs or is separable from that of the public interest. In fact, before this action by the railroads the Commission itself had taken the view that the welfare of dismissed employees must be considered in passing upon proposed consolidations, and in its sixth annual report in 1892 it declared in recognition of the same principle, that "relations existing between railway corporations and their employees are always of public interest". The Federal Coördinator of Railroads, in his fourth annual report to Congress in 1936, recommended the enactment of a comprehensive system of dismissal compensation, stating that such a system "would enhance the safety or efficiency of railroad service". . . .

The now extensive history of legislation regulating the relations of railroad employees and employers plainly evidences the awareness of Congress that just and reasonable treatment of railroad employees is not only an essential aid to the maintenance of a service uninterrupted by labor disputes, but that it promotes efficiency, which suffers through loss of employee morale when the demands of justice are ignored. Title 3 of the Transportation Act of 1920, which was enacted at the same time as the provisions of § 5(4)(b), set up a "Labor Board" to decide railroad labor disputes involving grievances, rules and working conditions, and declared in § 301 "it shall be the duty of all carriers and their officers and employees and agents, to make every reasonable effort and adopt every available means to avoid any interruption to the operation of any carrier growing out of any dispute between the carriers or employees or subordinate officials." Congress has passed successive measures for arbitration of railroad disputes between railroad employees and employers, all aimed at the prevention of interruptions of railroad service through such disputes, and culminating in the passage of the Railway Labor Act of 1926 . . . and in its amendments in 1934. . . . By the Wagner Labor Relations Act of 1935 it recognized and sought to prevent the interference with interstate commerce which may ensue from labor disputes arising in industry not engaged in transportation. See . . . *National Labor Relations Board* v. *Fainblatt* [page 84, this volume].

The Safety Appliance Act of 1893, the Hours of Service Act of 1907, and the Federal Employers Liability Act of 1908 were designed mainly to insure the safety and welfare of railroad employees and the constitutionality of those measures was sustained in part on the ground that they fostered the commerce in which the employees were engaged. In passing the Adamson Act of 1916, fixing the wages of railroad employees, Congress thought that it was safeguarding the railroads of the country from interruption which might result from labor disputes, and the constitutionality of the Act was sustained on that ground. . . . And in the [Railroad Retirement] Act of 1934, as amended in 1937, providing for a retirement and pension plan for railroad employees, Congress declared in terms that the plan was adopted for the purpose of "promoting efficiency and safety in interstate transportation".

In the last regular session of Congress, an act to amend the Interstate Commerce Act was passed by the Senate, S 2009, 76th Cong., 1st Sess. The House passed a substitute bill embodying extensive changes . . . Both bills are now in conference. But both as passed contain a provision carrying into effect the recommendation of the Committee of Six . . . by directing the Commission to require "as a prerequisite to its approval of any proposed transaction [consolidation or lease under § 5(4)(b)] a fair and equitable arrangement to protect the interests of the employees affected". Both bills as enacted declare it "to be the national transportation policy of Congress * * * to encourage fair wages and equitable working conditions, all to the end of developing, coördinating and preserving a national transportation system * * * by * * * rail * * * adequate to meet the needs of the commerce of the United States * * * " Congress has thus declared that fair and equitable provision for the compensation of losses thrown upon employees as the result of an authorized consolidation or lease promotes the national transportation policy by developing, coördinating and preserving the railroad transportation system.

In the light of this record of practical experience and congressional legislation, we cannot say that the just and reasonable conditions imposed on appellees in this case will not promote the public interest in its statutory meaning by facilitating the national policy of railroad consolidation; that it will not tend to prevent interruption of interstate commerce through labor disputes growing out of labor grievances, or that it will not promote that efficiency of service which common experience teaches is advanced by the just and reasonable treatment of those who serve. In the light of that record, too, we do not doubt that Congress, by its choice of the broad language of § 5(4)(b) intended at least to permit the Commission, in authorizing railroad consolidations and leases, to impose upon carriers conditions related, as these are, to the public policy of the Transportation Act to facilitate railroad consolidation and to promote the adequacy and efficiency of the railroad transportation system.

The fact that a bill has recently been introduced in Congress and approved by both its houses, requiring as a matter of national railway transportation policy the protection of employees such as the Commission has given here, does not militate against this conclusion. Doubts which the Commission at one time entertained but later resolved in favor of its authority to impose the conditions, were followed by the recommendation of the Committee of Six that fair and equitable arrangements for the protection of employees be "required". It was this recommendation which was embodied in the new legislation. . . . We think the only effect of this action was to give legislative emphasis to a policy and a practice already recognized by § 5(4)(b) by making the practice mandatory instead of discretionary, as it had been under the earlier act.

It is said that the statute, as we have construed it, is unconstitutional because not within the congressional power to regulate interstate commerce and is a denial of due process. It is true that in [the *Railroad Pension* case], in declaring the Railroad Retirement Act of June 27, 1934, not to be a valid regulation of interstate commerce, it was said, among other reasons advanced to support that conclusion, that a compulsory retirement system for railroad employees can have no relation to the promotion of efficiency, economy or safety of railroad operation. But notwithstanding what was said there and even if we were doubtful whether the particular provisions made here for the protection of employees could have the effect which we have indicated upon railroad consolidation and upon the adequacy and efficiency of the railroad transportation system, we could not say that the congressional judgment that those conditions have a relation to the public interest as defined by the statute is without rational basis. . . .

If we are right in our conclusion that the statute is a permissible regulation of interstate commerce, the exercise of that power to foster, protect and control the commerce with proper regard for the welfare of those who are immediately concerned in it, as well as the public at large, is undoubted. . . . Nor do we perceive any basis for saying that there is a denial of due process by a regulation otherwise permissible, which extends to the carrier a privilege relieving it of the costs of performance of its carrier duties, on condition that the savings be applied in part to compensate the loss to employees occasioned by the exercise of the privilege. That was decided in principle in *Dayton-Goose Creek Ry. Co.* v. *United States,* 263 U. S. 456. There it was held that the Fifth Amendment does not forbid the compulsory application of income, attributable to a privilege enjoyed by a railroad as a result of Commission action, to specified purposes "in the furtherance of the public interest in railroad transportation". . . . Moreover, we cannot say that this limited and special application of the principle, fully recognized in our cases sustaining workmen's compensation acts, that a business may be required to carry the burden of employee wastage incident to its operation, infringes due process. . . .

United States v. *Lowden et al.*
Decided December 4, 1939

APPRAISING LEGISLATIVE ACTION

THE Court upheld a city ordinance of Marysville, Kansas, requiring all gasoline and kerosene storage tanks with more than ten-gallon capacity to be buried at least three feet underground. The opinion by Justice Stone, excerpted below, was the first to point out the difference between the function which a court exercises in the trial of an ordinary lawsuit and that which it exercises in appraising the facts supporting legislative action.

THE MASTER made elaborate findings of fact from which he inferred generally that it is more dangerous, from the standpoint of public safety, to store underground than above, gasoline or kerosene in quantities of ten gallons or more. From this he drew the legal conclusion, adopted by the district court, that the ordinance was so arbitrary and capricious as not to be a permissible exercise of the police power.

We need not labor the point, long settled, that where legislative action is within the scope of the police power, fairly debatable questions as to its reasonableness, wisdom and propriety are not for the determination of courts, but for that of the legislative body on which rests the duty and responsibility of decision. . . . To determine that the present ordinance was a permissible exercise of legislative discretion, as thus defined, we need not go beyond those findings of the master to which petitioners offer no serious challenge. * * *

The facts * * * were properly for the consideration of the city council in determining whether the ordinance should be enacted, but they fall far short of withdrawing the subject from legislative determination or establishing that the decision made was arbitrary or unreasonable. The passage of the ordinance was within the delegated powers of the city council . . . , and it acted within its constitutional province in dealing with the matter as one affecting public safety. * * *

We may not test in the balances of judicial review the weight and sufficiency of the facts to sustain the conclusion of the legislative body, nor may we set aside the ordinance because compliance with it is burdensome.

Standard Oil Co. v. *Marysville*
279 U. S. 582 Decided May 20, 1929

[In the course of an opinion sustaining the Filled Milk Act, and answering the question whether the Act transcended the power of Congress to regulate interstate commerce or infringed the Fifth Amendment, Justice Stone said:]

THE EXISTENCE of facts supporting the legislative judgment is to be presumed, for regulatory legislation affecting ordinary commercial transactions is not to be pronounced unconstitutional unless in the light of facts made known or generally assumed it is of such a character as to preclude the assumption that it rests upon some rational basis within the knowledge and experience of the legislators.

There may be narrower scope for operation of the presumption of constitutionality when legislation appears on its face to be within a specific prohibition of the Constitution, such as those of the first ten amendments, which are deemed equally specific when held to be embraced within the Fourteenth. . . .

It is unnecessary to consider now whether legislation which restricts those political processes which can ordinarily be expected to bring about repeal of undesirable legislation, is to be subjected to more exacting judicial scrutiny under the general prohibitions of the Fourteenth Amendment than are most other types of legislation. [Cases cited: restrictions upon the right to vote, restraints upon the dissemination of information, interferences with political organizations, prohibition of peaceable assembly.]

Nor need we enquire whether similar considerations enter into the review of statutes directed at particular religions, or national, or racial minorities . . . ; whether prejudice against discrete and insular minorities may be a special condition, which tends seriously to curtail the operation of those political processes ordinarily to be relied upon to protect minorities, and which may call for a correspondingly more searching judicial inquiry. * * *

Where the existence of a rational basis for legislation whose constitutionality is attacked depends upon facts beyond the sphere of judicial notice, such facts may properly be made the subject of judicial inquiry . . . and the constitutionality of a statute predicated upon the existence of a particular state of facts may be challenged by showing to the court that those facts have ceased to exist. . . . Similarly we recognize that the constitutionality of a statute, valid on its face, may be assailed by proof of facts tending to show that the statute as applied to a particular article is without support in reason because the article, although within the prohibited class, is so different from others of the class as to be without the reason for the prohibition . . . though the effect of such proof depends on the relevant circumstances in each case, as for example the administrative difficulty of excluding the article from the regulated class.

United States v. *Carolene Products Co.*
304 U. S. 144 Decided April 25, 1938

Index

Index

Index

Index